DIGITAL TRANSFORMATION FOR ENTREPRENEURSHIP

Digital Transformation: Accelerating Organizational Intelligence

Print ISSN: 2811-0552
Online ISSN: 2811-0560

Series Editor: Jay Liebowitz *(Seton Hall University, USA)*

According to a report released by Veritis in 2021 "the global digital transformation market size is anticipated to reach USD 1009.8 billion by 2025 from USD 469.8 billion in 2020. The demand for digital transformation services is expected to rise at a Compound Annual Growth Rate (CAGR) of around 16.5% over the forecast period from 2021 to 2025. The growing adoption of digital technologies, including Artificial Intelligence (AI), cloud computing, big data, the Internet of Things (IoT), and Machine Learning (ML), is driving the growth of the digital transformation market." To be competitive in today's fast-changing marketplace, organizations need to apply the "alphabet" of digital transformation.

The focus of the book series is unique and will cover the various perspectives on organizational digital transformation, namely business & management, technology, legal and ethics, and social aspects.

Published:

Vol. 5 *Digital Transformation for Entrepreneurship*
edited by Susanne Durst and Aive Pevkur

Vol. 4 *Digital Strategies and Organizational Transformation*
edited by G Reza Djavanshir

Vol. 3 *Doing Well and Doing Good: Human-Centered Digital Transformation Leadership*
by Cheryl Flink, Liora Gross and William Pasmore

Vol. 2 *Digital Transformation Demystified*
by Frank Granito

Vol. 1 *Digital Transformation for the University of the Future*
edited by Jay Liebowitz

More information on this series can be found at https://www.worldscientific.com/series/dtaoi

Digital Transformation
Accelerating Organizational Intelligence
– Volume 5

Series Editor: **Jay Liebowitz**

DIGITAL TRANSFORMATION FOR ENTREPRENEURSHIP

Editors

Susanne Durst
Reykjavik University, Iceland

Aive Pevkur
Tallinn University of Technology, Estonia

World Scientific

W JERSEY • LONDON • SINGAPORE • BEIJING • SHANGHAI • HONG KONG • TAIPEI • CHENNAI • TOKYO

Published by

World Scientific Publishing Co. Pte. Ltd.
5 Toh Tuck Link, Singapore 596224
USA office: 27 Warren Street, Suite 401-402, Hackensack, NJ 07601
UK office: 57 Shelton Street, Covent Garden, London WC2H 9HE

Library of Congress Cataloging-in-Publication Data
Names: Durst, Susanne, editor. | Pevkur, Aive, editor.
Title: Digital transformation for entrepreneurship / editors: Susanne Durst, Reykjavik University, Iceland, Aive Pevkur, Tallinn University of Technology, Estonia.
Description: New Jersey : World Scientific, [2024] | Series: Digital transformation: accelerating organizational intelligence, 2811-0552; volume 5 | Includes bibliographical references and index.
Identifiers: LCCN 2023022300 | ISBN 9789811270161 (hardcover) | ISBN 9789811270178 (ebook) | ISBN 9789811270185 (ebook other)
Subjects: LCSH: Entrepreneurship. | Information technology--Economic aspects. | Business--Data processing. | New business enterprises.
Classification: LCC HB615 .D45 2024 | DDC 338/.04--dc23/eng/20230614
LC record available at https://lccn.loc.gov/2023022300

British Library Cataloguing-in-Publication Data
A catalogue record for this book is available from the British Library.

For any available supplementary material, please visit
https://www.worldscientific.com/worldscibooks/10.1142/13244#t=suppl

Desk Editors: Balasubramanian Shanmugam/Nicole Ong

Typeset by Stallion Press
Email: enquiries@stallionpress.com

To all curious people in the world

https://doi.org/10.1142/9789811270178_fmatter

About the Editors

Susanne Durst is a full professor of management at the Department of Business Administration at Reykjavik University (Iceland), a full professor of business administration at the University of Skövde, Sweden and an adjunct professor at the Department of Business Administration at Tallinn University of Technology (Estonia). Her research interests include knowledge (risk) management, innovation management, responsible digitalization, and sustainable business development in the context of small entrepreneurial companies. She has been conducting several national and international research projects. Her work has been awarded different awards and published in international peer-reviewed journals. Before joining academia, she worked with private enterprises.

Aive Pevkur (DPhil in practical philosophy) is a senior lecturer at Tallinn University of Technology and a national and international expert in professional and public ethics and integrity. Dr. Pevkur has more than 25 years of experience in philosophy and ethics-related consultancy projects and courses and ethics research projects in Estonia and internationally. She is an author and co-author of articles and books on ethics and values in the public sphere, engineering, and professional life.

https://doi.org/10.1142/9789811270178_fmatter

About the Contributors

Tommaso Aguzzi is a PhD candidate in the Innovative Training Network MARKETS program (EU-MSCA fellowship) at the Department of Business Administration of Tallinn University of Technology (TalTech), Estonia. He holds a double MA degree in global studies from the University of Vienna and Roskilde University. His research interests focus on the informal economy in the former Soviet region; in particular, his investigation focuses on the (il)logics and motivations of informal entrepreneurship, the construction of social norms, and the diverging moralities between states and individuals in the Central Asian region.

Lidia Davies is a PhD candidate in the Department of Business Administration at Tallinn University of Technology, Estonia. Before joining academia, she worked in international marketing research agencies, sharpening her expertise in strategic marketing and qualitative research. Her academic interests include risk and knowledge management, small- and medium-sized enterprise management, business model innovation, and corporate governance.

Samuel Foli holds a master's degree in business administration (MBA). He is currently a PhD student and also an early-stage researcher at the Department of Business Administration at Tallinn University of Technology, Estonia. He has published in several internationally recognized peer-reviewed journals, such as *Management Review Quarterly* (MRQ), *Journal of Entrepreneurship in Emerging Economies* (Emerald), and *VINE Journal of Information and Knowledge Management Systems*

(Emerald). His research interests include knowledge (risk) management, business sustainability, supply chain risk management, and statistical modeling.

Basel Hammoda is a PhD candidate at the Department of Business Administration at Tallinn University of Technology in Estonia. He focuses on innovative models in entrepreneurship in his research. Prior to working in academia, he worked in several managerial roles in the technology, consulting, healthcare, and education sectors.

Elisabeth Kraut has set herself the goal of helping companies in the transformation process to a more sustainable, circular economy. She is a doctoral candidate at the Department of Business Administration at Tallinn University of Technology, Estonia, and her research is focused on the transformation models toward a more circular economy. Previously, she studied international business administration for her bachelor's and applied sustainability for her master's degree. She is the founder of 7step-solution, a sustainability consultancy. Furthermore, she works as a lecturer at the Heilbronn University of Applied Sciences.

Velli Parts (MSc in psychology) is a lecturer at Tallinn University of Technology, where she teaches future HRM professionals. Her research focuses on personality, well-being, and competence-related issues in the contexts of work, HRM, and entrepreneurship. She is also a PhD student at the Department of Business Administration, investigating the darker side of student entrepreneurs or how personality traits considered dysfunctional in everyday life can boost entrepreneurial success.

Johann Timo Theisen is a PhD student in corporate entrepreneurship, leverages 15+ years of experience. With a solid foundation in product development, he brings practical knowledge to research. He holds an MSc in entrepreneurship from the University of Liechtenstein. Currently pursuing his PhD at Reykjavik University, his research explores waste's impact on value co-creation. Johann believes waste represents missed value opportunities and approaches innovation with empathy, science, engineering, storytelling, and mindset convergence. Committed to positive change, he challenges consumer behavior and implements sustainable business strategies. Johann's dedication shapes a better future through rigorous research and academic pursuits.

Talshyn Tokyzhanova is a PhD student and an early-stage researcher at the Department of Business Administration at Tallinn University of Technology, Estonia. Prior to that, Talshyn has worked as a lecturer at the university and a consulting analyst for business development projects in Almaty, Kazakhstan. Her academic interests include business ethics, technology adoption, and the informal economy.

Fabian Zimmermann is a management consultant and an experienced advisor in business development, business model innovation, merger analysis, and financial regulation. He holds a master's degree in international business & alternative investments from the University of St. Andrews and a BSc in business administration & international financial services from the University of Liechtenstein. In his PhD research, he focuses on the financial service sector, with a special emphasis on the developments in wealth and asset management.

https://doi.org/10.1142/9789811270178_fmatter

Contents

About the Editors vii

About the Contributors ix

Chapter 1 Introduction 1
Susanne Durst

Chapter 2 Digital Transformation for Entrepreneurship 5
Susanne Durst

Chapter 3 Ethical Challenges in Digital Transformation for Entrepreneurship 17
Aive Pevkur

Chapter 4 The Role of Knowledge Management in the Preparedness of Small- and Medium-Sized Enterprises for Digital Transformation 31
Lidia Davies

Chapter 5 Discovering the Hidden String Connecting Knowledge Risks and the Digital Entrepreneurial Ecosystem 51
Samuel Foli

Chapter 6 Digital Technology in Entrepreneurship Education: An Overview of the Status Quo 71
Basel Hammoda

Chapter 7 From Technostress to Digital Well-being 95
Velli Parts

Chapter 8 We Want to Work Smart Now! How Digitalization Challenges Entrepreneurial Leadership 117
Velli Parts

Chapter 9 Disruptive Services as an Opportunity for Digital Entrepreneurs 135
Johann Timo Theisen

Chapter 10 Transformation of Entrepreneurial Business Finance 151
Fabian Zimmermann

Chapter 11 Moving to New Digital Platforms: A Case Study of Kazakhstani Small- and Medium-Sized Enterprises 175
Talshyn Tokyzhanova

Chapter 12 Digitalizing Micro-Business in Times of Disruption: Insight into Innovative Strategies in the Kazakh Economy 195
Tommaso Aguzzi

Chapter 13 Sustainability Transformation Journey of Small- and Medium-Sized Enterprises: The Path of a Design Company 215
Elisabeth Kraut

Chapter 14 Conclusions and Outlook 243
Aive Pevkur and Susanne Durst

Index 249

https://doi.org/10.1142/9789811270178_0001

Chapter 1

Introduction

Susanne Durst

*Department of Business Administration,
Reykjavik University, Menntavegi 1,
102 Reykjavík, Iceland*

*Department of Business Administration,
Tallinn University of Technology, Ehitajate tee 5,
Tallinn 19086, Estonia*

susanned@ru.is

Abstract

This book is primarily composed of contributions from PhD students in the Entrepreneurship and International Business group at the Faculty of Business Administration, Tallinn University of Technology, Estonia. The PhD students — who form a talented group of individuals from different countries, such as Egypt, Estonia, Germany, Ghana, Italy, Kazakhstan, and Russia — explore various topics related to digital transformation for entrepreneurship. In this way, the topic of entrepreneurship is addressed by a new generation of researchers working in the field of entrepreneurship and related areas. The topic is discussed not only from different angles and perspectives but also from those that reflect this generation's thinking on the subject.

1.1. Structure of the Book

Throughout the book, interested readers will obtain a broad overview of digital transformation and its possible application in the broad context of entrepreneurship. Recent research will be presented mainly by early-stage researchers (i.e., doctoral students) whose doctoral studies are linked to digital transformation for entrepreneurship or related fields, which will help readers develop and/or expand their understanding of this (still) emerging phenomenon.

The chapters covered in this book have decision makers of small entrepreneurial firms (start-ups and mature ones) as the primary target group and give this group insights into recent (fresh) research findings produced by doctoral students as part of their doctoral studies.

The broad approach of this book can also help broaden or even change the way readers think about the topic under study and its application. In doing so, this book focuses on the applications of digital transformation to different types of companies while also taking different cultural and geographical settings into account.

In order to achieve the above-mentioned, the book consists of 13 chapters that are divided into four parts.

The idea behind Part 1 is to introduce the main concepts covered in this book, namely digital transformation and entrepreneurship. This is followed by Part 2, which provides theoretical and conceptual research insights into the application of digital transformation for entrepreneurship. In Part 3 of the book, an empirical insight into digital transformation for entrepreneurship in different types of smaller firms will be presented. The book concludes with Part 4, which highlights promising future directions for exploring digital transformation for entrepreneurship derived from the insights conveyed in this book.

In the following, the content of each chapter is briefly outlined.

1.1.1. *Part 1*

In Chapter 2, "Digital Transformation for Entrepreneurship," Susanne Durst introduces the readers to the concepts of entrepreneurship and digital transformation and the linkage between the two concepts. It also provides some ideas on how digital transformation could and does happen in different modes of entrepreneurship.

1.1.2. *Part 2*

This part continues with contributions that address digital transformation for entrepreneurship from theoretical and conceptual perspectives.

Chapter 3, "Ethical Challenges in Digital Transformation for Entrepreneurship" by Aive Pevkur, addresses the ethical issues and challenges that can arise from digital transformation for entrepreneurship.

The following three chapters highlight the issues of knowledge and learning (i.e., education) in the given context.

Lidia Davies, in Chapter 4, "The Role of Knowledge Management in the Preparedness of Small- and Medium-Sized Enterprises for Digital Transformation," shows how systematic knowledge management can better prepare smaller entrepreneurial firms for digital transformation. While Chapter 5, "Discovering the Hidden String Connecting Knowledge Risks and the Digital Entrepreneurial Ecosystem," by Samuel Foli draws attention to the so-called knowledge risks and proposes a conceptual model that illuminates the relationship and nature of potential knowledge risks in the digital entrepreneurial ecosystem. In Chapter 6, "Digital Technology in Entrepreneurship Education: An Overview of the Status Quo," Basel Hammoda gives an overview of the changes in entrepreneurial education and the role of digital technologies in this context.

Velli Parts has contributed two chapters, Chapters 7 and 8, that deal with the impact of digital transformation on work and leadership in smaller entrepreneurial firms.

Chapter 7, "From Technostress to Digital Well-being," provides an overview of the impact of the increased use of digital technologies on work-related stress in companies. It identifies ways that can lead to the improvement of digital well-being in the workplace. Chapter 8, "We Want to Work Smart Now! How Digitalization Challenges Entrepreneurial Leadership," addresses "smart working" and shows the challenges that digital transformation brings to leadership in small entrepreneurial firms.

Chapter 9, "Disruptive Services as an Opportunity for Digital Entrepreneurs," by Johann Timo Theisen, shows the kind of opportunities the shift toward innovative service or service-oriented business models offer for entrepreneurial companies.

Eventually, Chapter 10, "Transformation of Entrepreneurial Business Finance," by Fabian Zimmermann, rounds off this part of the book by giving a comprehensive overview of new financing methods and what to look out for in these forms of financing.

1.1.3. *Part 3*

The third part of the book covers chapters that provide insight into digital transformation for entrepreneurship as it is practiced in smaller companies located in different parts of the world.

Two of the chapters lead readers to Kazakhstan. Talshyn Tokyzhanova, in Chapter 11, "Moving to New Digital Platforms: A Case Study of Kazakhstani Small- and Medium-Sized Enterprises," investigates the motivations of smaller firms in this country to turn to digital platforms and the challenges these companies faced at the beginning of transforming their traditional businesses into more digital ones. While Chapter 12, "Digitalizing Micro-Business in Times of Disruption: Insight into Innovative Strategies in the Kazakh Economy," by Tommaso Aguzzi, explores how selected owners of micro-businesses use digitalization to transform their businesses as a consequence of the COVID-19 pandemic.

Finally, Elisabeth Kraut gives, in Chapter 13, "Sustainability Transformation Journey of Small- and Medium-Sized Enterprises: The Path of a Design Company," an insight into the implementation process of a small German company moving toward sustainability management.

1.1.4. *Part 4*

In the final and concluding chapter, Chapter 14, "Conclusions and Outlook," Aive Pevkur and Susanne Durst present several promising future directions for the topic of digital transformation for entrepreneurship.

1.2. Conclusion

In summary, we, the people involved, are very proud to have created this book. We are convinced that this book can be considered a useful tool for decision makers of entrepreneurial companies in their daily work to improve the long-term success of their organizations. Other actors may find the content presented useful as well. Last but not least, we hope that this book will also encourage researchers to conduct research projects on digital transformation for entrepreneurship.

https://doi.org/10.1142/9789811270178_0002

Chapter 2

Digital Transformation for Entrepreneurship

Susanne Durst

Department of Business Administration,
Reykjavik University, Menntavegi 1,
IS-102 Reykjavík, Iceland

Department of Business Administration,
Tallinn University of Technology, Ehitajate tee 5,
Tallinn 19086, Estonia

susanned@ru.is

Abstract

The aim of this chapter is to set the frame for the book's topic, namely digital transformation for entrepreneurship. In order to do so, the chapter starts broadly and introduces the topics of entrepreneurship and digital transformation, first individually and then combined. The outcome shows that there is a clear need for more systematic research, so this chapter opens the door for the subsequent chapters presented in this book and is intended to further our understanding of the need for digital transformation for entrepreneurship.

2.1. Introduction

This chapter is a general introduction to the topic and provides the background for the book. Therefore, this chapter provides an overview of the relevant terms and explores the meaning and scope of the key concepts that are discussed in this book, namely entrepreneurship and digital transformation.

The book is designed to give you, dear reader, an opportunity to think broadly rather than to provide specific plans to suit certain situations. It considers the theme of digital transformation for entrepreneurship from different angles and perspectives, showing its importance within organizations and society in general.

The chapter is structured as follows. In the following sections, the two main concepts are first presented individually before being brought together to underline the relevance of the topic and thus of the book.

2.2. Entrepreneurship

Entrepreneurship is seen as a key issue in most countries around the world and is receiving increasing attention in many government policies. It is now widely recognized that entrepreneurial firms drive global economic development (Acs & Audretsch, 2010; Premand *et al.*, 2016) and contribute to the renewal process (Kuratko, 2005). However, defining entrepreneurship is not easy because, as with other inflationary terms that are used, it is often unclear what people actually mean when they use the term. Therefore, the following is a brief attempt to define entrepreneurship and briefly discuss the different forms of entrepreneurial activity.

By considering the absence of a generally accepted definition of the term "entrepreneurship," Bridge *et al.* (2003) propose a narrow and a broader definition of entrepreneurship. From a narrow perspective, entrepreneurship is equal to starting a business, being in a business, and growing and developing a business, while the broader definition has a stronger orientation toward the aspect of change, emphasizing the involvement of innovative attributes and behavior. Shane and Venkataraman (2000, p. 218) associate entrepreneurship with "the processes of discovery, evaluation, and exploitation of opportunities." Regarding the exploitation of opportunities, Fueglistaller *et al.* (2004) punctuate that this exploitation is not limited to new businesses but includes, among others, business transfers too. Similarly, Shane and Venkataraman (2000) argue that business opportunities can be sold to other people.

According to Bruyat and Julien (2000, p. 173), entrepreneurship encompasses "a process of change, emergence and creation." This includes the creation of new value (i.e., innovation and/or a new venture) and, at the same time, the change and creation of individuals. The authors further argue that entrepreneurship, in order to be understood, has to focus on studying the dialogue between the individual and new value creation. Mole (2012) stresses that entrepreneurship is more than what an entrepreneur does. It also involves the circumstances that enable an entrepreneur to start and the processes that help some places be more entrepreneurial.

Bruyat and Julien see entrepreneurship primarily in the founding stage. In the period of growth and establishment, leadership often replaces innovative behavior. Moreover, it is reasoned that firms operating in the later stages of business development require different abilities and skills compared to those needed in the foundation stage of a company (Fueglistaller *et al.*, 2004).

The definitions presented above also indicate that there are different modes of entrepreneurship (Cooper & Dunkelberg, 1986). In this chapter, the focus is placed on the two main entrepreneurial options, namely starting a company from scratch or taking over an already existing company.

The study of entrepreneurial activity (including entrepreneurship education) tends to focus on the former (Dilli *et al.*, 2018; Lim *et al.*, 2010; Urbano & Alvarez, 2014). This is not really a good situation, as there is evidence that the survival rate of business start-ups through business successions or takeovers is higher than that of new start-ups (Xi *et al.*, 2020). There is also evidence that more jobs are created by previously established firms than by new ones (Pasanen & Laukkanen, 2006). Furthermore, and more importantly, one cannot overlook the increasing number of small- and medium-sized enterprises (SMEs) waiting to be transferred to new owners, for example, in Europe. In absolute terms, it means that every year, around 450,000 firms and over two million employees are transferred to new owners (European Commission, 2019).

Several authors have underlined the differences between these two modes of entry into entrepreneurship. For instance, Durst and Gueldenberg (2010) stress the importance for a successor to have distinctive leadership skills since changes to the company's existing structure and culture have to be actively pursued. Activities that play no significant role in a new company. Block *et al.* (2013, p. 1100), on the other hand, state that starting a business from scratch can be perceived as "more entrepreneurial, more exciting, more complex, and riskier than taking over an existing business with an already-developed business model and an established customer base."

They argue that both risk-averse individuals and individuals with a greater internal locus of control will develop a preference for business takeovers as a mode of entry, but the authors also point out the influence of "country-level variables," i.e., innovation, regulation, finance, and culture, on the distribution of new venture creations and takeovers in societies. Social and financial capital can also affect the mode of entry (Bastié *et al.*, 2013). The latter has a more significant correlation with takeovers, whereas the former is more often associated with starting from scratch. Parker and Van Praag (2012), in a seminal paper on entrepreneurial entry modes, concluded that "important differences exist between the characteristics of entrepreneurs who opt for different modes of entry" (p. 31). Among the main findings of this study were that greater managerial experience increases the probability of becoming an entrepreneur through a takeover and that there is a positive correlation between higher levels of education and the new venture creation mode. Bastié *et al.* (2013) found that individuals with entrepreneurs around them, for example, in their families or in their immediate social network, are less likely to take over existing businesses than other individuals.

Based on these findings, it is clear that the decision to start a new venture or to take over an already existing company requires not only different skills and knowledge but also different approaches (Durst & Gueldenberg, 2010; Parker & Van Praag, 2012; Cadieux *et al.*, 2014). In the former case, the entrepreneur will need to develop an attractive product and/or service, identify customers who are willing to buy this product, inform them about the availability of the product and its benefits (i.e., informative advertising), start hiring personnel, and develop and implement systems and structures to make possible a smooth running of all business functions. While in the case of a business transfer, the entrepreneur will need the skills and competencies that are required to keep the company running and then develop it further. The way in which the business is transferred matters as well (Bastié *et al.*, 2018), e.g., transfer within the family, to members of the company, or to people coming from outside the company. Business transfers usually involve several changes, such as the voluntary resignation of (key) employees, shifts in strategy and structure, and promotions and demotions (Kesner & Sebora, 1994; Pitcher *et al.*, 2000; Ballinger *et al.*, 2009), which may also lead to company instability. Thus, it can be concluded that, compared to a start-up, a business transfer requires more managerial skills from the entrepreneur.

To further our understanding, one should also turn to the distinction between necessity- and opportunity-based entrepreneurship (Amorós *et al.*, 2019). Necessity-based entrepreneurship covers entrepreneurial activities (more precisely, business creations) by individuals who are faced with a job loss, dissatisfaction with their current positions, or a lack of career opportunities. Thus, these individuals are pushed to start a venture. Opportunity-based entrepreneurship, on the other hand, refers to the situation where individuals start an entrepreneurial activity because of the attractiveness of the business idea and its personal implications. These individuals may seek independence, increased earnings, and opportunities to realize their own business ideas. Existing research suggests that opportunity-based entrepreneurship is often procyclical, while necessity-based entrepreneurship is strongly countercyclical; that is, crises foster necessity-based entrepreneurship. Opportunity-based entrepreneurship is also often associated with more growth-oriented businesses (Aparicio *et al.*, 2016).

Moreover, it is important to mention that entrepreneurship can also take place in established companies. This leads us to the term "corporate entrepreneurship," which can be described as the strategic intent of an established organization to be more proactive, innovative, and risk-taking (Miller, 1983; Kaya, 2006; Hayton *et al.*, 2013), with the aim of discovering, evaluating, and ultimately exploiting entrepreneurial opportunities (Hayton *et al.*, 2013; Amberg & McGaughey, 2019).

The introductory chapter has stressed that the primary target group of this book is decision makers in entrepreneurial firms. By taking a broad perspective of entrepreneurship, our understanding of entrepreneurial firms includes smaller firms that are run by forward-looking individuals or groups of individuals who are continuously interested in developing their companies further to be in a better position to cope with current and upcoming organizational and societal challenges. These individuals recognize that their activities are influenced by the external environment (their formal and informal institutions), but they also know that the strategic decisions made within the organization also offer room for maneuver.

2.3. Digital Transformation

The term digital transformation presents a similar picture as the term entrepreneurship: Many people use it, and it is often unclear what a person actually means by the term. Therefore, we will proceed in a similar way as before and also try to define the term and distinguish it from other terms. Let us deal with the main terms which are often used interchangeably, namely (1) digitization, (2) digitalization, and (3) digital transformation.

The Gartner IT Glossary defines digitization as the process of changing from analog to digital form. There is also research (e.g., Hess *et al.*, 2016; Horváth & Szabó, 2019) that views the automation of processes through information technologies as digitization.

However, developments since the turn of the millennium have led to digital conversions being made possible, for example, by distributed computing or digital cellular networks that are more advanced than digitization and are associated with the term digitalization. This term calls for new ways of communication and collaboration at the workplace and refers to the use of digital technologies and data (digitized and digital data) to create new or additional revenues, improve businesses, and replace or transform business processes. Thus, it encompasses activities that go beyond simple digitization.

Digital transformation has been discussed as the integration of digital technologies into all aspects and operations of organizations, which typically leads to infrastructural changes in how organizations operate, create, and deliver value to their customers (Vial, 2019). These changes can also lead to completely new business models (Bouncken *et al.*, 2021). Therefore, to be prepared for the digital transformation, organizations are required to change in leadership, culture and mindsets, and attitudes toward risks; must adopt new technologies and ways of working; and show a willingness to accept ambiguity and constant change (Kane *et al.*, 2015); thus, radical changes are needed that can question the original existence of the organization.

Recently, there has also been an increase in the discussion of possible negative effects of digital transformation, including the relevance of responsible approaches for the management of digital transformation (O'Halloran & Griffin, 2019) as well as social and ethical issues (Royakkers *et al.*, 2018).

Against the background outlined above, it is not surprising that there is still no generally accepted definition of the term digital transformation (Knudsen, 2020; Schallmo *et al.*, 2019). Table 2.1 provides an overview of some definitions that have been published recently in management and business journals.

The definitions illustrate very well, on the one hand, the possible consequences for the companies, but also what efforts must be made within the companies in order to be able to profit from the positive consequences.

Table 2.1. Definitions of digital transformation.

Author(s)	Definition
Matt *et al.* (2015, p. 339)	Digital transformation strategies take on a different perspective and pursue different goals. Coming from a business-centric perspective, these strategies focus on the transformation of products, processes, and organizational aspects owing to new technologies.
Hess *et al.* (2016)	Digital transformation (also known as digitalization), however, is concerned with the changes that digital technologies can bring about in a company's business model, products, processes and organizational structure.
Hinings *et al.* (2018, p. 53)	Digital Transformation is the combined effects of several digital innovations bringing about novel actors (and actor constellations), structures, practices, values, and beliefs that change, threaten, replace or complement existing rules of the game within organizations, ecosystems, industries or fields.
Vial (2019, p. 121)	Digital transformation is a process that aims to improve an entity by triggering significant changes to its properties through combinations of information, computing, communication, and connectivity technologies.
Warner and Wäger (2019, p. 344)	Digital transformation is an ongoing process of strategic renewal that uses advances in digital technologies to build capabilities that refresh or replace an organization's business model, collaborative approach, and culture.

2.4. Now Let Us Bring the Pieces Together

The different modes of entrepreneurship presented earlier appear interesting to show the possible application and implication of digital transformation. Thus, Table 2.2 was developed with the intention of displaying several application areas for the different modes of entrepreneurship. Considering the primary modes of entrepreneurship, i.e., starting a new company and taking over an existing company, as discussed before, the emphasis is put on these two options. Moreover, considering the focus of this book, the focal point is placed on smaller entrepreneurial firms, even though the options provided could be of interest for larger organizations as well. The examples have been derived based on the author's experience and the themes discussed in this book.

Table 2.2. Digital transformation for different modes of entrepreneurship.

Mode of entrepreneurship	Digital transformation in practice
Start-up	Foundation of an e-business, i.e., the underlying notion of digital transformation is in its DNA from the very beginning.
	Creation of a digital company infrastructure that integrates all business processes and functions. Based on a modular character so that the relevant functions and processes evolve with the company.
	Constant training and further education of the members regarding e-skills and competences.
	Introduction of a knowledge management that has a key function in the company to control current and future knowledge needs.
	Conscious use of data and information for improved decisions on strategic and operational levels.
	Better allocation of financial and nonfinancial resources.
	Development and use of digital twins, i.e., virtual replicas of physical entities and their interactions, to support decision-making, e.g., in the area of supply chains or for smart buildings.
	Active use of dashboards supported by visualizations and simulations to support the firms' risk management and other business functions of critical importance.
	Use of 3D printing to reduce product development time and costs.
Takeover	Gradual transfer of a traditional company or semi-e business into an advanced e-business, i.e., step-by-step adjustment of overall company strategy, organizational structure, mindset, upskilling of employees.
	Analysis of the planned steps regarding the company's products and services, the relationships with the various stakeholders, and thus the business models of the company.
	Development of a new risk culture (as part of the company culture) that is aware of the new risks that digital transformation brings with it and always has a set of countermeasures available and uses them if necessary.
	Constant training and further education of the members regarding e-skills and competencies.
	Update of the company's knowledge management to better control current and future knowledge needs.

(*Continued*)

Table 2.2. (*Continued*)

Mode of entrepreneurship	Digital transformation in practice
	Deliberate introduction of new technologies, such as blockchain or artificial intelligence, for improved and/or new processes and products, consequently increasing opportunities for innovation.
	Introduction of a knowledge management that has a key function in the company to control current and future knowledge needs.
	Conscious use of data and information for improved decisions on strategic and operational levels.
	Better allocation of financial and nonfinancial resources.
	Start using digital twins to support decision-making, e.g., in supply chains or smart buildings, manufacturing or retail.
	Active use of dashboards supported by visualizations and simulations to make better decisions in critical business areas.
	Use of 3D printing to reduce product development time and costs.

2.5. Conclusion

This chapter has provided a short introduction to the key terms of this book, namely entrepreneurship and digital transformation. After that, both terms were integrated with the intention to show how digital transformation can possibly foster entrepreneurship in all its diversity and thus address the main theme of this book. By using the term diversity, this chapter and the following ones aim to make it clear that entrepreneurship is so much more than just starting a company — it can support any kind of business, regardless of age or stage of development, in order to counteract the effects of the current situation and upcoming challenges. The same applies to digital transformation; if approached wisely, it can also support companies in becoming better step by step.

The current book emphasizes the relevance of digital transformation for entrepreneurship in general and provides fresh theoretical and empirical insight into the different aspects of the theme, which ideally prompts decision makers of (smaller) entrepreneurial firms to develop and initiate concrete activities.

To conclude, this book addresses digital transformation for entrepreneurship and hopes that, through the chosen approach, it will contribute to the topic and its relevance.

References

Acs, Z. & Audretsch, D. (2010). Introduction to the 2nd edition of the handbook of entrepreneurship research. In Acs Z., Audretsch D. (eds.) *Handbook of Entrepreneurship Research. International Handbook Series on Entrepreneurship*, Vol. 5. Springer, New York.

Amberg, J. J. & McGaughey, S. L. (2019). Strategic human resource management and inertia in the corporate entrepreneurship of a multinational enterprise. *The International Journal of Human Resource Management* 30(5), 759–793.

Amorós, J. E., Ciravegna, L., Mandakovic, V., & Stenholm, P. (2019). Necessity or opportunity? The effects of state fragility and economic development on entrepreneurial efforts. *Entrepreneurship Theory and Practice* 43(4), 725–750. Doi: 10.1177/1042258717736857.

Aparicio, S., Urbano, D., & Audretsch, D. (2015). Institutional factors, opportunity entrepreneurship and economic growth: Panel data evidence. *Technological Forecasting and Social Change* 102, 45–61. Doi: 10.1016/j.techfore.2015.04.006.

Ballinger, G. A., Schoorman, F. D., & Lehman, D. W. (2009). Will you trust your new boss? The role of affective reactions to leadership succession. *The Leadership Quarterly* 20, 219–232.

Bastié, F., Cieply, S., & Cussy, P. (2018). Does mode of transfer matter for business performance? Transfers to employees versus transfers to outsiders. *Small Business Economics* 50(1), 77–89.

Bastié, F., Cieply, S., & Cussy, P. (2013). The entrepreneur's mode of entry: The effect of social and financial capital. *Small Business Economics* 40(4), 865–877.

Block, J., Thurik, R. Van Der Zwan, P., & Walter, S. (2013). Business takeover or new venture? Individual and environmental determinants from a cross-country study. *Entrepreneurship Theory and Practice* 37(5), 1099–1121.

Bouncken, R. B., Kraus, S., & Roig-Tierno, N. (2021). Knowledge- and innovation-based business models for future growth: Digitalized business models and portfolio considerations. *Review of Managerial Science* 15(1), 1–14. Doi: 10.1007/s11846-019-00366-z.

Bridge, S., O'Neill, K., & Cromie, S. (2003). *Understanding Enterprise, Entrepreneurship and Small Business*. 2nd ed. Palgrave Macmillan, Basingstoke, New York.

Bruyat, C. & Julien, P.-A. (2000). Defining the field of research in entrepreneurship. *Journal of Business Venturing* 16, 165–180.

Cadieux, L., Gratton, P., & St-Jean, É. (2014). La carrière repreneuriale: Contexte et défis. *Revue de l'entrepreneuriat* 13(1), 35–50.

Cooper, A. C. & Dunkelberg, W. C. (1986). Entrepreneurship and paths to business ownership. *Strategic Management Journal* 7, 53–68.

Dilli, S., Elert, N., & Herrmann, A. M. (2018). Varieties of entrepreneurship: Exploring the institutional foundations of different entrepreneurship types through "Varieties-of-Capitalism" arguments. *Small Business Economics* 51, 293–320.

Durst, S. & Gueldenberg, S. (2010). What makes SMEs attractive to external successors? *VINE* 40(2), 108–135.

European Commission (2019). Transfer of businesses. https://single-market-economy.ec.europa.eu/smes/supporting-entrepreneurship/transfer-businesses_en.

Fueglistaller, U., Müller, C., & Volery, T. (2004). *Entrepreneurship*. Wiesbaden, Gabler.

Hayton, J. C., Hornsby, J. S., & Bloodgood, J. (2013). Part II: The contribution of HRM to corporate entrepreneurship: A review and agenda for future research. *Management* 16(4), 357–432.

Hess, T., Benlian, A., Matt, C., & Wiesböck, F. (2016). Options for formulating a digital transformation strategy. *MIS Quarterly Executive* 15(2), 123–139.

Hinings, B., Gegenhuber, T., & Greenwood, R. (2018). Digital innovation and transformation: An institutional perspective. *Information and Organization* 28(1), 52–61.

Horváth, D. & Szabó, R. Z. (2019). Driving forces and barriers of Industry 4.0: Do multinational and small and medium-sized companies have equal opportunities? *Technological Forecasting and Social Change* 146, 119–132. Doi: 10.1016/j.techfore.2019.05.021.

Kane, G. C., Palmer, D., Phillips, A. N., Kiron, D., & Buckley, N. (2015). Strategy, not technology, drives digital transformation. *MIT Sloan Management Review* 14, 1–25.

Kaya, N. (2006). The impact of human resource management practices and corporate entrepreneurship on firm performance: Evidence from Turkish firms. *The International Journal of Human Resource Management* 17(12), 2074–2090.

Kesner, I. F. & Sebora, T. C. (1994). Executive succession: Past, present, & future. *Journal of Management* 20, 327–372.

Knudsen, D.-R. (2020). Elusive boundaries, power relations, and knowledge production: A systematic review of the literature on digitalization in accounting. *International Journal of Accounting Information Systems* 36, 100441.

Kuratko, D. F. (2005). The emergence of entrepreneurship education: Development, trends, and challenges. *Entrepreneurship Theory and Practice* 29(5), 577–598.

Lim, D. S. K., Morse, E. A., Mitchell, R. K., & Seawright, K. K. (2010). Institutional environment and entrepreneurial cognitions: A comparative business systems perspective. *Entrepreneurship: Theory and Practice* 34(3), 491–516.

Matt, C., Hess, T., & Benlian, A. (2015). Digital transformation strategies. *Business & Information Systems Engineering* 57(5), 339–343.

Miller, D. (1983). The correlates of entrepreneurship in three types of firms. *Management Science* 29(7), 770–791.

Mole, K. (2012). *Perspectives in Entrepreneurship*. In Mole, K. and Ram, M. (eds.), Chapter 1 "Introduction" Palgrave Macmillan, Basingstoke, pp. 1–10.

O'Halloran, D. & Griffin, W. (2019). Our Shared Digital Future: Responsible Digital Transformation. World Economic Forum.

Parker, S. C. & Van Praag, C. M. (2012). The entrepreneur's mode of entry: Business takeover or new venture start? *Journal of Business Venturing* 21(1), 31–46.

Pasanen, M. & Laukkanen, T. (2006). Team-managed growing SMEs: A distinct species? *Management Research News* 29(11), 684–700.

Pitcher, P., Chreim, S., & Kisfalvi, V. (2000). CEO succession research: Methodological bridges over troubled waters. *Strategic Management Journal* 21, 625–648.

Premand, P., Brodmann, S., Almeida, R., Grun, R., & Barouni, M. (2016). Entrepreneurship education and entry into self-employment among university graduates. *World Development* 77, 311–327.

Royakkers, L., Timmer, J., Kool, L., & van Est, R. (2018). Societal and ethical issues of digitization. *Ethics and Information Technology* 20(2), 127–142.

Schallmo, D., Williams, C. A., & Boardman, L. (2017). Digital transformation of business models — Best practice, enablers, and roadmap. *International Journal of Innovation Management* 21(8), 1–17.

Shane, S. & Venkataraman, S. (2000). The promise of entrepreneurship as a field of research. *Academy of Management Review* 25(1), 217–226.

Urbano, D. & Alvarez, C. (2014). Institutional dimensions and entrepreneurial activity: An international study. *Small Business Economics* 42(4), 703–716.

Vial, G. (2019). Understanding digital transformation: A review and a research agenda. *Journal of Strategic Information Systems* 28(2), 118–144. Doi: 10.1016/j.jsis.2019.01.003.

Warner, K. S. & Wäger, M. (2019). Building dynamic capabilities for digital transformation: An ongoing process of strategic renewal. *Long Range Planning* 52(3), 326–349.

Xi, G., Block, J., Lasch, F., Robert, F., & Thurik, R. (2020). The survival of business takeovers and new venture start-ups. *Industrial and Corporate Change* 29(3), 797–826. Doi: 10.1093/icc/dtz076.

https://doi.org/10.1142/9789811270178_0003

Chapter 3

Ethical Challenges in Digital Transformation for Entrepreneurship

Aive Pevkur

Tallinn University of Technology,
Department of Business Administration,
Ehitajate tee 3, Tallinn, Estonia

aive.pevkur@taltech.ee

Abstract

Digital transformation (DT), as a phenomenon, has been studied for around a decade. Its impact on the values, principles, and ethics of organizations has been studied even less. The ethics of entrepreneurial activity in the context of DT has been examined in academic literature with little attention. At the same time, societal awareness of risks and new challenges due to the digitalization of our everyday lives and business activities is rising. Entrepreneurs developing new technologies are at the forefront of DT. This chapter provides an overview of the issues of entrepreneurship and ethics, DT and ethics, and the challenges and outcomes when entrepreneurship meets the challenges of DT and faces ethical questions that impact not only the entrepreneurial activity but the society at large. Considering the basic ethical principles seems to be the next challenge in the DT ethics debates.

3.1. Introduction

Digital transformation (DT) as an academic field of study does not have a very long history. The systematic exploration of ethical issues in DT requires at least some extent of practical and theoretical literature before making any normative or general statements in the field. While a couple of years ago, ethics was mentioned in the DT literature as one of the aspects of challenges (Vial, 2021; Saarikko *et al.*, 2020), today we can observe that DT ethics has become a separate study field (Van Driel, 2019; Rosha, 2021; Saurabh *et al.*, 2022). It is worthy of note that, despite the value-laden essence of the DT, ethics has not been established as an inevitable part of DT studies (Rodriguez-Lluesma *et al.*, 2021; Skrynnyk, 2021). In Skrynnyk's (2021) study, she provides the results of an analysis of the most used keywords in the literature in the field of social and organizational acceptance of DT. Her study reveals that the keywords with the highest weightings indicating human behavior values and attitudes were "organizational culture(s)," "human," "male," and "female," but not ethics.

DT is often interpreted with a positive connotation, marking the phenomenon as something good and value-adding to an enterprise. For a meaningful discussion about DT, entrepreneurship, and ethics, practitioners and researchers need to differentiate the scale they are using to assess the ethical challenges. There are many prisms through which ethics can be looked at. This chapter introduces the main approaches to how ethical issues are addressed in conjunction with business, entrepreneurship, and technology; analyzes the pros and cons of those approaches; and makes preliminary proposals on how to implement ethical considerations in DT. In this chapter, the following questions will be discussed: First, who should be addressed while discussing the issues of entrepreneurial ethics? Second, how do organizational, business, and technological ethics issues differ from entrepreneurial ethics questions? And third, what should be the relevant ethical questions for entrepreneurs facing DT? The chapter will address these questions and, based on the answers, make some proposals for future academic studies and the actions of entrepreneurs.

3.2. Business, Entrepreneurship, and Ethics

Every choice and action can be assessed from an ethical point of view whether we can say something about the goodness or badness of that choice or action. Ethics is about the assessment of human behavior. More than a hundred years ago, Emile Durkheim gave lectures concerning professional ethics and civic morals (Durkheim, 2019). Among others, he described the main features of morality. For Durkheim, ethics is one of the most important determinants for dividing societies into different fields of activity. While individual ethics prescribes and regulates the personal sphere, civic morals regulate our relationship with the state. But the plurality of morals comes from professional ethics: "…there are many forms of morals as there are different callings, and since, in theory, each individual carries on only one calling, the result is that these different forms of morals apply to entirely different groups of individuals" (Durkheim, 2019, p. 5).

Durkheim sees professional ethics as one of the fundamental conditions of morality. Durkheim's concern was that the activity of doing business was left without solid ethics systems. "Nevertheless — and this is the comment that matters most — there is a whole category of functions that do not satisfy this condition [group ethics and control] in any way: these are the economic functions, both industry and trade" (Durkheim, 2019, p. 9).

Today, the commonly accepted approach is that business ethics covers all ethical aspects of doing business. In the literature, there is no tradition to separate ethics questions in business and entrepreneurship based on who is responsible for the ethical choices or the type of business where ethical issues emerge. That has caused the usage of business ethics in a broad sense. At the same time, looking at business activities, there are two distinctive roles. There are businessmen, who transact business and are mainly understood as business executives. And there are entrepreneurs, who organize, manage, and assume the risks of a business or an enterprise. Solymossy and Masters (2002) claim that entrepreneurs differ from other individuals in the moral issues they face and in their moral judgments and behaviors concerning those issues. By referring to the previous studies, they emphasize that entrepreneurs differ from others involved in business in that the entrepreneur operates with self-interest, has uncertainty tolerance, and has the foresight and willingness to assume and tolerate risk. The definitive values of entrepreneurs are opportunism and orientation toward achievement, autonomy, field independence, and a locus of control (Solymossy & Masters, 2002).

Despite the fact that businessmen and entrepreneurs are players in the field of business, they have distinctive functions and, therefore, different duties and responsibilities and different ethics. As the exchange is fundamental to business, "business ethics can thus be understood as the study of the ethical dimensions of the exchange of goods and services, and of the entities that offer goods and services for exchange. This includes related activities such as the production, distribution, marketing, sale, and consumption of goods and services" (Moriarty, 2021, p. 1). That definition allows for the inclusion of different aspects under the umbrella of business ethics discussions. At the same time, this approach is too broad to demonstrate the opportunities and limitations of entrepreneurial activity, which is about exploring new horizons, taking risks, and failing and learning from that.

Entrepreneurial ethics is about the value choices entrepreneurs make in establishing and developing their businesses. Moriarty provides a definition of business ethics as a study of professional practices and the effectiveness of the codes of conduct designed to guide the actions of people engaged in business activity (Moriarty, 2021). By analogy, entrepreneurial ethics could be defined as the study of professional practices and ethical norms designed to guide the actions of people engaged in entrepreneurial activity. The challenge is that entrepreneurship as a separate activity with its tasks and challenges has not gathered much attention from practical and professional ethicists. Only a few studies consider entrepreneurship as a separate field of activity with its ethical norms (Solymossy & Masters, 2002), while most studies see entrepreneurial activity through the lens of business ethics (Bucar *et al.*, 2003; De George, 1999; Robinson *et al.*, 2007; Tlaiss, 2015).

Before the start-up era arrived, entrepreneurs were seen mainly as small-business owners (Solymossy & Masters, 2002). The development of new technologies allowed the extensive growth of many small enterprises into international companies which influence people's everyday lives. The importance of ethics in entrepreneurship must accompany that growth.

Durkheim (2019) saw entrepreneurship as a risk to societal morality because of the lack of moral norms in entrepreneurs and the lack of codes of ethics. Today, the situation concerning codes of ethics for entrepreneurs has not changed much. Entrepreneurship, as a field of freedom of activities in a liberal market, might not need codes of ethics, but society needs certain boundaries to protect itself from harm and to encourage entrepreneurs to do good. This concern has gained new dimensions by introducing new digital technologies and by expecting DT in business activities.

Considering the emphasis that is being put on entrepreneurship and entrepreneurial activity in all countries and the new challenges due to technology, the environment, and society, we should talk about entrepreneurial ethics in depth.

3.3. Business Paradigms and Ethics

When thinking about business, two different paradigms can be pointed out: the old, industrial economies and the new, advanced, post-industrial, or digital economies. The industrial economy concerns those activities combining factors of production (facilities, supplies, work, and knowledge) to produce material goods intended for the market, while in the post-industrial economy, the relative importance of manufacturing is reducing and that of services, information, and research is growing. Such economies are often marked by a declining manufacturing sector, resulting in deindustrialization. New economies are more in line with an entrepreneurial mindset.

The digital economy belongs to the business sphere but seems to operate on different principles, which seem to resemble more professional activities. For example, old industries focus on organizations, whereas new industries focus rather on pursuing some humanistic values, such as interconnectivity (telecommunication), mobility (mobility services), or freedom (money transfer, work bites, gig economy). That causes the difference in ethical problems and challenges. Despite studies on the ethical challenges of the digital economy trying to use a traditional matrix of business ethics (Rosha, 2021), the traditional business ethics frame has not been very successful in explaining and resolving certain issues.

Individual societies, as well as international organizations, have proposed aspirational goals to pursue, which should positively benefit life on the planet. The United Nations' Sustainable Development Goals (SDGs) are probably the best known. Business ethics is focusing on challenges from the business organization perspective and offering scenarios on how to be "a good company" by following the principles of corporate social responsibility (CSR), being sustainable, and following the SDGs. As a new approach to tackle the expanding trend of digitalization, organizations are implementing the principles of corporate digital responsibility (CDR) (Weber-Lewerenz, 2021). All these principles prescribe companies to be responsible. In academic writings and practical studies, approaches to how to be socially responsible toward employees, stakeholders, the environment, and society are developed, but knowledge about how to be digitally responsible when facing Big Data, the Internet of Things (IoT), artificial intelligence (AI), data privacy, and data protection and how to manage data is still in the emerging phase. Following the principles of CSR that influence the company and community, the principles of CDR have wider, often global, outcomes, as the examples of Amazon and Meta have demonstrated.

3.4. Digital Domains and Ethics

DT cannot emerge without previous changes in digitization and digitalization. As the words to describe the phenomenon are often used interchangeably, Saarikko and his colleagues see the necessity of distinguishing different phenomena in digital domains to understand the main challenges. The same problem applies to discussions about ethical challenges in DT. It is important to note that DT, as a defined phenomenon, has a history beginning in 2011, when the MIT Center for Digital Business coined the term "digital transformation." The history of academic studies is shorter, and the study of the ethical issues of DT as a specific field marks the first steps in establishing it as a topic for scientific studies.

Digitization is defined as a "technical process of converting analogue signals to digital signals" (Saarikko *et al.*, 2020, p. 828). As a purely technical process, it is difficult to see the ethical challenges involved.

Digitalization is "the sociotechnical process of leveraging digitized products or systems to develop new organizational procedures, business models, or commercial offerings" (*ibid*, p. 828), and as this domain concerns human behavior and relations, it can be assessed through ethical lenses and via the ethical categories of good and bad.

DT, according to Saarikko and his colleagues, is "the sociocultural process of adapting firms to the new organizational forms and skill sets needed to remain viable and relevant in a digital landscape" (p. 829). The relations between the three phenomena are illustrated in Figure 3.1.

DT is often seen as the application of digital technologies to fundamentally impact all aspects of business and society to replace the existing culture within the company with a new one (Von Leipzig *et al.*, 2017; Saarikko *et al.*, 2020). The important term here is "culture," as DT embeds the whole organization and its practices, habits, norms, values, and ethics.

"Transformation" means that the organization is either going through or has gone through fundamental changes that have brought fundamentally different challenges to the organization, including principally different ethical challenges.

Ethical questions come into play as soon as human beings interact with technology, make decisions about what to do, and decide between good and bad. Technology itself does not have value. Technology can be assessed from a value point of view it provides to humans. Looking at the digital domains, Figure 3.1 can be supplemented with aspects of ethical considerations, presented in Figure 3.2.

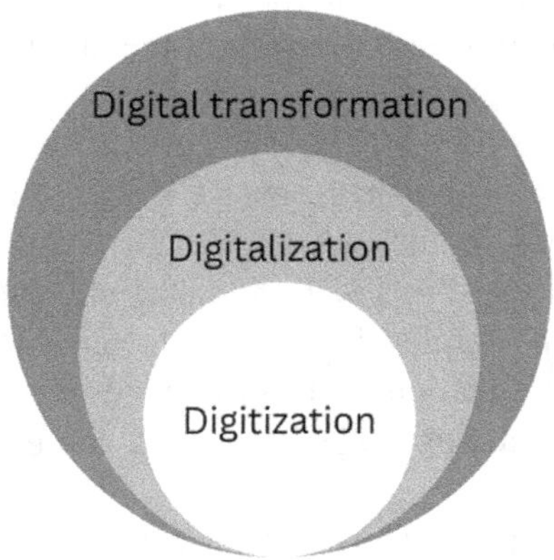

Fig. 3.1. Digital domains based on Saarikko *et al.* (2020).

Fig. 3.2. Digital domains and ethical issues (author's additions to Saarikko *et al.*, 2020).

In general, changes in technology bring about two types of ethical challenges for enterprises. The first one concerns the nature of technology, which is about the digitization of products or systems. The second one concerns changed business models, which require changes toward traditional organizational settlements and human resource processes and changes in the ethical dilemmas entrepreneurs have in developing their enterprises. Both need a separate look.

3.5. Technology and Ethics

Technology compounds its ethical challenges. The development of tools and machinery used in business determines the main ethical challenges of that time and field of activity. All the big changes in the industry (Industrial Revolutions 1.0–4.0) brought about fundamental changes in manufacturing and doing business, as well as in attitudes toward work labor and ethical issues. While Industry 3.0 gave flight to the ideology of CSR, both being born in the 1970s, Industry 4.0 pushed enterprises to identify six design principles for its implementation: interoperability, virtualization, decentralization, real-time capability, service orientation, and modularity (Hermann *et al.*, 2015), which can be related to the ideas of CDR.

Technologies used in the Third Industrial Revolution kept the focus on ethical challenges at the organizational level, and in providing solutions, the central player was the organization and its management. Organizations had to be economically, legally, ethically, and philanthropically responsible (A. Carroll, 2016; A. B. Carroll, 1991). As A. Carroll wrote, "In general, CSR has typically been understood as policies and practices that business people employ to be sure that society, or stakeholders, other than business owners, are considered and protected in their strategies and operations" (A. Carroll, 2016, p. 2). A company's interests, tasks, and operations were its first priority, and other considerations had to be in line with the company's aims. Ethics was seen as a part of organizational responsibilities. Technology, the machinery used before the Fourth Industrial Revolution, was never subject to ethical considerations.

The situation has changed in Industry 4.0, which is described as a union between physical assets and advanced digital technologies, such as the IoT, AI, robots, drones, autonomous vehicles, 3D printing, and cloud computing. Technology itself, for example, AI (Saurabh *et al.*, 2022), IoT

(Saarikko *et al.*, 2020), or digital ethics in all digital domains (Ashok *et al.*, 2022) started to drive ethics discussions. Ethics is no longer just a part of demands for organizational responsibilities but is seen as a separate category in analyzing and assessing changes in organizations going through DT (Vial, 2021).

The European Commission came out with the idea of Industry 5.0, which "provides a vision of an industry that aims beyond efficiency and productivity as the sole goals and reinforces the role and the contribution of industry to society. It places the wellbeing of the worker at the centre of the production process and uses new technologies to provide prosperity beyond jobs and growth while respecting the production limits of the planet" (European Commission, 2021).

In that sense, understanding DT as a sociocultural process rather than a technical feat (Saarikko *et al.*, 2020) coheres with the European Commission's approach where the human is placed at the center. In that sense, ethics gathers more importance than in the previous industrial revolutions, where technology was the promoter and definitive factor of changes, but never a subject of ethical considerations.

In the context of DT, we can observe a controversy between two different tendencies: beneficial innovation and harmful disruption (Saarikko *et al.*, 2020; Vial, 2021). The latter concerns researchers and makes them worry about ethical challenges (*ibid*). Saarikko and his colleagues state that DT "causes enterprises to rethink the very foundation of who and what they are" (Saarikko *et al.*, 2020, p. 826). Implicitly, that includes the need to reconsider the foundations of ethics in organizations. From being socially responsible, organizations need to become digitally conscious, "that is, by developing an understanding of the opportunities, implications, and limitations in moving from a generic technological paradigm to a specific application, and by understanding how they are contingent upon concurrent social, cultural, and judicial systems – firms can become better equipped to take on new and transformative technologies" (Saarikko *et al.*, 2020, p. 827).

Technology, previously a means or tool for enterprises, now influences the whole culture of organizations. It is not just a matter of access to technology; it is about attitudes toward digitalization and DT, which is often a complex phenomenon demanding solutions beyond the capacities of one individual organization. Ethics challenges accompanied by DT are even more complex to handle with accustomed approaches to CSR. Researchers admit the overall lack of common standards, and ethical risks from the development of digital technologies, such as privacy, data ownership, misuse of data, recording personal data, data-driven decisions, algorithmic discrimination, and digital surveillance (Rosha, 2021; Saarikko *et al.*, 2020), are still waiting for eligible and adequate solutions.

3.6. DT, Entrepreneurship, and Ethics

The development of technologies and especially the success of digital technologies have a great impact on entrepreneurship. While at the beginning of this century, in the studies of entrepreneurship, ethical entrepreneurs were seen mainly as small-business owners (Solymossy & Masters, 2002), digital technologies have opened new perspectives to entrepreneurs due to low barriers to entry and even small entrepreneur who are more agile and have few restrictions to transforming innovative ideas to viable market offerings (Saarikko *et al.*, 2020). That explains the importance of technological-ethical considerations in discussing entrepreneurship ethics in DT.

Comparing new digital enterprises with old businesses, we can observe the difference in the impact of individual preferences and choices of entrepreneurs on the business. The business ethics framework widely used as a model (Rosha, 2021; Saurabh *et al.*, 2022) seems unsatisfactory, as researchers propose additional aspects to the concept. Business ethics focuses on business but misses the new ethical challenges that emerged from new technologies, such as risks to privacy, autonomy, and security, as well as other undesirable outcomes. DT demands a fundamental redesign of the whole organizational culture (Saarikko *et al.*, 2020; Skrynnyk, 2021; Vial, 2021), implicitly expecting to (re)consider the fundamental values and principles. Doing business in the digital era is not only about exchanging goods and services but also about impacting interhuman relations and societal settlements.

3.7. A Quest for New Ethics for Entrepreneurs in the Digital Era

The development of digital technologies has opened new frontiers for all types of businesses. As small and medium enterprises are more agile to meet new challenges, they often see an opportunity in DT. New technologies are accompanied by new kinds of ethical challenges for organizations going through the process of DT. The main issues are about the missing broader and commonly accepted framework to assess ethical risks and standards to handle the problems. Digital consciousness and CDR are concepts that need to be filled with thicker content. The impact of DT goes beyond an individual organization, extending to the whole society and even further. Ashok and his colleagues point to 14 digital ethics themes and implications, namely intelligibility, accountability, fairness, promoting prosperity, solidarity, and moral sensitivity, empathy, appreciation for human rights, autonomy, dignity and well-being, sustainability, privacy, security, regulatory impact, financial and economic impact, and individual and societal impact (Ashok *et al.*, 2022). Most of the listed ethical implications cannot be grasped by traditional means of corporate responsibilities. Attempts to turn to classical normative ethical theories, such as consequentialist or deontological theories (Saurabh *et al.*, 2022; Vial, 2021), have limits as they overlook the role of new technologies. Laws that provide a framework for accustomed situations for business activities do not work anymore, as, since digitalization, technology is always ahead of the traditional systems of law-making (Van Driel, 2019). Every individual entrepreneur needs to be more conscious of ethical risks than ever before. Benefits need to be balanced with ethical considerations. The theories of common morality and principlism could be revitalized to help draft a new framework.

Beauchamp defines common morality as "the set of norms shared by all persons committed to the objectives of morality. The objectives of morality, I will argue, are those of promoting human flourishing by counteracting conditions that cause the quality of people's lives to worsen" (Beauchamp, 2003, p. 260).

Beauchamp and Childress (2001) propose four principles, also called principlism, as the basis of moral considerations. These principles are autonomy, non-maleficence, beneficence, and justice. Considering the ethical risks of digitalization (Ashok *et al.*, 2022), entrepreneurs could take the following principles as a starting point for ethical decision-making:

- Be sensitive to moral considerations.
- Avoid doing harm.
- Promote human flourishing.
- Respect the autonomy of every individual.
- Strive for just decisions.

The proposed principles are too general and need to be elaborated upon for them to claim to be a sufficient basis of ethics for entrepreneurs in DT. Nevertheless, considering ethical risks and challenges, a “new principlism” seems to be a promising start for future studies.

3.8. Conclusions

Enterprises face a complexity of challenges due to the globalization of the business environment, and DT adds a dimension to it. Discussions over values and ethics are often seen as unnecessary and resource-consuming activities that do not support the core business. At the same time, having a strong value basis and a vision of how the company wants to impact society helps to create a sustainable business model, to choose appropriate means for implementing that, and to earn customers’ trust and loyalty.

New digital technologies are a strong driving force for many companies. DT is an opportunity, especially for new companies, to expand their businesses. In that situation, overlooking basic human rights, autonomy, privacy, and dignity might cause the loss of customers’ trust. At the same time, raising awareness among customers not only about their rights but also about their expectations of social and environmental sustainability and promoting the common good by companies enforce thinking about values and ethics. “Customers today no longer only expect companies to respond to their expressed demands, but implicitly expect companies to anticipate and address their future needs before they themselves have realised them” (Von Leipzig *et al.*, 2017, p. 518).

Defining a business via technology might disrupt the business when the technology changes. Being aware of the different approaches to values and ethics provided in this chapter in conjunction with business, entrepreneurship, and technology and knowing the pros and cons of those approaches empowers enterprises to successfully deal with the complexity of contemporary challenges. Those companies that have made value and ethical considerations an inevitable part of their core business are more resilient to changes in the external environment and have a competitive advantage in the local market and globally. Some good examples of that can be found in this book.

References

Ashok, M., Madan, R., Joha, A., & Sivarajah, U. (2022). Ethical framework for Artificial Intelligence and Digital technologies. *International Journal of Information Management* 62, 102433. Doi: 10.1016/j.ijinfomgt.2021.102433.

Beauchamp, T. L. & Childress, J. F. (2001). *Principles of Biomedical Ethics*. 5th ed. Oxford University Press, Oxford.

Beauchamp, T. L. (2003). A defense of the common morality. *Kennedy Institute of Ethics Journal* 13(3), 259–274.

Bucar, B., Glas, M., & Hisrich, R. (2003). Ethics and entrepreneurs — An international comparative study. *Journal of Business Venturing* 18(2), 261–281. Doi: 10.1016/S0883-9026(01)00083-0.

Carroll, A. (2016). Carroll's pyramid of CSR: Taking another look. *International Journal of Corporate Social Responsibility* 1, 3. Doi: 10.1186/s40991-016-0004-6.

Carroll, A. B. (1991). The pyramid of corporate social responsibility: Toward the moral management of organizational stakeholders. *Business Horizon* 34(4), 39–48. Doi: 10.1016/0007-6813(91)90005-G.

De George, R. (1999). Entrepreneurs, multinationals, and business ethics. In G. Enderle (ed.), *International Business Ethics: Challenges and Approaches.* pp. 271–280. WOS:000168874100021.

Durkheim, E. (2019). *Professional Ethics and Civic Morals*. Routledge, Paper book.

European Commission, Directorate-General for Research and Innovation, Industry 5.0: Human-centric, sustainable and resilient, Publications Office, 2021, https://data.europa.eu/doi/10.2777/073781.

Hermann, M., Pentek, T., & Otto, B. (2015). Design principles for Industrie 4.0 scenarios: A literature review. Working paper No. 1, pp. 1–16. Doi: 10.13140/RG.2.2.29269.22248.

Moriarty, Jeffrey, "Business Ethics", The Stanford Encyclopedia of Philosophy (Fall 2021 Edition), Edward N. Zalta (ed.). https://plato.stanford.edu/archives/fall2021/entries/ethics-business/.

Robinson, D., Davidsson, P., van der Mescht, H., & Court, P. (2007). How entrepreneurs deal with ethical challenges — An application of the business ethics synergy star technique. *Journal of Business Ethics* 71(4), 411–423. Doi: 10.1007/s10551-006-9148-8.

Rodriguez-Lluesma, C., Garcia-Ruiz, P., & Pinto-Garay, J. (2021). The digital transformation of work: A relational view. *Business Ethics, The Environment & Responsibility* 30(1), 157–167. Doi: 10.1111/beer.12323.

Rosha, A. (2021). Exploring the role of ethical issues in the context of digital transformation. *Trends Economics and Management* 15, 23–33. Doi: 10.13164/trends.2021.38.23.

Saarikko, T., Westergren, W., & Blomquist, T. (2020). Digital transformation: Five recommendations for the digitally conscious firm. *Business Horizons* 63(6), 825–839. Doi: 10.1016/j.bushor.2020.07.005.

Saurabh, K., Arora, R., Rani, N., Mishra, D., & Ramkumar, M. (2022). AI led ethical digital transformation: Framework, research and managerial implications. *Journal of Information Communication & Ethics in Society* 20(2), 229–256. Doi: 10.1108/JICES-02-2021-0020.

Skrynnyk, O. (2021). Literature review on social and organizational acceptance of digital transformation. *Business Ethics and Leadership* 5, 110–117. Doi: 10.21272/bel.5(4).110-117.2021.

Solymossy, E. & Masters, J. (2002). Ethics through an entrepreneurial lens: Theory and observation. *Journal of Business Ethics* 38(3), 227–241. Doi: 10.1023/A:1015832123366.

Tlaiss, H. (2015). How Islamic business ethics impact women entrepreneurs: Insights from four Arab Middle Eastern countries. *Journal of Business Ethics* 129(4), 859–877. Doi: 10.1007/s10551-014-2138-3.

Van Driel, P. (2019). Ethics and digital transformation: The role of democratic institutions. Proceedings of the 15th European Conference on Management, Leadership and Governance, ECMLG, pp. 509–511. Doi: 10.34190/MLG.19.046.

Vial, G. (2021). Understanding digital transformation: A review and a research agenda. In Managing Digital Transformation: Understanding the Strategic Process, pp. 13–66.

Von Leipzig, T., Gamp, M., Manz, D., Schöttle, K., Ohlhausen, P., Oosthuizen, G., Palm, D., & von Leipzig, K (2017). Initializing customer-orientated digital transformation in enterprises. *Procedia Manufacturing* 8, 517–524.

Weber-Lewerenz, B. (2021). Corporate digital responsibility (CDR) in construction engineering-ethical guidelines for the application of digital transformation and Artificial Intelligence (AI) in user practice. *SN Applied Sciences* 3(10), 1–25. Doi: 10.1007/s42452-021-04776-1.

https://doi.org/10.1142/9789811270178_0004

Chapter 4

The Role of Knowledge Management in the Preparedness of Small- and Medium-Sized Enterprises for Digital Transformation

Lidia Davies

Tallinn University of Technology, Department of Business Administration, Akadeemia tee 3, Tallinn 19068, Estonia

lidia.davies@taltech.ee

Abstract

The recent global pandemic has forced companies to move operations online, and rapidly changing market conditions have increased the business need for digital transformation. This chapter evaluates the general characteristics of small- and medium-sized enterprises and considers the common barriers and supporting factors these organizations face during a digital transformation. To address those challenges, knowledge management is proposed as a useful framework. A set of practical recommendations follows that SMEs might employ as they plan digital transformation.

4.1. Introduction

Companies, whatever their size, scope, or industry, often strive to use available technological means to obtain a more competitive position in the marketplace. According to Trenkle (2019), small- and medium-sized enterprises (SMEs) have no choice but to digitally transform their businesses in order to remain competitive. Digital transformation (DT) affords an opportunity to create new business processes or remodel current business processes through the use of digital technology to meet market requirements. In the ideal case, as a result of these transformational processes, SMEs could optimize operations, achieve economies of scale, increase the potential for innovation, obtain access to business intelligence and process automation, and widen (and internationalize) their customer base (Kergroach, 2020; OECD, 2021).

Recent global public health regulations have exponentially accelerated the transition to digital technologies for many companies and pushed SMEs to digitize their main products and/or services and find new ways to reach customers (Savastano *et al.*, 2022). This chapter considers the definition of DT to be a companywide change "at all levels and all functions" (Priyono *et al.*, 2020) that aims to achieve new (and more competitive ways) of doing business. More precisely, it implies strategy-driven (Vial, 2019) fundamental changes in existing organizational structures, company culture, business processes, routines, and capabilities (Verhoef *et al.*, 2021) through the use of digital technologies.

DT can be challenging for corporations with established management practices and access to capital (Kindermann *et al.*, 2020; Volberda *et al.*, 2021). For SMEs, that challenge is much greater because they often lack a comprehensive view of commercial goals, the appropriate skills, and a comprehensive understanding and/or availability of resources at their disposal (Horváth & Szabó, 2019; Thrassou *et al.*, 2020). Moreover, decision-making power is most often concentrated in the hands of owner-managers (Rodrigues *et al.*, 2021). These entrepreneurs perform multiple functions within their companies and are often overloaded with the pressing exigencies of daily operations (Kindström *et al.*, 2022), without the time to plan long-term business changes (Maříková *et al.*, 2022). Other main barriers to a successful DT among SMEs include significant financial constraints (Klein & Todesco, 2021; Bowman, 2019), limited (Durst & Henschel, 2021) or insufficiently used internal resources, and difficulties to develop and follow any systematic transformational strategy (Pierenkemper & Gausemeier, 2021).

On the other hand, SMEs have a strong potential to conduct the digital transformational process efficiently for several reasons, including their flat organizational structure, ability to adapt, and propensity for rapid and independent decision-making (Clauss *et al.*, 2022; Eggers, 2020). Desouza and Awazu (2006), the knowledge and experience of the owner and the employees are more significant for success than capital.

Therefore the field of knowledge management (KM) can offer a promising framework to address the challenges of DT in SMEs because it allows companies to outline organizational knowledge and develop a concise transformational strategy. According to McInerney and Koenig (2011), KM is a multidisciplinary approach expounded within the past 30 years that studies the attempts to improve useful knowledge among company constituents to improve operations performance in an increasingly dynamic business environment.

The aim of this chapter is to explain how systematic KM can provide helpful guidance and support DT for SMEs, ultimately enabling improved business performance. In terms of chapter structure, the topic of DT for SMEs is introduced first. Next, the parameters of SMEs as a business segment are considered, leading to a consideration of success factors for SMEs and the role of KM in enhancing the process of DT for SMEs. The chapter concludes with practical recommendations for owners or managers of SMEs to develop strategies for more effective DT.

4.2. DT in SMEs: The Business Need and the Potential

The increasing use of digital tools for business engagement with suppliers and customers, as well as optimizing intracompany operations through technology, have been the predominant theme of changes in business during the past half-century (Verhoef *et al.*, 2021). Some pundits have described this period as the "Information Age" or "Digital Age" or have even gone as far as marking this period as the Fourth Industrial Revolution (Bai *et al.*, 2020). Although changes have often come slowly to SMEs, by the same token, some small companies have utilized innovations to harness massive economies of scale and springboard their companies into far-flung business empires (think of Amazon in 1994 or Square in 2009).

The recent global pandemic has wrought compulsory changes in lifestyle and consumption (Ratten, 2020) and reconfigured basic economic activities (Klein & Todesco, 2021). Such a cataclysmic shift in the business landscape accelerated the use of digital technologies by SMEs (Kraft *et al.*, 2022). Many SMEs quickly began to employ easily accessible, often open-source, technologies to perform essential communication and management activities (Klein & Todesco, 2021). The choice became mandatory: adopt digital tools or face business failure.

To operate virtually, common steps for SMEs might include using an online messaging service for their business, joining an online platform, or downloading a free rudimentary ERP for tracking suppliers. But in light of the fact that these tools are readily available and easy to duplicate, these steps do not portend a better position in the market.

DT, on the contrary, can provide an opportunity for small and medium businesses to outperform their competitors. The realization of a successful DT goes beyond the mere adoption of technologies (Konopik *et al.*, 2022) and may require the redesign of the whole company "at all levels and [in] all functions" (Priyono *et al.*, 2020). This impacts employees, processes, tasks, and organizational structures alike. To conduct DT in an efficient manner, a concise transformational strategy is needed that is in alignment with the overall company strategy (Hess *et al.*, 2016) and requires that management practices be adjusted to oversee operational changes alongside digitization (Matt *et al.*, 2015).

Given the more elaborate changes necessary in this approach to DT, involving comprehensive structural and business process redesign, some of the key features of the unique business category of SMEs merit analysis. This review is beneficial given that the characteristics of an organization in combination with resources, processes, and values define strategic development (Hanelt *et al.*, 2020). By first evaluating the common characteristics of smaller businesses, this chapter aims to chart a practical "hands-on" set of steps and issues to increase the probability of successful DT in SMEs and for this transformation to improve the chances of gaining a competitive advantage.

4.3. Characteristics of SMEs

SMEs are widely recognized as a vital business segment in every world economy, playing a significant role in job creation, innovation, and the diffusion of entrepreneurial skills (Thrassou *et al.*, 2020). The impact of smaller businesses extends beyond just the economic sphere, as SMEs are also crucial in building inclusive and resilient societies (OECD, 2021). Before reviewing the factors for success among SMEs in DT, the precarious nature of the fundamental characteristics of SMEs bears deeper consideration.

SMEs are a highly heterogenous segment with a multitude of different forms and features (Miller *et al.*, 2020; Curran & Blackburn, 2001) and operate in diverse business ecosystems (Kergroach, 2020). The vast range of business types in the segment cuts across a multitude of factors: size, industry, life-cycle stage, ownership structure, customer base, technological intensity, and level of internationalization. This makes every sector and sub-segment unique in terms of operational capabilities and perceptions of the strategic opportunities (OECD, 2021; Torrès & Julien, 2005).

One commonality among SMEs that has been identified by researchers is that SMEs are prone to rely on a short-term strategic approach (Klein & Todesco, 2021; Bouncken & Schmitt, 2022). The corollary of this approach is that SMEs are most often reactive rather than proactive in terms of management style (Maříková *et al.*, 2022). Several scholars have pointed out the constrained resources available to SMEs (Bouncken & Schmitt, 2022; Durst & Henschel, 2021), in terms of not only organizational capabilities (Eller *et al.*, 2020) but also access to external financing (Bowman, 2019). Another common feature of note is that incumbent SMEs may be reluctant to organizational changes (Horváth & Szabó, 2019).

Nonetheless, the fact that ownership or management of SMEs is most often centralized among one or two individuals means that quick, decisive changes are possible (Eggers, 2020), and the oftentimes flat organizational structure may benefit changes (Pati *et al.*, 2018; Durst & Edvardsson, 2012). Research suggests that there are a number of adherents to the notion that SMEs are considered more flexible, dynamic, and easier to adapt to changes (Clauss *et al.*, 2022; Eggers, 2020; Bartz & Winkler, 2016). The smaller size allows SMEs to respond faster to threats as well as opportunities (Eggers, 2020) and contribute to their sustainability in a dynamic environment (Durst & Henschel, 2021; Ter Wengel & Rodriguez, 2006).

An overview summary of several general characteristics common among SMEs and how they relate to some business challenges posted by DT are presented in Table 4.1. More precisely, it highlights the supporting

Table 4.1. Supporting factors of DT among SMEs.

Supporting factors	Potential effects on DT
Exceptional role of owner-managers (centrality) as the influential or sole decision maker as well as an opinion leader (Tidor *et al.*, 2012).	A highly motivated owner-manager possesses strong potential as a transformational leader, communicating new processes, articulating the potential of implemented technologies, activating employees as change agents, sharing knowledge of trends and updates on competitors' activities (Canhoto *et al.*, 2021).
Organic organizational culture supporting shared values, high level of trust among employees, and informal work communications (Tidor *et al.*, 2012) and supporting or being open to changes and knowledge development (Li *et al.*, 2016).	Developed DT strategy can be easily communicated to all company personnel. Informal organizational culture fosters the acceptance and engagement of the whole organization with the DT process.
Flat organizational structure (Pati *et al.*, 2018).	Simplifies an organizational transformation, i.e., implementation of changes and information flow.
Fast decision-making and recognition of opportunities (Eggers, 2020).	Helps to implement decisions quickly and to adjust transformational strategy and action steps as needed.
Small size enables competitive advantages through flexibility, strategic agility, and increased opportunities for innovation (Arbussa *et al.*, 2017).	Organizational agility, which simultaneously enables a balance between the exploration and exploitation of company resources, is a necessary condition for a successful transformation (Hess *et al.*, 2016). Organizational agility allows the adjustment of transformational strategy if needed: the ability to "build" and "configure" needed capabilities (Grover, 2022).

function of these essential characteristics of SMEs and the means by which they influence the process of DT.

It is also worthwhile to consider the opposite case, namely the drawbacks and limitations inherent in many SMEs which could impact a successful DT (Table 4.2).

Table 4.2. Hindering factors of DT among SMEs.

Hindering factors	**Potential effects on DT**
Lack of strategic vision and poor planning (Gutierrez *et al.*, 2009) and limited management, leadership, and strategic capabilities (Pati *et al.*, 2018).	Lack of understanding and experience in strategic management among SMEs' managers can be a serious obstacle to the development of a DT strategy (Pierenkemper & Gausemeier, 2021).
Limited managerial expertise (Klein & Todesco, 2021).	SMEs' owners or managers tend to rely on an intuitive approach in decision-making and ignore outside sources of knowledge. The failure to recognize the transformation of an organization as a managerial task can lead to stagnation in the transformation process (Peter *et al.*, 2020).
Organizational inertia (Cenamor *et al.*, 2019; Cardoso and Ramos, 2016) and embedded cultural resilience to change.	Lack of motivation and limited involvement of employees in the transformation process can be an obstacle and can lead to resource waste. Employee motivation can be weakened by a lack of understanding of new roles or responsibilities and by a fear that they do not fit into the new organization (Horváth & Szabó, 2019).
Lack of understanding of the linkages between digital technologies, information and communication technology, and business performance (Cenamor *et al.*, 2019).	A limited understanding of the potential of digital tools and their contribution to company performance can cause resource waste and the wrong selection of technologies. In addition, the lack of integration between technologies also negatively reflects on performance and resource allocation.
Lack of formalized processes (Kitsios & Kamariotou, 2019; Williams *et al.*, 2022).	Lack of formalized processes can hinder DT among SMEs since clear and transparent processes are essential to the development of strategic goals.
Unstructured approach to organizational learning (Edvardsson & Durst, 2013).	DT requires new skills for employees, and this process requires regular evaluation and continuous personnel development.

From the above tables of supporting and hindering factors, it is clear that SMEs possess the potential for a successful DT, but the realization of this potential depends on the ability of owners or managers to envision their strategy and to employ available resources efficiently, among other factors. While some skills and knowledge may be lacking among employees, for example, an equally compelling advantage to correcting this gap is that SMEs can adapt quickly. The very nature of many SMEs, i.e., a flexible and agile organizational structure, concentrated decision-making power, and a transparent operations structure, can support an efficient transformation process. However, there is the risk that decision-makers in SMEs have a limited understanding of intangible resources and lack an overview of processes and organizational knowledge.

To improve this understanding, systematic KM can be a useful approach to mapping organizational knowledge for this exact purpose in order to facilitate better strategic decision-making. With consideration of KM, the following section will elaborate on the mechanics of the essential first steps for SMEs in order to increase the probability of a successful DT.

4.4. KM as an Integrative Framework for DT

The lack of a strategy and the limited understanding of resources at their disposal can present significant challenges to the successful realization of DT for small- and medium-sized business decision-makers. To accommodate potential business needs during the transformational process, the field of KM presents itself as an instructive framework by allowing companies to outline organizational knowledge.

A couple of decades ago, KM practices were employed by organizations in which the main outcomes were knowledge-based (Grover & Davenport, 2001), e.g., consulting and research, insurance, financial services, information technology, and communications. More recently, companies from a variety of industries have been seeking to realize the benefits of the effective management of knowledge in order to gain a competitive advantage and contribute to organization sustainability (Durst & Zieba, 2020). The need and value of KM implementation in SMEs were elaborated by Durst *et al.* (2022), though the adoption of KM practices among SMEs remains limited (Mishra, 2019).

To manage knowledge is especially crucial for small organizations since, within small companies, knowledge is usually implicit (Giampaoli *et al.*, 2021). Meanwhile, for the purpose of DT among SMEs, knowledge should be explicit and codifiable. Therefore, taking inventory of organizational knowledge for SMEs presents itself as a logical initial step. ISO and IAF (2016, p. 1) define organizational knowledge as the "specific knowledge of the organization, coming either from its collective experience or from the individual experience of its persons. In an explicit or implicit way, this knowledge is, or can be, used to attain the organization's objectives."

At its essence, KM allows an organization to identify and store, utilize, and reuse knowledge, as well as create, transfer, and exchange it (Dayan & Evans, 2006). For the purpose of this chapter, KM is defined as a combination of organizational activities aimed at achieving goals through the use of knowledge (Groff & Jones, 2012). This use is realized, in turn, via a systematic process of acquiring, organizing, sustaining, applying, sharing, and renewing both the tacit and explicit knowledge of employees. Ultimately, the effect is to enhance organizational performance and create value (Davenport & Prusak, 2001).

From a physical perspective, the resources to which KM refers take the form of documents and other repositories, such as organizational databases. By contrast, from a process perspective, knowledge exists in organizational routines, activities, and outcomes or emerges from the interaction of a person with knowledge (McInerney & Koenig, 2011). Although there are many taxonomies of knowledge, one conventional approach in the field of KM identifies two types of knowledge. One is explicit knowledge ("knowing what") that can be expressed in formal and structured language and shared in the form of data or documents, such as specifications and manuals (Nonaka *et al.*, 2000). The other primary type of knowledge is implicit ("knowing how"), i.e., practical knowledge that cannot be openly expressed and requires some process of discovery (Wagner, 1987).

Assuming that DT would be appropriate for a given SME, the first step toward a thorough initiative of DT should be a documented evaluation, or audit, of organizational knowledge and its subsequent mapping. Liebowitz (2005) has been instructive in detailing the features of "audit" activity (p. 77) and has defined the following three main steps: (1) identification of existing knowledge in the targeted area, (2) identification of missing knowledge in the targeted area, and (3) development of recommendations. After this evaluation, the next step is to document the results in some form of a knowledge repository.

An outcome of the knowledge audit is the development of a knowledge map, which visualizes the sources, flows, constraints, and stopping points of knowledge. This, in turn, can serve as input for the development of a digital strategy. A follow-up step involves a clear formulation of the purpose of systematic organizational change. To develop a competitive strategy premised on DT, an organization must assess all its activities and consequent outcomes. The next step might include the strategic revision of organizational knowledge and the development of a digital strategy aligned with an overall company strategy. From the very beginning, the strategy must include measurable performance indicators. For smaller organizations with fewer personnel, new roles and responsibilities should be clearly defined and communicated.

In addition, another logical step is the establishment of a knowledge repository to serve as an internal library. This repository might consist of implicit knowledge, such as research reports, techniques, methods and policies, memos, presentations, and articles. It can also include informal internal knowledge (tacit knowledge), such as a discussion database or know-how forums, and other experience-related records (Semertzaki, 2011).

Systematic KM offers a blueprint for a DT among SMEs to include what knowledge currently exists in a given company, how it flows, and where and with whom it is located, as well as its subsequent documentation (Liebowitz, 2005). Clear, concise, and systematized knowledge allows the strategically driven selection of content for digitalization (Schumann & Tittmann, 2015), defines an optimal organizational structure, helps establish a system of performance monitoring, and provides an evaluation of organizational competencies. Moreover, systematic KM allows efficient management of the transformational process, incorporating the following outcomes:

(1) to monitor knowledge needs during the transformational process and establish patterns for continuous learning to satisfy such needs;
(2) to accommodate efficient integration of newly developed knowledge into the organizational structure;
(3) to support better decision-making and resource allocation based on data-based intelligence.

If the transformation process is launched without a well-developed understanding of what knowledge is relevant, what is the level of knowledge integration, and where this knowledge currently resides, the digitalized knowledge may be incomplete or irrelevant to achieve transformational goals. The key decisions of DT involve exactly what needs to be digitalized (content) and for what purpose (sustainable competitive advantage).

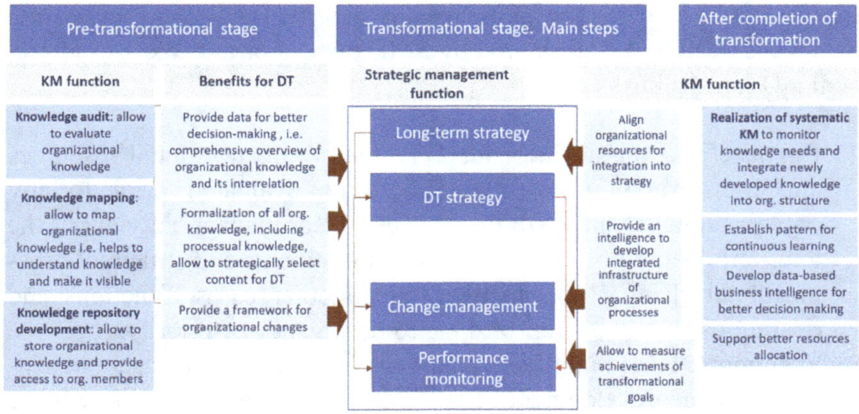

Fig. 4.1. KM as a framework for DT.

Systematic KM as a detailed framework for DT is outlined in Figure 4.1.

As Figure 4.1 demonstrates, the digital transformational process must be initiated with a strategic view of where the results may lead. The process of DT requires a sound understanding of what knowledge a company has and how it plans to employ available knowledge in the transformational process. Because of their smaller scale, SMEs have no choice but to obtain the maximum value from their limited resources in optimizing any process (Edvardsson *et al.*, 2019), including DT.

The direct benefits of applying KM to DT in SMEs spawn a host of related positive outcomes: a mindset to apply organizational processes, targeted existing process improvements, process integration, the development of organizational knowledge, productivity increases, and ultimately, sales growth. Indirect benefits are no less substantial because this approach can contribute to employee development (skills improvement, continuous learning, and job satisfaction), with a likely increase in customer satisfaction.

4.5. Practical Recommendations for Implementation of DT in SMEs via KM

SMEs are a highly heterogenous business segment; therefore, the need for digitalization, the resources available, and the level of digital literacy vary significantly. There is no easy recipe for success for SMEs, but several main steps need to be considered by SME owners or managers to implement a DT, as follows:

(1) **Purpose and possibilities for DT:** SMEs' organizational resources and transformation potential should be evaluated prior to any organizational changes. In the case of a clear managerial view of the long-term benefit of this process, the investments and structural organizational changes are justified. In all other cases, functions and operations should be digitized based on urgency or priority.
(2) **Systematic KM:** Small- and medium-sized organizations should benefit from the development of systematic management of knowledge within an organization.
(3) **Transformation management:** DT managers within SMEs should pay close attention to the process of transformation itself and actively manage it (not only focusing on the completion of the process). In other words, the transformational process should be outlined, explained to organizational members, and systematically monitored. It is especially valid for SMEs since they are prone to informal practices.
(4) **Changes in the organizational process:** These changes should be logically defined, and the interconnections between the old and new ways of working must be clarified to all employees. A new organizational structure should facilitate changes and be flexible enough for adaptation.
(5) **Performance monitoring:** This is a necessary function to evaluate the achievement of intermediate transformational goals. It allows for timely correction and necessary changes in processes and strategy.

4.6. Conclusion

This chapter aimed to consider the challenges and potential of incumbent small- and medium-sized organizations to undergo DT, with an analysis of their general characteristics. The following two main factors hinder effective DT strategy development and realization: (1) a lack of expertise in strategic management and a reliance on short-term approaches and (2) a limited understanding of organizational knowledge and the absence of its systematic evaluation. A systematic approach to KM is proposed as an integrative framework to manage and align the organizational knowledge of SMEs for better realization of DT. As a contribution, practical guidelines are outlined to support SMEs on their transformational journey.

References

Arbussa, A., Bikfalvi, A., & Marquès, P. (2017). Strategic agility-driven business model renewal: The case of an SME. *Management Decision* 55(2), 271–293. Doi: 10.1108/md-05-2016-0355.

Bai, C., Dallasega, P., Orzes, G., & Sarkis, J. (2020). Industry 4.0 technologies assessment: A sustainability perspective. *International Journal of Production Economics* 229(229), 107776. Doi: 10.1016/j.ijpe.2020.107776.

Bartz, W. & Winkler, A. (2016). Flexible or fragile? The growth performance of small and young businesses during the global financial crisis — Evidence from Germany. *Journal of Business Venturing* 31(2), 196–215. https://doi.org/10.1016/j.jbusvent.2015.10.002.

Bouncken, R. & Schmitt, F. (2022). SME family firms and strategic digital transformation: Inverting dualisms related to overconfidence and centralization. *Journal of Small Business Strategy* 32(3), 1–17.

Bouwman, H., Nikou, S., & de Reuver, M. (2019). Digitalization, business models, and SMEs: How do business model innovation practices improve performance of digitalizing SMEs? *Telecommunications Policy* 43(9), 1–18. https://doi.org/10.1016/j.telpol.2019.101828.

Canhoto, A. I., Quinton, S., Pera, R., Molinillo, S., & Simkin, L. (2021). Digital strategy aligning in SMEs: A dynamic capabilities perspective. *The Journal of Strategic Information Systems* 30(3), 101682. Doi: 10.1016/j.jsis.2021.101682.

Cardoso, M. & Ramos, I. (2016). The resilience of a small company and the grounds of capitalism: Thriving on non-knowledgeable ground. *Sustainability* 8(1), 74. https://doi.org/10.3390/su8010074.

Cenamor, J., Parida, V., & Wincent, J. (2019). How entrepreneurial SMEs compete through digital platforms: The roles of digital platform capability, network capability and ambidexterity. *Journal of Business Research* 100, 196–206. https://doi.org/10.1016/j.jbusres.2019.03.035.

Clauss, T., Breier, M., Kraus, S., Durst, S., & Mahto, R. V. (2021). Temporary business model innovation — SMEs' innovation response to the COVID-19 crisis. *R&D Management* 52(2), 294–312. Doi: 10.1111/radm.12498.

Centobelli, P., Cerchione, R., & Esposito, E. (2017). Knowledge management systems: The hallmark of SMEs. *Knowledge Management Research & Practice* 15(2), 294–304. Doi: 10.1057/s41275-017-0054-x.

Curran, J. & Blackburn, R. (2001). *Researching the Small Enterprise*. SAGE Publications Ltd, London. Doi: 10.4135/9781849209847.

Dabic, M., Vlacic, E., Ramanathan, U., & Egri, C. (2019). Evolving absorptive capacity: The mediating role of systematic knowledge management. *IEEE Transactions on Engineering Management* 67, 1–11. Doi: 10.1109/tem.2019.2893133.

Davenport, T. H. & Grover, V. (2001). Special issue: Knowledge management. *Journal of Management Information Systems* 18(1), 3–4. Doi: 10.1080/07421222.2001.11045674.

Davenport, T. H. & Prusak, L. (2000). *Working Knowledge: How Organisations Manage What They Know*. Harvard Business School Press, Boston.

Dayan, R. & Evans, S. (2006). KM your way to CMMI. *Journal of Knowledge Management* 10(1), 69–80. Doi: 10.1108/13673270610650111.

Desouza, K. C. & Awazu, Y. (2006). Knowledge management at SMEs: Five peculiarities. *Journal of Knowledge Management* 10(1), 32–43. https://doi.org/10.1108/13673270610650085.

Durst, S. & Edvardsson, I. R. (2012). Knowledge management in SMEs: A literature review. *Journal of Knowledge Management* 16(6), 879–903. Doi: 10.1108/13673271211276173.

Durst, S., Foli, S., & Edvardsson, I. R. (2022). A systematic literature review on knowledge management in SMEs: Current trends and future directions. *Management Review Quarterly*. https://link.springer.com/article/10.1007/s11301-022-00299-0#citeas.

Durst, S. & Henschel, T. (2021). COVID-19 as an accelerator for developing strong(er) businesses? Insights from Estonian small firms. *Journal of the International Council for Small Business* 2(1), 1–29. Doi: 10.1080/26437015.2020.1859935.

Durst, S. & Zieba, M. (2020). Knowledge risks inherent in business sustainability. *Journal of Cleaner Production* 251, 119670. Doi: 10.1016/j.jclepro.2019.119670.

Edvardsson, I. R. & Durst, S. (2013). The benefits of knowledge management in small and medium-sized enterprises. *Procedia — Social and Behavioral Sciences* 81(4), 351–354. Doi: 10.1016/j.sbspro.2013.06.441.

Edvardsson, I. R., Durst, S., & Oskarsson, G. K. (2019). Strategic outsourcing in SMEs. *Journal of Small Business and Enterprise Development* 27(1), 73–84. Doi: 10.1108/jsbed-09-2019-0322.

Eggers, F. (2020). Masters of disasters? Challenges and opportunities for SMEs in times of crisis. *Journal of Business Research* 116, 199–208. https://doi.org/10.1016/j.jbusres.2020.05.025.

Eller, R., Alford, P., Kallmünzer, A., & Peters, M. (2020). Antecedents, consequences, and challenges of small and medium-sized enterprise digitalization. *Journal of Business Research* 112, 119–127. https://doi.org/10.1016/j.jbusres.2020.03.004.

Giampaoli, D., Sgrò, F., Ciambotti, M., & Bontis, N. (2021). Integrating knowledge management with intellectual capital to drive strategy: A focus on

Italian SMEs. *VINE Journal of Information and Knowledge Management Systems*. https://www.emerald.com/insight/content/doi/10.1108/VJIKMS-04-2021-0059/full/html.

Groff, T. & Jones, T. (2012). *Introduction to Knowledge Management*. https://doi.org/10.4324/9780080495781y First published by Butterworth-Heinemann. This edition published 2011 by Routledge, New York, NY 10017, USA.

Grover, V. (2022). Digital agility: Responding to digital opportunities. *European Journal of Information Systems* 31(6), 709–715. Doi: 10.1080/0960085x.2022.2096492.

Grover, V. & Davenport, T. H. (2001). General perspectives on knowledge management: Fostering a research agenda. *Journal of Management Information Systems* 18(1), 5–21. Doi: 10.1080/07421222.2001.11045672.

Gutierrez, A., Orozco, J., & Serrano, A. (2009). Factors affecting IT and business alignment: a comparative study in SMEs and large organisations. *Journal of Enterprise Information Management* 22(1/2), 197–211. https://doi.org/10.1108/17410390910932830

Hanelt, A., Bohnsack, R., Marz, D., & Antunes, C. (2020). A systematic review of the literature on digital transformation: Insights and implications for strategy and organizational change. *Journal of Management Studies* 58(5), 1159–1197. Doi: 10.1111/joms.12639.

Hess, T., Matt, C., Benlian, A., & Wiesböck, F. (2016). Options for formulating a digital transformation strategy. *MIS Quarterly Executive* 15, 103–119.

Hessels, J. & Parker, S. C. (2013). Constraints, internationalization and growth: A cross-country analysis of European SMEs. *Journal of World Business* 48(1), 137–148. Doi: 10.1016/j.jwb.2012.06.014.

Horváth, D. & Szabó, R. Zs. (2019). Driving forces and barriers of Industry 4.0: Do multinational and small and medium-sized companies have equal opportunities? *Technological Forecasting and Social Change* 146, 119–132. Doi: 10.1016/j.techfore.2019.05.021.

ISO & IAF (2016). Auditing Practices Group Guidance on: Organizational Knowledge.

Kergroach, S. (2020). Giving momentum to SME digitalization. *Journal of the International Council for Small Business* 1(1), 28–31. Doi: 10.1080/26437015.2020.1714358.

Kindermann, B., Beutel, S., Garcia de Lomana, G., Strese, S., Bendig, D., & Brettel, M. (2020). Digital orientation: Conceptualization and operationalization of a new strategic orientation. *European Management Journal* 39(5), 645–657. Doi: 10.1016/j.emj.2020.10.009.

Kindström, D., Carlborg, P., & Nord, T. (2022). Challenges for growing SMEs: A managerial perspective. *Journal of Small Business Management* 1–24. https://doi.org/10.1080/00472778.2022.2082456.

Kitsios, F. & Kamariotou, M. (2019). Information systems strategy and strategy-as-practice: Planning evaluation in SMEs. In *Proceedings of Americas Conference on Information Systems*. AMCIS2019, Cancun, Mexico, pp. 1–10.

Klein, V. B. & Todesco, J. L. (2021). COVID-19 crisis and SMEs responses: The role of digital transformation. *Knowledge and Process Management* 28(2), 117–133. Doi: 10.1002/kpm.1660.

Konopik, J., Jahn, C., Schuster, T., Hoßbach, N., & Pflaum, A. (2021). Mastering the digital transformation through organizational capabilities: A conceptual framework. *Digital Business* 2(2), 100019. Doi: 10.1016/j.digbus.2021.100019.

Kraft, C., Lindeque, J. P., & Peter, M. K. (2022). The digital transformation of Swiss small and medium-sized enterprises: Insights from digital tool adoption. *Journal of Strategy and Management* 15, 468–494. Doi: 10.1108/jsma-02-2021-0063.

Li, W., Liu, K., Belitski, M., Ghobadian, A., & O'Regan, N. (2016). E-leadership through strategic alignment: An empirical study of small- and medium-sized enterprises in the digital age. *Journal of Information Technology* 31(2), 185–206. Doi: 10.1057/jit.2016.10.

Liebowitz, J. (2005). Linking social network analysis with the analytic hierarchy process for knowledge mapping in organizations. *Journal of Knowledge Management* 9(1), 76–86. Doi: 10.1108/13673270510582974.

Maříková, M., Rolínek, L., Vrchota, J., & Řehoř, P. (2022). Determination of the level of strategic management in SMEs. *Central European Business Review* 11(3), 55–78. Doi: 10.18267/j.cebr.296.

Matt, C., Hess, T., & Benlian, A. (2015). Digital transformation strategies. *Business & Information Systems Engineering* 57(5), 339–343. Doi: 10.1007/s12599-015-0401-5.

McAdam, R. & Reid, R. (2001). SME and large organization perceptions of knowledge management: Comparisons and contrasts. *Journal of Knowledge Management* 5(3), 231–241. Doi: 10.1108/13673270110400870.

McInerney, C. R. & Koenig, M. E. D. (2011). *Knowledge Management (KM) Processes in Organizations: Theoretical Foundations and Practice*. Morgan and Claypool Publishers, pp. 1–96. Doi: 10.2200/s00323ed1v01y201012icr018.

Miller, K., McAdam, M., Spieth, P., & Brady, M. (2020). Business models big and small: Review of conceptualizations and constructs and future directions for SME business model research. *Journal of Business Research* 131, 619–626. Doi: 10.1016/j.jbusres.2020.12.036.

Mishra, N. (2019). Knowledge management practice for effective operations in SMEs. *Production Planning & Control* 30(10–12), 795–798. Doi: 10.1080/09537287.2019.1582108.

Nonaka, I., Toyama, R., & Konno, N. (2000). SECI, Ba and Leadership: A unified model of dynamic knowledge creation. *Long Range Planning* 33(1), 5–34. Doi: 10.1016/s0024-6301(99)00115-6.

OECD (2021). *The Digital Transformation of SMEs. OECD Studies on SMEs and Entrepreneurship*. OECD. Doi: 10.1787/bdb9256a-en.

Pati, R. K., Nandakumar, M. K., Ghobadian, A., Ireland, R. D., & O'Regan, N. (2018). Business model design–performance relationship under external and internal contingencies: Evidence from SMEs in an emerging economy. *Long Range Planning* 51(5), 750–769. https://doi.org/10.1016/j.lrp.2018.01.001.

Peter, M. K., Kraft, C., & Lindeque, J. (2020). Strategic action fields of digital transformation. *Journal of Strategy and Management* 13(1), 160–180. Doi: 10.1108/jsma-05-2019-0070.

Pierenkemper, C. & Gausemeier, J. (2021). Developing strategies for digital transformation in SMEs with maturity models. In Schallmo, D. R. A. & Tidd, J. (eds.) *Digitalization. Management for Professionals.* Springer, Cham. pp. 103–124. Doi: 10.1007/978-3-030-69380-0_7.

Priyono, A., Moin, A., & Putri, V. N. A. O. (2020). Identifying digital transformation paths in the business model of SMEs during the COVID-19 pandemic. *Journal of Open Innovation: Technology, Market, and Complexity* [online] 6(4), 104. Doi: 10.3390/joitmc6040104.

Quinton, S. & Simkin, L. (2016). The digital journey: Reflected learnings and emerging challenges. *International Journal of Management Reviews* 19(4), 455–472. Doi: 10.1111/ijmr.12104.

Ratten, V. (2020). Coronavirus (COVID-19) and entrepreneurship: Changing life and work landscape. *Journal of Small Business & Entrepreneurship* 32(5), 1–14. Doi: 10.1080/08276331.2020.1790167.

Rodrigues, M., Franco, M., Silva, R., & Oliveira, C. (2021). Success factors of SMEs: Empirical study guided by dynamic capabilities and resources-based view. *Sustainability* 13(21), 12301. Doi: 10.3390/su132112301.

Rogers, D. L. (2016). *The Digital Transformation Playbook: Rethink Your Business for the Digital Age.* Columbia University Press, New York Chichester, West Sussex.

Savastano, M., Zentner, H., Spremić, M., & Cucari, N. (2022). Assessing the relationship between digital transformation and sustainable business excellence in a turbulent scenario. *Total Quality Management & Business Excellence*, 1–22. https://www.tandfonline.com/doi/epdf/10.1080/14783363.2022.2063717needAccess=true&role=button.

Schumann, C. A. & Tittmann, C. (2015). Digital business transformation in the context of knowledge management. Proceedings of the European Conference on Knowledge Management, *ECKM* 671–675.

Semertzaki, E. ed. (2011). Components of a knowledge management system at a special library. In E. Semertzaki, (ed.), *Chandos Information Professional*

Series, Special Libraries as Knowledge Management Centres. Chandos Publishing, pp. 121–186.

Serrat, O. (2017). Building a Learning Organization. In *Knowledge Solutions*. Springer, Singapore. Doi: 10.1007/978-981-10-0983-9_11.

Thrassou, A., Vrontis, D., Weber, Y., Riad Shams, S. M., and Tsoukatos, E. (2020). *The Changing Role of SMEs in Global Business: Volume I: Paradigms of Opportunities and Challenges*. Springer International Publishing, Cham.

Tidor, A., Gelmereanu, C., Baru, P., & Morar, L. (2012). Diagnosing organizational culture for SME performance. *Procedia Economics and Finance* 3, 710–715. Doi: 10.1016/s2212-5671(12)00218-3.

Torrès, O. & Julien, P.-A. (2005). Specificity and denaturing of small business. *International Small Business Journal: Researching Entrepreneurship* 23(4), 355–377. Doi: 10.1177/0266242605054049.

Verhoef, P. C., Broekhuizen, T., Bart, Y., Bhattacharya, A., Qi Dong, J., Fabian, N., & Haenlein, M. (2021). Digital transformation: A multidisciplinary reflection and research agenda. *Journal of Business Research* 122, 889–901. Doi: 10.1016/j.jbusres.2019.09.022.

Volberda, H. W., Khanagha, S., Baden-Fuller, C., Mihalache, O. R., & Birkinsh, J. (2021). Strategizing in a digital world: Overcoming cognitive barriers, reconfiguring routines and introducing new organizational forms. *Long Range Planning* 54(5), 102110. Doi: 10.1016/j.lrp.2021.102110.

Vial, G. (2019). Understanding digital transformation: A review and a research agenda. *The Journal of Strategic Information Systems* 28(2), 118–144. Doi: 10.1016/j.jsis.2019.01.003.

Wagner, R. K. (1987). Tacit knowledge in everyday intelligent behavior. *Journal of Personality and Social Psychology* 52(6), 1236–1247. Doi: 10.1037/0022-3514.52.6.1236.

Wang, J. & Rusu, L. (2018). Factors hindering business-IT alignment in small and medium enterprises in China. *Procedia Computer Science* 138, 425–432. Doi: 10.1016/j.procs.2018.10.060.

Wang, J. & Rusu, L. (2018). Factors Hindering Business-IT Alignment in Small and Medium Enterprises in China. Procedia Computer Science, [online] 138, pp. 425–432. doi: 10.1016/j.procs.2018.10.060.

Wengel, J. T. & Rodriguez, E. (2006). SME export performance in Indonesia after the crisis. *Small Business Economics* 26(1), 25–37. Doi: 10.1007/s11187-004-6491-y.

Williams, C., Krumay, B., Schallmo, D., & Scornavacca, E. (2022). An interaction-based Digital Maturity Model for SMEs. PACIS 2022 Proceedings. https://aisel.aisnet.org/pacis2022/254.

Yew Wong, K. & Aspinwall, E. (2005). An empirical study of the important factors for knowledge-management adoption in the SME sector. *Journal of Knowledge Management* 9(3), 64–82. Doi: 10.1108/13673270510602773.

Zambon, I., Cecchini, M., Egidi, G., Saporito, M. G., & Colantoni, A. (2019). Revolution 4.0: Industry vs. agriculture in a future development for SMEs. *Processes* 7(1), 36. Doi: 10.3390/pr7010036.

https://doi.org/10.1142/9789811270178_0005

Chapter 5

Discovering the Hidden String Connecting Knowledge Risks and the Digital Entrepreneurial Ecosystem

Samuel Foli

Department of Business Administration,
Tallinn University of Technology, Ehitajate tee 5,
Tallinn 19086, Estonia

samuel.foli@taltech.ee

Abstract

With the advent of digital transformation, a growing number of firms have become digital businesses, increasing the risk of cybercrime and other risks associated with their competitive knowledge, thus making the ecosystem in which they function more vulnerable. However, how these knowledge risks relate to the digital entrepreneurial ecosystems (DEEs) is not well understood. This chapter, therefore, situates the discussion of knowledge risks within the DEE and argues that such risks may have possible consequences for the ecosystem. These potential risks are identified through a critical analysis of existing knowledge on knowledge risks and the DEE. It has been determined that unlearning, cyberattacks, digitalization risks, knowledge leakage, and knowledge censoring are possible risks in the ecosystem. As a consequence of the unique effects of these risks, a conceptual model has been developed to better understand their nature. In addition, several recommendations were offered on how stakeholders, including government institutions, policymakers, and entrepreneurs, can contribute to the creation of an ecosystem that is digital, vibrant, and sustainable.

5.1. Introduction

There is widespread recognition of the importance of entrepreneurship in the development of regional and national economies (Gu & Wang, 2022; Audretsch & Belitski, 2017). One of the recurring questions in entrepreneurship literature, however, is "What types of risks do entrepreneurs face?" (Bhimani, 2022; Shishido, 2009). This question has become even more relevant and timely following the recent shift in entrepreneurship scholarship from individual-centered to digital-ecosystem-based (Shen *et al.*, 2015; Sussan & Acs, 2017; Acs, 2022), also referred to as a digital entrepreneurial ecosystem (DEE).

From the perspective of an entrepreneur, a DEE can be considered a double-edged sword since, on the one hand, it creates new opportunities by providing a conducive environment for the development and growth of new ventures through the engagement of key stakeholders and the use of digital technologies (Ratten & Thompson, 2020). On the other hand, a DEE may also present additional and new types of risks, particularly as technology advances. These risks are likely to manifest in the form of cyberattacks (Durst, 2021; Foli *et al.*, 2022), insufficient or outdated skills, knowledge, and competence (Sumbal *et al.*, 2020; Temel & Durst, 2020), or inappropriate use of digital technologies (Borgia & La Torre, 2022). Taking a practical example, if taxi drivers had refused to upgrade their skills to sign up for the Bolt app, such an ecosystem would have failed to survive; the same applies to Airbnb users. Several other possible risks may also exist within a DEE, such as reinventing the wheel and the depletion of knowledge stock due to leakage or loss of knowledge.

Despite the repercussions these risks may have (Durst *et al.*, 2019; Zieba *et al.*, 2022), there is little discussion in the literature regarding how knowledge risks relate to the DEE. Thus, an integrated framework is necessary for a more comprehensive understanding of how knowledge risks interact with the various DEE compartments. By developing such a framework, stakeholders, including entrepreneurs and policymakers, would be better able to comprehend the threat associated with these risks and appreciate the need to implement proactive measures to mitigate these risks.

This chapter aims to fill this gap by developing a conceptual model that highlights the relationship and nature of potential knowledge risks with those of DEEs. This overall aim is achieved by providing answers to the following questions: What are the compartments of the DEE? What are the potential knowledge risks associated with the ecosystem? How do these risks relate to the various compartments of the ecosystem?

This chapter is divided into seven sections. Section 5.2 presents the concept of a DEE. In Section 5.3, a review of the literature on knowledge risks is provided. Section 5.4 presents the method, followed by Section 5.5 which describes the development of the conceptual framework, and Section 5.6 presents the conceptual model. The conclusion is provided in Section 5.7.

5.2. Digital and Entrepreneurial Ecosystem

This section introduces the concept of DEE. To accomplish this, an overview of digital and entrepreneurial ecosystems will be provided to set the necessary foundation for integration.

5.2.1. *Digital ecosystem*

An extension of a business ecosystem is the digital ecosystem that places special emphasis on the importance of digital transformation – a trend widely recognized across various sectors and industries (Kraus *et al.*, 2022; Rajnai & Kocsis, 2018). Throughout the last decade, digital ecosystems have been continuously defined, redefined, and studied, as shown in Table 5.1. Following Acs *et al.*'s (2021) definition, the author of this chapter defines a digital ecosystem as a self-regulating and socio-complex system consisting of entities that leverage digital technologies through collaboration and competition for co-creation. These entities comprise suppliers, customers, trading partners, applications, third-party data service providers, and all associated technologies. The ability of a digital ecosystem to maintain communication and connectivity in a coordinated manner is an important aspect. In other words, this is to suggest that controlling or managing a digital ecosystem is equally important as creating it. Managing or controlling an ecosystem includes orchestrating,

Table 5.1. Definitions of a digital ecosystem.

Authors	Definitions
Katz and Callorda (2018, pp. 662–663)	A digital ecosystem is defined as a set of interconnected components (or pillars) operating within a socioeconomic context.
Abebe *et al.* (2015, p. 1)	Digital ecosystem refers to a network of companies, individual contributors, institutions, and customers that interact to promote collaboration and maintain mutual value.
Li *et al.* (2012, p. 117)	Digital ecosystems refer to complex and interdependent systems and their underlying infrastructures by which all constituents interact and exhibit as a whole self-organizing, scalable, and sustainable behaviors.
Kreuzer *et al.* (2022, p. 50)	Digital ecosystems refer to multiple actors, e.g., organizations and customers, who interact by means of an exchange of data, information and knowledge, and through the consumption of focal value propositions in a self-organizing, scalable and DT-mediated system, e.g., on digital platforms.
Kotilainen *et al.* (2016, p. 48)	A digital ecosystem can be described as a self-organizing digital infrastructure for creating a digital environment for organizations that supports the cooperation, the knowledge sharing, the development of open and adaptive technologies and evolutionary business models.

delivering, and monetizing services, as well as communicating with customers and managing data, which are easier within a digital framework.

Now that many organizations are incorporating digital transformation into their strategies, it is essential that a digital ecosystem be created in order to improve performance and facilitate cooperation between companies. Through the digital ecosystem, an organization can focus on facilitating business value without having to deal with outdated legacy business-to-business (B2B) services. In addition, digital ecosystems can enable organizations to adhere to service-level agreements consistently and with ease, provide quick fixes, and quickly identify customer expectations. Several sectors have adopted a digital ecosystem concept. Modern banking applications are an example of a typical digital ecosystem in the financial industry, as they integrate all services and applications into a single platform, including expense managers, digital wallets, online banking, and digital passbooks. Apart from that, many healthcare organizations are investigating how to integrate artificial intelligence (AI) and blockchain technologies into their systems in order to improve client or patient experiences and decision-making.

In the reading of the literature (as also emphasized by Sussan and Acs, 2017), a digital ecosystem hinges on two foundational pillars: digital infrastructure and users; many other scholars (e.g., Dini *et al.*, 2011; Li *et al.*, 2012) have established this as well. As a result, I will be focusing on these pillars in this chapter. Here, digital infrastructure is a digitally enabled social tool that supports innovation and entrepreneurship through communication, collaboration, and computing (Nambisan, 2017). On the other hand, users are considered persons who directly interact with digital technologies (Sussan & Acs, 2017).

5.2.2. *Entrepreneurial ecosystem*

Prior to defining what an entrepreneurial ecosystem is, it is necessary to define entrepreneurship (or the term "entrepreneurial") in this chapter in recognition of the fact that entrepreneurship has been defined in multiple ways (Ratten, 2020; Sohns & Revilla Diez, 2018) and from various perspectives (Brünjes & Revilla Diez, 2012; Carter *et al.*, 1996) over the past few years. Entrepreneurship is defined here as the identification and exploitation of opportunities that lead to wealth creation or social change at all levels of society, from regions to organizations to individuals (Shane & Venkataraman, 2000; Schumpeter, 1934). The definition given here, as broadly defined, provides a comprehensive understanding of what entrepreneurship actually entails. Furthermore, this definition emphasizes the underappreciated aspect of entrepreneurship (Sussan & Acs, 2017), which is ecosystem building, compared to the self-employment aspects which have dominated existing literature (Ratten & Shahriar, 2020).

According to Roundy *et al.* (2018), an entrepreneurial ecosystem is defined as "a self-organized, adaptive, and geographically bounded community of complex agents operating at multiple, aggregated levels, whose nonlinear interactions result in the patterns of activities through which new ventures form and dissolve over time" (p. 5). From Spigel's (2017) point of view, an entrepreneurial ecosystem can be considered a community characterized by economic, political, social, and cultural factors that provide a framework for creating new ventures. It is this community that symbolizes the unit within which actors, including large corporations, universities, financial institutions, and public organizations, can interact to promote the growth of new entrepreneurs (Brown & Mason, 2017). As part of their attempt to conceptualize the entrepreneurial ecosystem, Sussan and Acs (2017) divided these actors into two pillars: agents and institutions. The authors refer to this institution as the economic institution that ensures that property rights are enforced in order to encourage investors to invest and therefore allocate funds appropriately. Agents, on the other hand, are viewed as entrepreneurs who, based on the scarcity of resources they possess, make decisions in order to gain a competitive advantage. Taking into consideration what has been discussed above, an entrepreneurial ecosystem can be broadly defined as a unique system of interdependent actors, typically agents and institutions, supporting new venture creation and growth.

5.2.3. *Digital entrepreneurial ecosystem*

Prior to discussing the concept of DEE, it is important to mention that this concept was developed at a time when entrepreneurship was arguably not well conceptualized in the digital space. This can be attributed to a lack of emphasis on recognizing the value of knowledge to the ecosystem (Munaiseche *et al.*, 2022). According to Sussan and Acs (2017), their work is the first to conceptualize the DEE, which combines both the digital ecosystem and the entrepreneurial ecosystem. Thus, it is logical to combine the definitions of the digital ecosystem and the entrepreneurial ecosystem and define the DEE as a set of elements within a region that facilitate the development and growth of innovative start-ups that utilize digital technologies to take advantage of new opportunities (Du *et al.*, 2018). Ultimately, Sussan and Acs (2017) conceptualized DEE in four dimensions, namely digital infrastructure governance, digital user citizenship, digital entrepreneurship, and digital marketplaces.

In a follow-up study, Song (2019) redefined two dimensions of the DEE framework that had been proposed by Sussan and Acs (2017). This is due to the fact that the previous framework failed to explicitly distinguish between users and agents. In addition, the redefined framework acknowledged the platform (digital marketplace) as the core of DEE. Accordingly, the following dimensions were proposed: digital citizenship, digital infrastructure governance, digital multi-sided platforms, and digital technology entrepreneurship.

5.3. Knowledge Risks

Since knowledge risk is gaining traction as a research area in knowledge management, it is not surprising that several definitions continue to develop over time. Bayer and Maier (2006) defined knowledge risk as an operational risk associated with the reliance on, loss of, or unsuccessful or accidental knowledge transfer. Due to the narrowness of the definition, which focuses primarily on operational levels within an organization, Perrot (2007) developed a more comprehensive version, defining knowledge risk as the likelihood of any loss from an event connected with the identification, storage, or protection of knowledge that may decrease the operational or strategic benefit of any party involved in the network. Even though this definition acknowledged that knowledge risks can also impact strategic levels within an organization, the severity of these risks was not recognized at all levels within the organization. For this reason, this chapter applies Durst and Zieba's (2019) definition, which defines knowledge risk as "a measure of the probability and severity of adverse effects of any activities engaging or related somehow to knowledge that can affect the functioning of an organization on any level" (p. 2).

According to the knowledge risk literature, organizations are exposed to a wide array of knowledge risks (Durst & Zieba, 2019) which have the potential to negatively impact their performance (Zieba *et al.*, 2022; Bratianu *et al.*, 2020). Due to this, studies on taxonomy have been exceptionally useful in ensuring that these risks are appropriately classified in order to gain a better understanding of how they manifest themselves in unique contexts. Among these studies is Durst and Zieba's (2017) work, which proposed a taxonomy of knowledge risks to illustrate the different ways in which knowledge risks can exist within and outside of an organization, as well as the intersection between the organization and its external environment (e.g., relational risk and knowledge outsourcing risks). The same authors (2018) developed a taxonomy of knowledge risks within the context of the sharing economy; however, their focus was only on risks from the outside and their intersection with external entities. North *et al.*'s (2020) conducted an exploratory study that focused on specific knowledge risks associated with supply chain interactions. There were three phases to these interactions, namely the preparation phase, the development and learning phase, and the operational phase. A majority of the risks associated with the first two phases were attributed to the risk of disclosing confidential knowledge that could result in a loss of competitiveness for the organization. Several potential knowledge risks were identified in the final phase, including unlearning, knowledge loss, high dependency on clients, knowledge leakage, and attrition. A broader view of knowledge risks was proposed by Durst and Zieba (2019), who divided them into three categories: human, technological, and operational. In the study, the authors argued that human knowledge risks can be attributed to human behavior, which is influenced by social, cultural, and psychological factors, whereas technological knowledge risks are a result of the misapplication or misuse of outdated technologies or of cyberattacks. Whereas, operational knowledge risks can arise from the day-to-day operations of the company, such as outsourcing.

Several aspects of knowledge risk research have also evolved, including perspectives, organizational contexts, research approaches, and techniques. As a response to Trkman and Desouza's (2012) exploratory study, Marabelli and Newell (2012) examined the risks associated with knowledge transfer across networks. Both studies were examined from a practice-based perspective, which argued that knowledge can be at risk, particularly in networked environments where knowledge sharing is common practice. There have been several recent studies that have used multi-criteria decision analysis techniques, such as interpretive structural modeling (Foli & Durst, 2022) and total interpretive structural modeling (Foli, 2022), in order to study knowledge risks, particularly in collaborative contexts.

In light of the above review, it is evident that there is a void of discussion and understanding of the knowledge risks associated with DEEs, a gap that this chapter intends to address.

5.4. Method

Taking other approaches that have been used in conceptual studies into account, this study employed a model-based approach. With the use of a model-based approach, it is possible to develop a conceptual model that ties knowledge risks into DEE areas, such as digital user citizenship, digital infrastructure governance, digital technology entrepreneurship, and digital multi-sided platforms, by drawing upon the literature on knowledge risks and DEE.

First, a review of the literature was conducted to collect relevant papers on knowledge risks. Following that, the author screened the papers and included only those that dealt with contexts related to DEEs, such as network structure, supply chain, and collaborative arrangements. Each paper was then examined in detail to identify the potential knowledge risks mentioned, and an additional risk was added based on the author's expertise and experience. These risks are summarized with their definitions and sources in Table 5.2.

Table 5.2. Potential knowledge risks in a DEE.

Knowledge Risk	**Definition**	**Supported Reference**
Knowledge leakage	…refers to the deliberate or accidental dissemination of confidential information to unauthorized personnel or third parties.	Annansingh (2020), Abdul Molok *et al.* (2018), and Sarigianni *et al.* (2015)
Digitalization risk	…refers to the risk associated with the use of digital technologies in order to change a business model and create new revenue and value generation opportunities.	Foli (2022), Luo (2022), and Ribeiro-Navarrete *et al.* (2021)
Unlearning	…is described as the process of reducing or eliminating preexisting knowledge or habits that would otherwise create formidable barriers to the acquisition of new knowledge.	Wilbert *et al.* (2018) and Klammer and Gueldenberg (2019)
Cyberattack	…refers to an attempt by a person or organization to breach another's computer system maliciously and deliberately.	Durst and Zieba (2019)
Knowledge censoring	…refers to a situation where either the founder or the co-founder withdraws from the ecosystem or when there are issues of knowledge incompatibility where newly created knowledge cannot be used within an ecosystem.	Author's construction

5.5. Conceptual Framework

This section presents arguments based on the prior literature linking the identified risks with the four compartments of the DEE. Consequently, a conceptual model is developed in order to illustrate the nature of the influence that these risks can have on DEEs.

5.5.1. *Knowledge leakage, digitalization risk, and digital multi-sided platform*

As a result of the advent of digital platforms, knowledge sharing has become more convenient and faster than in the past. In the Global Digital Report, published in July 2022, approximately 4.7 billion people worldwide are estimated to use digital platforms, equivalent to 59% of the population. With this, it becomes clear why Sussan and Acs (2017) were right in their suggestion that digitalization be incorporated into entrepreneurial ecosystems. Specifically, the digital multi-sided platform in the DEE is what enables all the key actors and market players to come together and interact on a single platform. As Song (2019) posits, the multi-sided platform breaks away from traditional business models — where only one side is involved — by providing direct connections between suppliers, manufacturers, and clients, as well as between entrepreneurs, institutions, and investors. Thus, it creates an environment where there is a high level of exchange of ideas, information, and knowledge, which makes actors more susceptible to knowledge leaks.

In fact, prior studies have confirmed the assertion that knowledge leakage is significantly more likely to occur in an interconnected environment. For instance, Abdul Molok *et al.* (2018) used a case study approach to investigate how and why the use of digital platforms can result in accidental knowledge leakage. It was found in their study that the occurrence of knowledge leakage through digital platforms is unavoidable, particularly if there is no comprehensive risk management strategy concerning the use of digital platforms in place. As Annansingh (2021) revealed, digital platforms can expose users to risks such as cyberattacks and knowledge leakage. Essentially, such digital platforms are the doorway to the ecosystem, thus creating a scenario in which knowledge shared inadvertently becomes public knowledge. Sarigianni *et al.* (2015) argued that digital platforms can present several potential knowledge risks, which can lead to knowledge leakage. On the basis of this premise, knowledge risks related to digital platforms were examined, and the authors concluded that knowledge risks can be induced by digital platforms, so practitioners should take these risks into account when managing risks. Hence, the author proposes the following:

> *P1. Digital multi-sided platforms create an undesired avenue for knowledge leakage.*

The existence and use of digitally enabled multi-sided platforms can magnify the digitalization risk by increasing the pursuit of technological advancements. Digitalization risk can be a concern at times, particularly among those who are averse to change and are technophobic. However, given the rate at which digitalization is permeating every industry, especially the financial, manufacturing, pharmaceutical, and education sectors, thanks to COVID-19, it would only be wise to view digitalization as a new opportunity and follow suit (Luo, 2022). As such, this risk is likely to be a positive risk that stimulates actors to improve their digital skills and competencies.

Ribeiro-Navarrete *et al.* (2021) studied the effect of digitalization on organizational performance. Their results showed that the use of digital platforms for corporate purposes and training in digital tools can improve performance. In other words, digitalization creates opportunities for employees to reorient themselves through training, unlearning, learning, and relearning activities in order to update their skills and knowledge, thereby improving the overall performance of their organizations. Hence, the author proposes the following:

> *P2. Digital multi-sided platforms support digitalization risk.*

5.5.2. *Unlearning and digital user citizenship*

Currently, unlearning is gaining attention within the knowledge management literature, and it is being largely considered a human knowledge risk (Durst *et al.*, 2020). Unlearning can be understood as a deliberate attempt to forget skills, knowledge, and competencies accumulated in the past but no longer necessary (Durst & Zieba, 2019). In the context of the DEE, where digitalization is at its heart, unlearning can be of particular importance for users to get rid of outdated knowledge, values, and practices. This is even more important due to rapid technological advancements. Effective unlearning can enhance the overall performance and functionality of the ecosystem, through full user participation.

Wilbert *et al.* (2018), in their exploratory study among shop floor agents in the Brazilian state of Catarina, concluded that national culture was an effective lens for exploring unlearning at an individual level. As a result, the unlearning process requires deliberate efforts to instill a culture of unlearning in order to be successful. A study by Klammer and Gueldenberg (2019) explored the factors of unlearning among teams responsible for new product development. Using a multiple case study approach, it was revealed that managing knowledge loss by promoting unlearning enhances creativity and flexibility. Hence, the author proposes the following:

P3. Unlearning can empower digital user citizenship.

5.5.3. *Cyberattack and digital infrastructure governance*

Digital infrastructure governance ensures that the activities of users and agents are compliant with regional laws and regulations. This provides a legal framework that, in a sense, encourages investors to place investments within the ecosystem. According to Song (2019), "the critical role of digital infrastructure governance is to keep the internet space open, transparent, and free for business enterprise" (p. 573). Munaiseche *et al.* (2022) assert that the smooth functionality of DEEs depends on the digital infrastructure, which should be free of attack and disruption. Furthermore, the digital infrastructure forms the DNA of a multi-sided digital platform.

This implies that if a cyberattack occurs, this infrastructure could be severely damaged, thereby halting the activities within the ecosystem. It has been shown by Durst and Zieba (2019) that cyberattacks can lead to a loss of competitive advantage and reputational damage. In the context of ecosystems, it is likely to have the same effect and cause stakeholders to withdraw their involvement. Hence, the author proposes the following:

P4. Cybercrime can negatively influence digital infrastructure governance.

5.5.4. *Knowledge censoring and digital technology entrepreneurship*

Censoring has its origins in the field of survival analysis; it involves the absence of observation of an entity, resulting in the loss of data, information, or knowledge (Huang *et al.*, 2020). Interestingly, the phenomenon can also arise within DEEs. The entrepreneur is regarded in this context as an agent of change within the ecosystem as well as a knowledge source (Sheriff & Muffatto, 2015). Based on the assumption that the entrepreneur in this case consists of multiple agents, including the founder and co-founders, it can be said that the viability and functionality of the ecosystem are dependent upon their ideas, experiences, and contributions, which constitute their overall knowledge stock, giving it a competitive edge over other ecosystems. Taking this into consideration, it is imperative that there be a concern about the ecosystem's survival when either the founder or co-founder withdraws from the ecosystem or when new knowledge cannot be applied within the ecosystem.

Particularly, in the case of censored knowledge due to withdrawal, such processes may result in a gradual erosion of the ecosystem due to diminishing knowledge stocks. The situation becomes even more critical if the one that champions the digital component of the ecosystem is the one that withdraws; this can easily lead to its collapse. Hence, the author proposes the following:

> *P5. Knowledge censored negatively affects digital technology entrepreneurship.*

5.6. Proposed Conceptual Model

On the basis of the propositions listed above, a conceptual model is proposed, as shown in Figure 5.1. By combining knowledge risks and the DEE literature as a theoretical base, the framework proposes that (1) unlearning can improve digital citizenship users. Digital multi-sided platforms may contribute to (2) knowledge leakage in an adverse manner, whereas (3) digitalization risks may boost the skills and competencies of users and agents. It is also assumed that in the event of (4) a cyberattack, the consequences can be devastating to the DEE via its digital infrastructure. In contrast, (5) knowledge censoring may be minimally disruptive to the DEE, depending on the agent that leaves.

Fig. 5.1. The proposed conceptual model.

5.7. Conclusion

While DDEs have become a prominent area of entrepreneurship research in recent years and is gaining wide recognition, there is a paucity of research discussing their relation to knowledge risks. Overall, this chapter proposes a framework to illustrate how knowledge risks relate to DEEs.

This is systematically achieved by first adopting Song's (2019) DEE model, which encompasses digital user citizenship, digital infrastructure governance, digital technology entrepreneurship, and multi-sided digital platforms. Next, potential knowledge risks are identified, namely unlearning, knowledge leakage, digitalization risks, cyberattacks, and knowledge censoring. Finally, arguments from the literature are subsequently used to explain the nature of the relationships.

5.7.1. *Implications*

By achieving the study's objectives, several contributions are made to theory and practice. From a theoretical standpoint, besides arguably being the first study to theorize the link between knowledge risks and DEE, this study proposes a theoretically grounded framework that illustrates the potential impact (knowledge) risks can have on the DEE. Additionally, the proposed framework shows that within the context of DEE, both positive and negative risks may coexist. Finally, it extends the knowledge risks literature by proposing a new risk.

Additionally, the study sheds light on the fact that the approach of the DEE is a positive one; however, attention must also be paid to these potential risks that may have an impact on the ecosystem as a whole. In the following section, some recommendations are outlined.

5.7.2. *Recommendations*

As previously established, DEEs may be vulnerable to knowledge risks, so the following set of guidelines is proposed to entrepreneurs in particular, as well as other relevant stakeholders, such as government institutions and policymakers to maintain the smooth operation and effectiveness of the ecosystem:

- Keeping up with technology is essential. Outdated software and failing connections hinder collaboration and innovation. A successful digital ecosystem invests in the latest technologies on the market as well as in people who are eager to learn, unlearn, and relearn.
- It is imperative that risk management be incorporated into the digital ecosystem framework.
- Formalizing a risk management approach that considers the risks associated with knowledge is recommended.
- Reporting critical knowledge risks, managing them over time, and thus learning how to handle a wide variety of risks are recommended.
- Developing a culture of open communication and collaboration between companies is essential for a successful and well-rounded digital ecosystem.
- Cybersecurity measures, such as antivirus software, not opening suspicious emails, and password management, are encouraged.

- Measures are continually monitored for effectiveness, and countermeasures are taken when a measure does not work as expected.

References

Abdul Molok, N. N., Ahmad, A., & Chang, S. (2018). A case analysis of securing organizations against information leakage through online social networking. *International Journal of Information Management* 43, 351–356.

Abebe, M. A., Getahun, F., Asres, S., & Chbeir, R. (2015). Event extraction for collective knowledge in multimedia digital EcoSystem. In AFRICON 2015, 14–17 September 2015, pp. 1–5.

Acs, Z. J. (2022). The global digital platform economy and the region. *The Annals of Regional Science* 70(1), 101–133.

Acs, Z. J., Szerb, L., Song, A., Komlosi, E., & Lafuente, E. (2021). The digital platform economy index 2020. Available at the Global Entrepreneurship and Development Institute.

Annansingh, F. (2021). Bring your own device to work: How serious is the risk? *Journal of Business Strategy* 42(6), 392–398.

Audretsch, D. B. & Belitski, M. (2017). Entrepreneurial ecosystems in cities: Establishing the framework conditions. *The Journal of Technology Transfer* 42(5), 1030–1051.

Bayer, F. & Maier, R. (2006). Knowledge risks in inter-organizational knowledge transfer. In Proceedings of I-KNOW'06, pp. 6–8.

Bhimani, A. (2022). *Financial Management for Technology Start-Ups: How to Power Growth, Track Performance and Drive Innovation.* London: Kogan Page Publishers.

Borgia, M. S. & La Torre, M. (2022). Anti-money laundering in banks: Towards a model for training evaluation. *Management* 10(2), 115–124.

Bratianu, C., Neştian, A. Ş., Tiţă, S. M., Voda, A. I., & Guţă, A. L. (2020). The impact of knowledge risk on sustainability of firms. *Amfiteatru Economic* 22(55), 639–652.

Brown, R. & Mason, C. (2017). Looking inside the spiky bits: A critical review and conceptualization of entrepreneurial ecosystems. *Small Business Economics* 49(1), 11–30.

Brünjes, J. & Diez, J. R. (2012). Opportunity entrepreneurs — potential drivers of non-farm growth in rural Vietnam? In Working Papers on Innovation and Space.

Carter, N. M., Gartner, W. B., & Reynolds, P. D. (1996). Exploring start-up event sequences. *Journal of Business Venturing* 11(3), 151–166.

Dini, P., Iqani, M., & Mansell, R. (2011). The (Im)possibility of interdisciplinarity: Lessons from constructing a theoretical framework for digital ecosystems. *Culture, Theory and Critique* 52(1), 3–27.

Du, W., Pan, S. L., Zhou, N., & Ouyang, T. (2018). From a marketplace of electronics to a digital entrepreneurial ecosystem (DEE): The emergence of a meta-organization in Zhongguancun, China. *Information Systems Journal* 28(6), 1158–1175.

Durst, S. (2021). A plea for responsible and inclusive knowledge management at the world level. *VINE Journal of Information and Knowledge Management Systems*.

Durst, S., Heinze, I., Henschel, T., & Nawaz, N. (2020). Unlearning: A systematic literature review. *International Journal of Business and Globalization* 24(4), 472–495.

Durst, S., Hinteregger, C., & Zieba, M. (2019). The linkage between knowledge risk management and organizational performance. *Journal of Business Research* 105, 1–10.

Durst, S. & Zieba, M. (2017). Knowledge risks-towards a taxonomy. *International Journal of Business Environment* 9(1), 51–63.

Durst, S. & Zieba, M. (2019). Mapping knowledge risks: Towards a better understanding of knowledge management. *Knowledge Management Research & Practice* 17(1), 1–13.

Foli, S. (2022). Total interpretive structural modelling (TISM) and MICMAC approach in analysing knowledge risks in ICT-supported collaborative project. *Vine Journal of Information and Knowledge Management Systems* 52(3), 394–410.

Foli, S. & Durst, S. (2022). Analysing drivers of knowledge leakage in collaborative agreements: A magnetic processing case firm. *Journal of Risk and Financial Management* 15(9), 389.

Foli, S., Durst, S., Davies, L., & Temel, S. (2022). Supply chain risk management in young and mature SMEs. *Journal of Risk and Financial Management* 15(8), 328.

Global Digital Reports (2022). Digital in 2022. https://datareportal.com/global-digital-overview in 24 September 2020.

Gu, W. & Wang, J. (2022). Research on index construction of sustainable entrepreneurship and its impact on economic growth. *Journal of Business Research* 142, 266–276.

Huang, J., Matthews, K., & Zhou, P. (2020). What causes Chinese listed firms to switch bank loan provider? Evidence from a survival analysis. *Emerging Markets Review* 43, 100678.

Katz, R. & Callorda, F. (2018). Accelerating the development of Latin American digital ecosystem and implications for broadband policy. *Telecommunications Policy* 42(9), 661–681.

Klammer, A. & Gueldenberg, S. (2020). Honor the old, welcome the new: An account of unlearning and forgetting in NPD teams. *European Journal of Innovation Management* 23(4), 581–603.

Kotilainen, K., Sommarberg, M., Järventausta, P., & Aalto, P. (2016). Prosumer centric digital energy ecosystem framework. In *Proceedings of the 8th International Conference on Management of Digital EcoSystems*, pp. 47–51.

Kraus, S., Durst, S., Ferreira, J. J., Veiga, P., Kailer, N., & Weinmann, A. (2022). Digital transformation in business and management research: An overview of the current status quo. *International Journal of Information Management* 63, 102466.

Kreuzer, T., Lindenthal, A. K., Oberländer, A. M., & Röglinger, M. (2022). The effects of digital technology on opportunity recognition. *Business & Information Systems Engineering* 64(1), 47–67.

Li, W., Badr, Y., & Biennier, F. (2012). Digital ecosystems: Challenges and prospects. In Proceedings of the International Conference on Management of Emergent Digital EcoSystems, Addis Ababa, Ethiopia. Doi: 10.1145/2457276.2457297.

Luo, Y. (2022). A general framework of digitization risks in international business. *Journal of International Business Studies* 53(2), 344–361.

Marabelli, M. & Newell, S. (2012). Knowledge risks in organizational networks: The practice perspective. *The Journal of Strategic Information Systems* 21(1), 18–30.

Munaiseche, M., Saroinsong, T., Rumambi, H., Kondoj, M., Rangkang, J., & Kumaat, A. (2022). The concept of digital entrepreneurial ecosystem for SMEs in North Sulawesi, Indonesia. *American Journal of Industrial and Business Management* 12(3), 405–419.

Nambisan, S. (2017). Digital entrepreneurship: Toward a digital technology perspective of entrepreneurship. *Entrepreneurship Theory and Practice* 41(6), 1029–1055.

North, K., De Carvalho, A. B., Braccini, A. M., Durst, S., Carvalho, J. Á., Gräslund, K., & Thalmann, S. (2020). 4.1 Knowledge risks in supply chain interactions of SMEs: An exploratory study. In 2019 Knowledge Management in Digital Work Environments.

Perrott, B. E. (2007). A strategic risk approach to knowledge management. *Business Horizons* 50(6), 523–533.

Rajnai, Z. & Kocsis, I. (2018). Assessing Industry 4.0 readiness of enterprises. In 2018 IEEE 16th World Symposium on Applied Machine Intelligence and Informatics (SAMI), 7–10 February 2018, pp. 000225–000230.

Ratten, V. (2020). Creating entrepreneurial opportunities through sport ecosystems. In Ratten, V. (ed.) *Sport Startups: New Advances in Entrepreneurship*, Emerald Publishing Limited, pp. 29–44.

Ratten, V. & Shahriar, A. Z. (2020). Planning and managing open innovative ecosystems, data and government. In Leitão, J., Ratten, V. and Barroca, J. (eds.), *A Guide to Planning and Managing Open Innovative Ecosystems*, Emerald Publishing Limited, pp. 1–12.

Ratten, V. & Thompson, A.-J. (2020). Digital sport entrepreneurial ecosystems. *Thunderbird International Business Review* 62(5), 565–578.

Ribeiro-Navarrete, S., Botella-Carrubi, D., Palacios-Marqués, D., & Orero-Blat, M. (2021). The effect of digitalization on business performance: An applied study of KIBS. *Journal of Business Research* 126, 319–326.

Roundy, P. T., Bradshaw, M., & Brockman, B. K. (2018). The emergence of entrepreneurial ecosystems: A complex adaptive systems approach. *Journal of Business Research* 86, 1–10.

Sarigianni, C., Thalmann, S., & Manhart, M. (2015). Knowledge risks of social media in the financial industry. *International Journal of Knowledge Management (IJKM)* 11(4), 19–34.

Schumpeter, J. A. (1934). *The Theory of Economic Development.* Harvard University Press, Cambridge.

Shane, S. & Venkataraman, S. (2000). The promise of entrepreneurship as a field of research. *Academy of Management Review* 25(1), 217–226.

Shen, K., Lindsay, V., & Xu, Y. (2015). Information Systems Journal special issue on: Digital entrepreneurship. *Information Systems Journal* 11–46.

Sheriff, M. & Muffatto, M. (2015). The present state of entrepreneurship ecosystems in selected countries in Africa. *African Journal of Economic and Management Studies* 6(1), 17–54.

Shishido, Z. (2009). Why Japanese entrepreneurs don't give up control to venture capitalists. Available at SSRN 1370519.

Sohns, F. & Revilla Diez, J. (2018). Explaining micro entrepreneurship in rural Vietnam — A multilevel analysis. *Small Business Economics* 50(1), 219–237.

Song, A. K. (2019). The digital entrepreneurial ecosystem — A critique and reconfiguration. *Small Business Economics* 53(3), 569–590.

Spigel, B. (2017). The relational organization of entrepreneurial ecosystems. *Entrepreneurship Theory and Practice* 41(1), 49–72.

Sumbal, M. S., Tsui, E., Durst, S., Shujahat, M., Irfan, I., & Ali, S. M. (2020). A framework to retain the knowledge of departing knowledge workers in the manufacturing industry. *VINE Journal of Information and Knowledge Management Systems* 50(4), 631–651.

Sussan, F. & Acs, Z. J. (2017). The digital entrepreneurial ecosystem. *Small Business Economics* 49(1), 55–73.

Temel, S. & Durst, S. (2020). Knowledge risk prevention strategies for handling new technological innovations in small businesses. *VINE Journal of Information and Knowledge Management Systems* 51(4), 655–673.

Trkman, P. & Desouza, K. C. (2012). Knowledge risks in organizational networks: An exploratory framework. *The Journal of Strategic Information Systems* 21(1), 1–17.

Wilbert, J. K., Durst, S., Aisenberg Ferenhof, H., & Selig, P. M. (2018). Unlearning at the individual level: An exploratory case study in a high power distance country. *Journal of Innovation Management* 6(3), 17–39.

Zieba, M. & Durst, S. (2018). Knowledge risks in the sharing economy. In Vătămănescu, E.-M. & Pînzaru, F. M. (eds.), *Knowledge Management in the Sharing Economy: Cross-Sectoral Insights into the Future of Competitive Advantage*, Springer International Publishing, Cham, pp. 253–270.

Zieba, M., Durst, S., & Hinteregger, C. (2022). The impact of knowledge risk management on sustainability. *Journal of Knowledge Management* 26(11), 234–258.

https://doi.org/10.1142/9789811270178_0006

Chapter 6

Digital Technology in Entrepreneurship Education: An Overview of the Status Quo

Basel Hammoda

Department of Business Administration,
Tallinn University of Technology, Ehitajate tee5,
Tallinn 19086, Estonia

basel.hammoda@taltech.ee

Abstract

Entrepreneurship is important for the socioeconomic development of our communities. The long-standing debate on whether entrepreneurial skills are acquired or inherited was settled with the growing literature showing the direct benefits entrepreneurship education has on developing entrepreneurial intentions, mindsets, and setting up businesses. However, there has been recent calls for renovating entrepreneurship education to make it more active, engaging, and suitable to the digitally savvy new generations. Technology has, for a long time, played an important role in developing and improving the learning process, and most recently, its application has expanded to entrepreneurship education. This chapter provides a review of the transformative changes in entrepreneurship education and the role digital technology plays in them, expounding on the goals, benefits, and challenges of applying them.

6.1. Introduction

Entrepreneurship education has been shown to have positive socioeconomic impacts in several studies (Katz, 2003; Roulin & Bangerter, 2013; Santos *et al.*, 2019). Traditionally, it heavily relied on theory-laden lectures and reading assignments, trying to impart knowledge to the students. However, these standardized methods fell short of activating students' interests and developing their practical entrepreneurial skills (Fayolle, 2018; Gibb, 2002; Neck & Greene, 2012). Hence, scholars and educators started exploring the potential of other pedagogies that are more engaging and can provide semi-real-life experiences to entrepreneurship students (Fellnhofer, 2019; Ferreira *et al.*, 2018). One of the promising sets of methods is the set of digital educational technologies. Early studies have shown their potential to improve students' learning motivations and develop their entrepreneurial competences in comparison to traditional methods (Antonaci *et al.*, 2015; Ratten & Usmanij, 2021; Schou *et al.*, 2022).

In this chapter, we investigate the role that digital educational technologies play in entrepreneurship education, comment on the challenges affecting their adoption and applications, and exhibit the opportunities they provide for renovating entrepreneurship education. The chapter has the following sections. In Section 6.2, we discuss how ontological and epistemological discourses in entrepreneurship education affect its emergence and pedagogical development. Following that, we expound on the adoption of digital technologies in education and how they are utilized in entrepreneurship education, with specific reference to the benefits they bring about and the obstacles to their incorporation in mainstream entrepreneurial curricula.

6.2. Entrepreneurship Education

6.2.1. *Can we teach people to become entrepreneurial?*

A conventional debate in literature that extended for ages among scholars, educators, and entrepreneurship ecosystem agents was how entrepreneurial orientation can be nurtured? And whether entrepreneurs are born or created? Scholars developed a general opinion toward the end of the past century that entrepreneurs can be taught and trained to varying levels and thus created (Ronstadt, 1985; Solomon & Fernald, 1991). On the practice side of entrepreneurship, as in venture creation, it is true that the journey entrepreneurs go through, from the early days of establishing a start-up, exposes and equips them with the required knowledge and skills to become more successful. Those experiences represent an unreplaceable asset in their survival and future growth (Peña, 2002).

From a statistical perspective, recent studies on start-ups' survival or failure rates found the lack of entrepreneurial competences among nascent entrepreneurs to be the single most important predictor of their success or failure. For example, a recent study from the University of Tennessee found that the main cause of start-up failures in nearly half of the cases is "incompetence," as in lacking vision, deficient planning, erratic pricing, neglected accounting and financial management activities, and a lack of required knowledge in different areas. This was followed by a "lack of managerial experience" in almost one-third of the cases, which manifested as unplanned growth, poor financing activities, and the inability to manage resources or expand sales channels (Cosenz & Noto, 2018). In their review of the entrepreneurship education literature, Nabi *et al.* (2017) confirm that entrepreneurship education is a core component of entrepreneurship development as it plays an important role in shaping the mindset, behaviors, and skills of learners and entrepreneurs. It helps establish their entrepreneurial identity and supports their endeavors in starting new businesses and launching innovative initiatives.

6.2.2. *Development of entrepreneurship education in research and practice*

In the past two decades, entrepreneurship education has garnered increasing attention from scholars, with a growing number of studies trying to shape the ontological, epistemological, and didactical assumptions of entrepreneurship education, in addition to defining its actors, components, assessment methods and frameworks, and contingencies. The aim is to better equip educators and learners with the tools necessary to promote entrepreneurship and entrepreneurial outcomes (Loi & Fayolle, 2021). This scholarly activity coincided with huge investments made by countries around the world in developing and promoting entrepreneurship education throughout the years (Fayolle *et al.*, 2006; Karimi *et al.*, 2016).

In turn, the range of programs offered to educate students on entrepreneurial skills has widened and spread to almost all educational fields, levels, and systems (Morris *et al.*, 2013; Neck & Greene, 2011). Students from various disciplines are increasingly exposed to educational and training courses and activities focused on entrepreneurship (Damásio & Bicacro, 2017; Yi & Duval-Couetil, 2018). The recent explosion in entrepreneurship education has extended beyond university borders to schools, colleges, and social organizations, with new initiatives and tailored programs erupting every day (European Commission: Entrepreneurship Action Plan, 2020). In Italy, for example, the growing relevance of and interest in entrepreneurship education is evidenced by a remarkable growth in the number of entrepreneurship courses and programs offered by universities (Curci & Micozzi, 2017; Iacobucci & Micozzi, 2012). Hence, entrepreneurship education has become a core part of the educational program across different systems, geographies, and disciplines (Kozlinska, 2011; Shane & Venkataraman, 2000).

6.2.3. *Entrepreneurship education aims*

The main purpose of entrepreneurship education is to prepare students, graduates, and social agents for the dynamic and rapidly changing professional environment with its economic and employability challenges (Fayolle, 2018). Entrepreneurship education helps shape the mindsets, attitudes, and behaviors of learners and social actors and equips them with the skills required to face such turbulent and challenging environments (Hytti & O'Gorman, 2004; Nabi *et al.*, 2017).

Entrepreneurship education can thus be said to have a set of primary objectives. These objectives were reported in several studies (e.g., Davis *et al.*, 2016; Fretschner & Weber, 2013; Hytti & O'Gorman, 2004; O'Connor, 2013):

- develop an entrepreneurial mindset,
- build entrepreneurial skills and competence,
- increase knowledge acquisition of management-related topics,
- improve entrepreneurial abilities and behaviors,
- enhance managerial and professional skills.

6.2.4. *Impact and importance of entrepreneurship education*

Entrepreneurship education provides its audience with a set of knowledge, skills, behaviors and attitudes which are deemed essential in a broad range of settings (Brännback *et al.*, 2007; Cheung, 2008; Dickson *et al.*, 2008; Krueger, 2007; Oosterbeek *et al.*, 2010; Peterman & Kennedy, 2003; Petridou & Glaveli, 2008; von Graevenitz *et al.*, 2010). In this way, it shapes their behaviors and opinions (Fretschner & Weber, 2013; Walter & Dohse, 2012). These help recipients fulfill several roles in their communities as competent and well-educated employees, citizens, clients, and leaders, especially within a start-up or small-business context (Thrane *et al.*, 2016). Entrepreneurship education also helps increase the number of those effective social actors (Matlay, 2008; O'Connor, 2013).

Entrepreneurship education programs provide value to learners from different backgrounds and in different situations. Hence, the impact of those programs is not limited by company formation or learners becoming entrepreneurs (Kuckertz, 2013). As an example, companies have been hiring entrepreneurship graduates in order to enhance the innovative abilities and professional capacities of their workforce (Daniel, 2016; Kuckertz, 2013).

6.2.5. *Innovating entrepreneurship education pedagogies*

According to Kuratko and Morris (2018), entrepreneurship education relies on several pedagogies and methods that can be generally classified into traditional teaching approaches, such as lectures and reading materials, and experiential learning approaches, such as case studies, business simulations and gaming, and extracurricular activities.

Entrepreneurship educators often feel that traditional educational approaches through lectures, readings, and essay assignments are not suitable for the dynamic and complex nature of entrepreneurship. These traditional methods in entrepreneurship education have been subjected to negative feedback from scholars, educators, and the students. They are regarded as being mainly theoretical or dry (Huebscher & Lendner, 2010; Fayolle, 2018; Loi & Fayolle, 2021). As a result, they were not able to fulfill the core purpose of entrepreneurship education, which is to instill practical entrepreneurial competencies, such as creative thinking and coping with risks, among learners (Hughes *et al.*, 2008).

Hence, entrepreneurship educators have been exploring and toying around with more effective and impactful methods in the hope of better developing entrepreneurial learners' knowledge application and affective competencies (Fayolle *et al.*, 2006; Kasurinen & Knutas, 2018; Taatila, 2010). Thus, these effective methods help teachers and lecturers get over the limiting constraints of entrepreneurship education.

Among researchers, there is similar agreement that innovative methods to teaching entrepreneurship can help educators overcome the challenges observed in entrepreneurship education, as these methods help the students not only acquire but also put into practice, through a variety of activities, the knowledge and skills they acquired (Ferreira *et al.*, 2018; Neck *et al.*, 2014).

Those new experiential approaches to entrepreneurship education are increasingly being adopted and spread, thus overtaking the traditional, lecture-based theoretical approach (Sousa *et al.*, 2019; Loi & Fayolle, 2021). Entrepreneurship students are also growing fond of these approaches as it engages them in the learning process (Sousa *et al.*, 2019), and allows them to study management without relying primarily on theory-laden textbooks and articles (Pratikto *et al.*, 2021). According to Zuo *et al.* (2021), this fits the description of entrepreneurship as a practice-inclined skill, and learning it should be based on actively getting the learner involved in acquiring and practicing it.

However, it is to be noted that a balance needs to be struck between active learning approaches and more theory-based methods. Modern methods can play a role that is complementary to and synergetic with more traditional methods by promoting the application of acquired knowledge and enhancing the development of cognitive and affective skills (Buzady & Almeida, 2019).

6.2.6. *Learning theories in entrepreneurship education*

Learning theories can be categorically classified into behavioral, cognitive, and simulative, according to Akgün *et al.* (2003). Corbett (2005) argues that behavioral learning theories are the least impactful in an entrepreneurial context, as they "reward those that follow routine and status quo the antithesis of entrepreneurship" (p. 482). He argues that learning through experience is essential for entrepreneurs. They must engage in the stimulative cognitive processes of thinking, empathizing, practicing, and observing (Corbett, 2005).

Entrepreneurship education is naturally more action oriented than general education (Fayolle, 2018). It focuses on the importance of practical activities and exposure to real-world scenarios and experiences (Kassean *et al.*, 2015; Neck & Greene, 2012; Neck *et al.*, 2014). Entrepreneurs and students are hence encouraged to put the knowledge they acquired through theoretical lectures into practice (Kriz & Hense, 2004). These practical activities can happen as a follow-up or concurrent engagement. They have been repeatedly proven to provide superior benefits to learners through their interactive approach (Cooper, 2007) and to help them with knowledge retention, comprehension, and application (Kriz & Hense, 2004).

Canaleta *et al.* (2014) argued that active learning approaches improve students' competences and educators' ability to assess the outcomes of the educational process. One of the core premises of active learning is the natural experiences it offers to learners, with all the complexities and unclarity that characterizes real-life situations. These experiences are essential for the cognitive and behavioral learning processes (Jones & Holt, 2008). Experiential learning enhances student learning and retention (Abrahams & Singh, 2013; Bruni-Bossio & Willness, 2016), as it concentrates on the "doing" part of the learning process (Corbett, 2005).

6.2.7. *Experiential learning theory of entrepreneurship education*

Experiential learning is defined by Kolb (1984) as "the process by which knowledge is created through the transformation of experience" (p. 41). He regards experience as a process of interaction between an individual and their environment. Specifically, Kolb (1984) identified that individuals learn through a continuous cycle of experience, reflection, thought, and experimentation, with reflection being the process by which learners process their experience in such a way that they know what they are doing and, more importantly, why they are doing it (Boud, 1999).

Entrepreneurship education has acknowledged the importance of experiential learning in the process of educating the nascent entrepreneur (Le Roux & Steyn, 2007). In the literature, experiential learning theory has grown into "the" theory of entrepreneurship education (Wang & Chugh, 2014), as it supports individual learners' experiences. Several authors have emphasized that developing entrepreneurial skills, attitudes, and behaviors necessitates the application of experiential learning methods. However, while experiential learning has provided many insights into the study of entrepreneurial learning, it has been criticized for insufficiently explaining how individuals learn with and from each other.

6.2.8. *Challenges of entrepreneurship education*

Entrepreneurship education as a research field and as a practice is facing several challenges. Multiple literature reviews have highlighted the increasing fragmentation of the field, with a lack of experimentally proven methodologies and frameworks. With the accelerated and expansive adoption of experiential learning methods, there is limited visibility on the applicability and effectiveness of these diverse approaches, methods, and tools (Gorman *et al.*, 1997; Naia *et al.*, 2014; Pittaway & Cope, 2007). In addition, there is a dire need for more research on the outcomes of using innovative methods in entrepreneurship education (Antonaci *et al.*, 2015).

Fayolle *et al.* (2006) suggest a few points to remedy this fragmentation and lack of clarity. He argues that entrepreneurship education scholars and practitioners need to:

- reflect a better understanding of the skills and competencies it aims to create,
- provide more effective methods for evaluating educational pedagogies, and
- undertake more rigorous studies of educational effectiveness.

6.3. Digital Technology in Entrepreneurship Education

6.3.1. *Digital technology in education*

6.3.1.1. *Transformational era*

Recent advances in information and communication technology have affected different aspects of our lives and various economic sectors. Digital technologies have become embedded in all our activities, providing unlimited chances for improvement and creativity (Vorbach *et al.*, 2019).

The education sector is affected by this change, similar to other sectors. Digital technologies are aimed at aiding the transformation of education by filling the gap between the present status and the desired future one. These reforms can gradually enhance the effectiveness and efficiency of the educational process (Papadakis *et al.*, 2017).

Universities today are on a fast track to enhancing their quality and effectiveness. This was primarily made possible by the widespread application of technology and communication systems in education (Teymurova *et al.*, 2020). It is expected that digitalization will create and continue to offer opportunities for leveraging digital tools in different parts of the educational process (Mavlutova *et al.*, 2020).

Modern digital and communication technologies have led to the development of worldwide connected learning systems and to the convergence of academic programs and disciplines. It has increased the attractiveness of the education system as it allows students to have better access, flexibility, and control over their learning journey, regardless of their location or circumstance (Gianesini *et al.*, 2018; Qureshi *et al.*, 2020).

6.3.1.2. *The need for change*

Most of the current students belong to Generation Z. Those young learners are used to interacting with a huge range of technological tools and applications in their daily lives. Hence, using similar technologies to teach them will bring a sense of familiarity and liking to the process. However, educators are required to keep up with technological updates and work on enhancing their digital skills (Mavlutova *et al.*, 2020). That is one of the reasons for the accelerated adoption of what is called a "student-focused approach" among educational institutions, which leverages modern digital and communication tools. These innovative digital solutions improve the student-focused approach, increase the attractiveness of courses and programs, and open up access to educational materials and resources, transcending space and time boundaries (Oyelere *et al.*, 2016).

6.3.1.3. *Accelerated adoption in education*

Information and communication technology is nowadays being used to make teaching methods more effective, moving away from the traditional lecture-focused approach to a competency-based one (Wu *et al.*, 2018). Teachers are adopting them to enhance their communication and delivery of educational messages to their students (Tess, 2013). Digital interaction during learning sessions motivates the students and makes them more interested in learning (Chen & Huang, 2012). They are becoming a central component of students' engagement (Stoney & Oliver, 1997). On a personal level, digital tools have a positive impact on students' quality of life and academic performance at universities (Coccoli *et al.*, 2014).

Tretyakova *et al.* (2021) conclude that as digital technologies become more widely available and accessible to the majority of stakeholders in the learning business, the link between technology and education will inevitably continue to grow. They predict that the education sector will certainly move in the direction of becoming heavily reliant on digital technologies.

6.3.2. *Digital technology in entrepreneurship education*

Digital technology represents a collection of digital tools, infrastructure components and services, and interactive platforms. It is regarded as a strong foundation for designing and applying digitally transformative experiences to entrepreneurial learning settings within universities and higher educational institutions (Secundo *et al.*, 2020). Digital technologies provide new avenues for transforming the way entrepreneurship is taught to students (Schou *et al.*, 2022). The entrepreneurship education landscape has gradually been witnessing the introduction of several methods and artifacts, whether in online or offline forms, to teach students.

However, only in recent years have researchers started devoting efforts to exploring their applications in entrepreneurship education (Wu *et al.*, 2018). Holinska *et al.* (2019) argue that scholars should focus more on digital technology applications in entrepreneurship education, as early studies have confirmed their value in improving its effectiveness. It has hence become important for scholars and educators to assess and define the possible methods of integrating digital technology in the process of entrepreneurship education, aiming at further enhancing the entrepreneurial competences of learners (Tretyakova *et al.*, 2021).

6.3.2.1. *A learner perspective on digital technology adoption in entrepreneurship education*

For any innovative educational solution in entrepreneurship to be adopted, attention must be paid to students' opinions and preferences (Neergaard & Christensen, 2017), especially if it is intended for broader propagation among the masses of entrepreneurship students (Cooper, 2007). In digital transformation initiatives, the inability or incapability of an educational institution to understand and meet students' needs appropriately can have costly consequences. One part of that is related to the cost of procuring and operating the educational technologies themselves, and the other part is due to the attrition of unsatisfied students (Reigeluth, 1999). Hence, the continually progressing notion of learners as customers (Cooper, 2007) is becoming of particular importance these days.

In an entrepreneurship education context, students prefer innovative and practical modalities, i.e., those involving some sort of technological tool, such as business model simulation, that can help with learning activities (Mavlutova *et al.*, 2020). That comes as no surprise, as most students are already heavily attached with digital products and technologies in their studies and daily lives (Philippe *et al.*, 2018).

6.3.2.2. *Are digital technologies the answer?*

Fayolle (2018) argues that using digital technologies to teach entrepreneurship to students could prove valuable. Digital technologies provide unmatched innovation opportunities to entrepreneurs and can become a source of inspiration and creativity when utilized by entrepreneurial learners (Cohen *et al.*, 2017; Urbinati *et al.*, 2017; Yoo, 2010).

Tretyakova *et al.* (2021) believe the introduction of digital technologies in educational institutions and their integration with other teaching methods in entrepreneurship education curricula could serve as the required solution to effectively educate and train nascent entrepreneurs. Hence, the use of innovative technologies in bringing about competent entrepreneurs is essential (Tretyakova *et al.*, 2021).

6.3.2.3. *The aim of applying digital technologies to entrepreneurship education*

Digital technologies are being deployed in entrepreneurship education for the purpose of fortifying the learning experience of students (Papadakis *et al.*, 2017). Their introduction into entrepreneurship education has provided a strong push for the research and practice of experiential learning approaches, as digital tools provide practical entrepreneurial experiences (Tretyakova *et al.*, 2021).

It is acknowledged that the entrepreneurship education curricula could benefit from including educational technology as it attracts and retains students, enhances their experiences, and improves the learning outcomes (Kuratko, 2005; Wu *et al.*, 2018). Hence, modern entrepreneurship pedagogies incorporate educational technologies to influence students' entrepreneurial intentions, mindset, and outcomes (Tretyakova *et al.*, 2021).

6.3.2.4. *Benefits of using digital technologies in entrepreneurship education*

Entrepreneurship education researchers have highlighted the importance of including digital technologies in entrepreneurship curricula. The literature has cited several benefits of deploying educational technologies for teaching entrepreneurship. These can be generally grouped into five categories: financial, convenience, student-centered, engagement, and outcomes:

- Financial:
  - Digital technologies represent a cost-effective measure in delivering entrepreneurship education, especially at scale (Russell, 1999).
  - They can be used to address issues involved in dealing with large class sizes in entrepreneurship education (Cooper, 2007).
- Convenience:
  - They offer learners personal control over time, pace, place, and direction of learning (Cooper, 2007).
  - They make it possible to involve not only young people but also all population categories in the study of entrepreneurship at a comfortable pace and with flexible terms (Maresch *et al.*, 2017).
  - They make collaborative entrepreneurship learning easy and flexible in terms of learning time and place (Tretyakova *et al.*, 2021).
- Student-centered:
  - They are effective in meeting the learners' needs of a student-focused approach (Reigeluth, 1999).
  - They are perceived as a better approach than lectures as they are more personal. They provide students with a direct feedback channel and are always available and accessible whenever required (Cooper, 2007).
- Engagement:
  - They can enhance interaction between students and course content, improve their motivation, and engage students in the educational experience (Wu *et al.*, 2018).

- Outcomes:
  - They promote the development and implementation of experiential learning that inspires students to think creatively (Tretyakova *et al.*, 2021).
  - They improve entrepreneurial competences (Wu *et al.*, 2018).
  - They increase the rates of setting up businesses (Tretyakova *et al.*, 2021).
  - They improve creativity and innovative drive of students (Cohen *et al.*, 2017; Urbinati *et al.*, 2017; Yoo, 2010).

6.3.2.5. *Challenges of adopting digital technologies in entrepreneurship education*

Although incorporating digital tools in entrepreneurship courses has proven to bring about positive outcomes from several perspectives — that of the learner, the educator, and the educational institute — there are still multiple challenges hindering further expansion in the usage of digital technologies in entrepreneurship education. Some of the most common obstacles cited by scholars include the following:

- The focus on the cost–benefit analysis or opportunity costs from an educational institution perspective might not be in favor of adopting digital tools required for entrepreneurship education (G. T. Henry *et al.*, 2004; C. Henry *et al.*, 2005).
- High-quality educational technologies, which provide the required effectiveness, are more expensive, whether developed inhouse or purchased, and hence constitute a risky decision (Cooper, 2007).
- Inadequate realization and utilization of the full functionalities and potential of digital educational technologies (Secundo *et al.*, 2020).
- Lack of awareness and basic level of understanding of educational technologies among educators and educational institutions (Secundo *et al.*, 2020).
- Most entrepreneurship education programs have not integrated or explored the potential of including digital technologies within their curricula (Ratten, 2020).
- There is limited research on the applicability and outcomes of digital technologies in entrepreneurship education (Wu *et al.*, 2018).

- Applying digital technologies in classes with a large number of students is likely to require a level of design specification which offers a wide range of choices to students to meet their varying needs and expectations (Cooper, 2007).
- There are certain conditions and circumstances that must be met, depending on the type of technology used, to fulfill the desired outcomes (Samašonok *et al.*, 2020).

6.4. Conclusion

As the expansion of entrepreneurship education is following a similar trajectory to digital technology inclusion in the educational process, it became essential to review the literature at the intersection of these two research fields to provide an overview of our understanding of the current applications and effectiveness of using digital technologies in entrepreneurship education. We reviewed the emergence of entrepreneurship education as a field of inquiry and the current challenges it faces. Then, we accounted for the educational technology cited in the entrepreneurship education literature and expounded on their applications, the benefits they provide, and the reported outcomes of using them. We did so by scoping and reviewing the important literary work at the nexus of entrepreneurship education and digital educational technology.

This chapter adds to our understanding as researchers of the role of digital technology in entrepreneurship education in terms of its benefits, challenges, and applications. It provides eye-opening and practical insights to educators willing to apply digital technologies in their entrepreneurship programs and courses and to incorporate them into their curricula. It can help them understand and plan for the several contingencies related to their introduction to entrepreneurship education. The review of the challenges and benefits of applying them can support educational institutions in their adoption and implementation plans in entrepreneurship education settings. Hence, this chapter can act as a foundation for those involved in entrepreneurship education planning and delivery to achieve more efficient and effective incorporation of digital technologies in its processes.

In addition, our proposition signals multiple areas for future research focused on the intersection of entrepreneurship education and digital technologies. For example, more studies are needed to understand the main reasons behind the reported challenges and to investigate how we, as researchers and educators, can overcome them. The reported benefits also need to be more rigorously studied, perhaps by applying longitudinal and experimental studies, which are currently deficient in entrepreneurship education research. Overall, we consider our review an essential piece of the puzzle that sheds some light on this under-researched interdisciplinary area between digital technology and entrepreneurship education, which is receiving increased interest from scholars and practitioners in this field.

For entrepreneurs and managers of small entrepreneurial firms, it provides them with much-needed guidance on using accessible and engaging educational tools that can help them develop and enhance their entrepreneurial competence. They might not have time for or access to standardized entrepreneurship education, and hence, digital educational technologies can be a valuable option in their learning endeavors. This will, in turn, help them better manage their entrepreneurial companies and improve their outcomes. Moreover, when digital educational applications are used in entrepreneurial settings, they extend the learning experience to a semi-real environment. Hence, it can also be useful to apply it to previous or existing business scenarios that entrepreneurs and managers face in their daily entrepreneurial lives.

References

Antonaci, A., Dagnino, F. M., Ott, M., Bellotti, F., Berta, R., De Gloria, A., Lavagnino, E., Romero, M., Usart, M., & Mayer, I. (2015). A gamified collaborative course in entrepreneurship: Focus on objectives and tools. *Computers in Human Behavior* 51, 1276–1283.

Akgün, A. E., Lynn, G. S., & Byrne, J. C. (2003). Organizational learning: A socio-cognitive framework. *Human Relations* 56(7), 839–868.

Abrahams, A. S. & Singh, T. (2013). Expeditionary learning in information systems: Definition, implementation, and assessment. *Decision Sciences Journal of Innovative Education* 11(1), 47–75.

Barba-Sánchez, V. & Atienza-Sahuquillo, C. (2018). Entrepreneurial intention among engineering students: The role of entrepreneurship education. *European Research on Management and Business Economics* 24(1), 53–61.

Boud, D. (1999). Situating academic development in professional work: Using peer learning. *The International Journal for Academic Development* 4(1), 3–10.

Brännback, M., Krueger, N. F., Carsrud, A. L., Kickul, J., & Elfving, J. (June 2007). 'Trying' to be an entrepreneur? A 'Goal-Specific' challenge to the Intentions Model. *SSRN Electronic Journal* 27. DOI:10.2139/ssrn.1135224.

Bruni-Bossio, V. & Willness, C. (2016). The "Kobayashi Maru" meeting: High-fidelity experiential learning. *Journal of Management Education* 40(5), 619–647.

Buzady, Z. & Almeida, F. (2019, July). FLIGBY — A serious game tool to enhance motivation and competencies in entrepreneurship. In *Informatics* (Vol. 6, No. 3, p. 27). MDPI.

Canaleta, X., Vernet, D., Vicent, L., & Montero, J. A. (2014). Master in teacher training: A real implementation of active learning. *Computers in Human Behavior* 31, 651–658.

Chen, C. C. & Huang, T. C. (2012). Learning in a u-Museum: Developing a context aware ubiquitous learning environment. *Computers & Education* 59(3), 873–883.

Cheung, C. K. (2008). Entrepreneurship education in Hong Kong's secondary curriculum: Possibilities and limitations, *Education + Training* 50(6), 500–515. https://doi.org/10.1108/00400910810901827.

Coccoli, M., Guercio, A., Maresca, P., & Stanganelli, L. (2014). Smarter universities: A vision for the fast changing digital era. *Journal of Visual Languages & Computing* 25(6), 1003–1011.

Cohen, J., Jones, W. M., Smith, S., & Calandra, B. (2017). Makification: Towards a framework for leveraging the maker movement in formal education. *Journal of Educational Multimedia and Hypermedia* 26(3), 217–229.

Cooper, B. (2007). Central issues in the use of computer-based materials for high volume entrepreneurship education. *Active Learning in Higher Education* 8(3), 201–217.

Corbett, A. C. (2005). Experiential learning within the process of opportunity identification and exploitation. *Entrepreneurship Theory and Practice* 29(4), 473–491.

Cosenz, F. & Noto, G. (2018). Fostering entrepreneurial learning processes through Dynamic Start-up business model simulators. *The International Journal of Management Education* 16(3), 468–482.

Curci, N. & Micozzi, A. (2017). Entrepreneurial activity and education in Italy. *L'industria* 38(3), 385–410.

Damasio, M. J., & Bicacro, J. (2017). Entrepreneurship education for film and media arts: How can we teach entrepreneurship to students in the creative disciplines? *Industry and Higher Education*, 31(4), 253–266.

Daniel, A. D. (2016). Fostering an entrepreneurial mindset by using a design thinking approach in entrepreneurship education. *Industry and Higher Education* 30(3), 215–223.

Davis, M. H., Hall, J. A., & Mayer, P. S. (2016). Developing a new measure of entrepreneurial mindset: Reliability, validity, and implications for practitioners. *Consulting Psychology Journal: Practice and Research* 68(1), 21.

Dickson, P. H., Solomon, G. T., & Weaver, K. M. (2008). Entrepreneurial selection and success: does education matter?. *Journal of small business and enterprise development* 15(2), 239–258.

European Economic and Social Committee (2013). Entrepreneurship 2020 Action Plan. European Commission. Available at: https://www.eesc.europa.eu/en/our-work/opinions-information-reports/opinions/entrepreneurship-2020-action-plan.

Fayolle, A. (2018). Personal views on the future of entrepreneurship education. In *A Research Agenda for Entrepreneurship Education*. Edward Elgar Publishing.

Fayolle, A., Gailly, B., & Lassas-Clerc, N. (2006). Assessing the impact of entrepreneurship education programmes: a new methodology. *Journal of European Industrial Training*, 30(9), 701–720.

Fellnhofer, K. (2019). Toward a taxonomy of entrepreneurship education research literature: A bibliometric mapping and visualization. *Educational Research Review* 27, 28–55.

Ferreira, J. J., Fayolle, A., Ratten, V., & Raposo, M. (eds.). (2018). *Entrepreneurial Universities*. Edward Elgar Publishing, Cheltenham, UK.

Fretschner, M. & Weber, S. (2013). Measuring and understanding the effects of entrepreneurial awareness education. *Journal of Small Business Management* 51(3), 410–428.

Gianesini, G., Cubico, S., Favretto, G., & Leitão, J. (2018). Entrepreneurial competences: Comparing and contrasting models and taxonomies. In *Entrepreneurship and the Industry Life Cycle*, pp. 13–32. Springer, Cham.

Gibb, A. (2002). In pursuit of a new 'enterprise' and 'entrepreneurship' paradigm for learning: Creative destruction, new values, new ways of doing things and new combinations of knowledge. *International Journal of Management Reviews* 4(3), 233–269.

Gorman, G., Hanlon, D., & King, W. (1997). Some research perspectives on entrepreneurship education, enterprise education and education for small business management: A ten-year literature review. *International Small Business Journal* 15(3), 56–77.

Grivokostopoulou, F., Kovas, K., & Perikos, I. (2019). Examining the impact of a gamified entrepreneurship education framework in higher education. *Sustainability* 11(20), 5623.

Henry, C., Hill, F., & Leitch, C. (2005). Entrepreneurship education and training: Can entrepreneurship be taught? Part I, *Education + Training* 47(2), 98–111. https://doi.org/10.1108/00400910510586524

Henry, G. T., Rubenstein, R., & Bugler, D. T. (2004). Is HOPE enough? Impacts of receiving and losing merit-based financial aid. *Educational Policy* 18(5), 686–709.

Holinska, T., Komarovska, O., Melnyk, O., Pet'ko, L., Shpitsa, R., Sova, O., & Strohal, T. (2019). Cloud technologies in art entrepreneurship education. *Journal of Entrepreneurship Education* 22(5), 1–6.

Huebscher, J. & Lendner, C. (2010). Effects of entrepreneurship simulation game seminars on entrepreneurs' and students' learning. *Journal of Small Business & Entrepreneurship* 23(4), 543–554.

Hughes, T., O'Regan, N., & Wornham, D. (2008). The credibility issue: Closing the academic/practitioner gap. *Strategic Change* 17(7–8), 215–233.

Hytti, U. & O'Gorman, C. (2004). What is "enterprise education"? An analysis of the objectives and methods of enterprise education programmes in four European countries. *Education + Training*, 46, 11–23.

Iacobucci, D. & Micozzi, A. (2012). Entrepreneurship education in Italian universities: trend, situation and opportunities. *Education + Training* 54(8/9), 673–696.

Jones, O., & Holt, R. (2008). The creation and evolution of new business ventures: an activity theory perspective. *Journal of Small Business and Enterprise Development* 15(1), 51–73.

Karimi, S., Biemans, H. J., Lans, T., Chizari, M., & Mulder, M. (2016). The impact of entrepreneurship education: A study of Iranian students' entrepreneurial intentions and opportunity identification. *Journal of Small Business Management* 54(1), 187–209.

Kassean, H., Vanevenhoven, J., Liguori, E., & Winkel, D. E. (2015). Entrepreneurship education: a need for reflection, real-world experience and action. *International Journal of Entrepreneurial Behavior & Research* 21(5), 690–708.

Kasurinen, J. & Knutas, A. (2018). Publication trends in gamification: A systematic mapping study. *Computer Science Review* 27, 33–44.

Katz, J. A. (2003). The chronology and intellectual trajectory of American entrepreneurship education: 1876–1999. *Journal of Business Venturing* 18(2), 283–300.

Kolb, D. A. (1984). The process of experiential learning. Experiential learning: Experience as the source of learning and development, pp. 20–38.

Kozlinska, I. (2011). Contemporary approaches to entrepreneurship education. *Journal of Business Management* 4, 205–220.

Kriz, W. C. & Hense, J. (2004). Evaluation of the EU-Project "Simgame" in business education. In Bridging the gap: transforming knowledge into action through gaming and simulation (Isaga 2004 Conference Proceedings) (pp. 352–363). Munchen: Sagsaga.

Krueger Jr, N. F. (2007). What lies beneath? The experiential essence of entrepreneurial thinking. *Entrepreneurship Theory and Practice* 31(1), 123–138.

Kuckertz, A. (2013). Entrepreneurship education–status quo and prospective developments. *Journal of Entrepreneurship Education* 16, 59–71.

Kuratko, D. F. (2005). The emergence of entrepreneurship education: Development, trends, and challenges. *Entrepreneurship Theory and Practice* 29(5), pp. 577–597.

Kuratko, D. F. & Morris, M. H. (2018). Examining the future trajectory of entrepreneurship. *Journal of Small Business Management* 56(1), 11–23.

Le Roux, I. & Steyn, B. (2007). Experiential learning and critical reflection as a tool for transfer of business knowledge: An empirical case study of a start-up simulation intervention for nascent entrepreneurs. *South African Journal of Economic and Management Sciences* 10(3), 330–347.

Loi, M., & Fayolle, A. (2021). Impact of entrepreneurship education: a review of the past, overview of the present, and a glimpse of future trends. *Annals of Entrepreneurship Education and Pedagogy–2021*, 170–193.

Maresch, D., Harms, R., Kailer, N., & Wimmer-Wurm, B. (2016). The impact of entrepreneurship education on the entrepreneurial intention of students in science and engineering versus business studies university programs. *Technological Forecasting and Social Change* 104, 172–179.

Matlay, H. (2008). The impact of entrepreneurship education on entrepreneurial outcomes. *Journal of Small Business and Enterprise Development* 15(2), 382–396. https://doi.org/10.1108/14626000810871745.

Mavlutova, I., Lesinskis, K., Liogys, M., & Hermanis, J. (2020). Innovative teaching techniques for entrepreneurship education in the era of digitalisation. *WSEAS Transactions on Environment and Development* 16(1), 725–733.

McCarthy, J. (2010). Blended learning environments: Using social networking sites to enhance the first year experience. *Australasian Journal of Educational Technology* 26(6), 729–740.

Morris, M. H., Webb, J. W., Fu, J., & Singhal, S. (2013). A competency-based perspective on entrepreneurship education: Conceptual and empirical insights. *Journal of Small Business Management* 51(3), 352–369.

Nabi, G., Liñán, F., Fayolle, A., Krueger, N., & Walmsley, A. (2017). The impact of entrepreneurship education in higher education: A systematic review and research agenda. *Academy of Management Learning & Education* 16(2), 277–299.

Naia, A., Baptista, R., Januário, C., & Trigo, V. (2014). A systematization of the literature on entrepreneurship education: Challenges and emerging solutions in the entrepreneurial classroom. *Industry and Higher Education* 28(2), 79–96.

Neck, H. M. & Greene, P. G. (2011). Entrepreneurship education: Known worlds and new frontiers. *Journal of Small Business Management* 49(1), 55–70.

Neck, H. M. & Greene, P. G. (2012). Entrepreneurship education: Known worlds and new frontiers. *IEEE Engineering Management Review* 40(2), 9–21.

Neck, H. M., Greene, P. G., & Brush, C. G. (eds.). (2014). *Teaching Entrepreneurship: A Practice-based Approach*. Edward Elgar Publishing, Cheltenham, UK.

Neergaard, H. & Christensen, D. R. (2017). Breaking the waves: Routines and rituals in entrepreneurship education. *Industry and Higher Education* 31(2), 90–100.

Oosterbeek, H., Van Praag, M., & Ijsselstein, A. (2010). The impact of entrepreneurship education on entrepreneurship skills and motivation. *European Economic Review* 54(3), 442–454.

Oyelere, S. S., Suhonen, J., Shonola, S. A., & Joy, M. S. (2016). Discovering students mobile learning experiences in higher education in Nigeria. In *2016 IEEE Frontiers in Education Conference (FIE)*. IEEE Press, pp. 1–7. https://doi.org/10.1109/FIE.2016.7757541.

O'Connor, A. (2013). A conceptual framework for entrepreneurship education policy: Meeting government and economic purposes. *Journal of Business Venturing* 28(4), 546–563.

Pacheco, D. F., Dean, T. J., & Payne, D. S. (2010). Escaping the green prison: Entrepreneurship and the creation of opportunities for sustainable development. *Journal of Business Venturing* 25(5), 464–480.

Palazzeschi, L., Bucci, O., & Fabio, A. D. (2018). High entrepreneurship, leadership, and professionalism (HELP): A new resource for workers in the 21st century. *Frontiers in Psychology* 9, 1480.

Papadakis, S., Kalogiannakis, M., & Zaranis, N. (2017). Designing and creating an educational app rubric for preschool teachers. *Education and Information Technologies* 22(6), 3147–3165.

Peña, I. (2002). Intellectual capital and business start-up success. *Journal of Intellectual Capital* 3(2), 180–198.

Peterman, N. E. & Kennedy, J. (2003). Enterprise education: Influencing students' perceptions of entrepreneurship. *Entrepreneurship Theory and Practice* 28(2), 129–144.

Petridou, E. & Glaveli, N. (2008). Rural women entrepreneurship within co-operatives: training support. *Gender in Management: An International Journal* 23(4), 262–277.

Philippe, S., Souchet, A. D., Lameras, P., Petridis, P., Caporal, J., Coldeboeuf, G., & Duzan, H. (2020). Multimodal teaching, learning and training in virtual reality: A review and case study. *Virtual Reality & Intelligent Hardware* 2(5), 421–442.

Pittaway, L. & Cope, J. (2007). Entrepreneurship education: A systematic review of the evidence. *International Small Business Journal* 25(5), 479–510.

Pratikto, H., Hanafiya, R., Ashar, M., Akbar, M. I., & Harsono, Y. T. (2021). Entrepreneurship game apps to enhancement student skill thinking analytic in class online. *International Journal of Interactive Mobile Technology* 15(8), 155–162.

Qureshi, M. I., Khan, N., Raza, H., Imran, A., & Ismail, F. (2021). Digital technologies in education 4.0. Does it enhance the effectiveness of learning?

Ratten, V. (2020). Cloud computing technology innovation advances: A set of research propositions. In *Disruptive Technology: Concepts, Methodologies, Tools, and Applications*, pp. 693–703. IGI Global.

Ratten, V. & Usmanij, P. (2021). Entrepreneurship education: Time for a change in research direction? *The International Journal of Management Education* 19(1), 100367.

Reigeluth, C. M. (1999). What is instructional-design theory and how is it changing. *Instructional-design Theories and Models: A New Paradigm of Instructional Theory* 2, 5–29.

Ronstadt, R. (1985). The educated entrepreneurs: A new era of entrepreneurial education is beginning. *American Journal of Small Business* 10(1), 7–23.

Roulin, N. & Bangerter, A. (2013). Students' use of extra-curricular activities for positional advantage in competitive job markets. *Journal of Education and Work* 26(1), 21–47.

Russell, R. D. (1999). Developing a process model of intrapreneurial systems: A cognitive mapping approach. *Entrepreneurship Theory and Practice* 23(3), 65–84.

Samašonok, K., Išoraitė, M., & Žirnelė, L. (2020). Education of entrepreneurship by participation in a business simulation enterprise activities: Conditions of effectiveness and opportunities for improvement. *Entrepreneurship and Sustainability Issues* 7, 3122–3144.

Santos, S. C., Neumeyer, X., & Morris, M. H. (2019). Entrepreneurship education in a poverty context: An empowerment perspective. *Journal of Small Business Management* 57, 6–32.

Schou, P. K., Bucher, E., & Waldkirch, M. (2022). Entrepreneurial learning in online communities. *Small Business Economics* 58(4), 2087–2108.

Secundo, G., Del Vecchio, P., & Mele, G. (2020). Social media for entrepreneurship: Myth or reality? A structured literature review and a future research agenda. *International Journal of Entrepreneurial Behavior & Research* 27(1), 149–177.

Shane, S., & Venkataraman, S. (2000). The promise of entrepreneurship as a field of research. *Academy of Management Review*, 25(1), 217–226.

Solomon, G. T. & Fernald Jr, L. W. (1991). Trends in small business management and entrepreneurship education in the United States. *Entrepreneurship Theory and Practice* 15(3), 25–40.

Sousa, M. J., Carmo, M., Gonçalves, A. C., Cruz, R., & Martins, J. M. (2019). Creating knowledge and entrepreneurial capacity for HE students with digital education methodologies: Differences in the perceptions of students and entrepreneurs. *Journal of Business Research* 94, 227–240.

Stoney, S. & Oliver, R. (1999). Can higher order thinking and cognitive engagement be enhanced with multimedia. *Interactive Multimedia Electronic Journal of Computer-Enhanced Learning* 1(2), 7.

Taatila, V. P. (2010). Learning entrepreneurship in higher education. *Education+ Training*.

Tess, P. A. (2013). The role of social media in higher education classes (real and virtual) — A literature review. *Computers in Human Behavior* 29(5), A60–A68.

Teymurova, V., Abdalova, M., Babayeva, S., Huseynova, V., Mammadov, E., & Islamova, N. (2020). Implementation of Mobile Entrepreneurial Learning in the Context of Flexible Integration of Traditions and Innovations. *International Journal of Interactive Mobile Technologies (iJIM)* 14(21), 118–135.

Thrane, C., Blenker, P., Korsgaard, S., & Neergaard, H. (2016). The promise of entrepreneurship education: Reconceptualizing the individual–opportunity nexus as a conceptual framework for entrepreneurship education. *International Small Business Journal* 34(7), 905–924.

Tretyakova, N., Lyzhin, A., Chubarkova, E., Uandykova, M., & Lukiyanova, M. (2021). Mobile-learning platform for the development of entrepreneurial competences of the students. *International Journal of Interactive Mobile Technologies* 15(9), 118–135.

Urbinati, A., Manelli, L., Frattini, F., & Bogers, M. L. (2022). The digital transformation of the innovation process: Orchestration mechanisms and future research directions. *Innovation* 24(1), 65–85.

Von Graevenitz, G., Harhoff, D., & Weber, R. (2010). The effects of entrepreneurship education. *Journal of Economic Behavior & Organization* 76(1), 90–112.

Voogt, J. & Roblin, N. P. (2010). 21st century skills. Discussienota. *Zoetermeer: The Netherlands: Kennisnet* 23(3), 2000.

Vorbach, S., Poandl, E. M., & Korajman, I. (2019). Digital entrepreneurship education: The role of MOOCs. *International Journal of Engineering Pedagogy* 9(3), 99–111.

Wang, C. L. & Chugh, H. (2014). Entrepreneurial learning: Past research and future challenges. *International Journal of Management Reviews* 16(1), 24–61.

Walter, S. G. & Dohse, D. (2012). Why mode and regional context matter for entrepreneurship education. *Entrepreneurship & Regional Development* 24(9–10), 807–835.

Wu, Y. J., Yuan, C. H., & Pan, C. I. (2018). Entrepreneurship education: An experimental study with information and communication technology. *Sustainability* 10(3), 691.

Yi, S., & Duval-Couetil, N. (2018). What drives engineering students to be entrepreneurs? Evidence of validity for an entrepreneurial motivation scale. *Journal of Engineering Education*, 107(2), 291-317.

Yoo, Y., Henfridsson, O., & Lyytinen, K. (2010). Research commentary — The new organizing logic of digital innovation: An agenda for information systems research. *Information Systems Research* 21(4), 724–735.

Zuo, L., Shestak, V., Vlasova, S., & Islamov, A. (2021). Efficiency of outsourcing and outstaffing mechanisms based on MOOCs in the market of entrepreneurial education services. *International Journal of Emerging Technologies in Learning (iJET)* 16(2), 135–148.

https://doi.org/10.1142/9789811270178_0007

Chapter 7

From Technostress to Digital Well-being

Velli Parts

Department of Business Administration,
Tallinn University of Technology, Ehitajate tee 5,
Tallinn 19086, Estonia

velli.parts@taltech.ee

Abstract

Technology can be a source of stress at work, contributing to a variety of mental health problems. Therefore, it is important to understand how to mitigate the effects of technology-related stress and promote digital well-being at work in the context of increasingly virtual workplaces. This chapter overviews the factors causing technostress in contemporary organizations and delineates ways of enhancing digital well-being. Virtual workplaces can inflict stress by increasing work-related stressors (overload, time pressure, poor communication) and intensifying technostress-creating conditions. Also, technostress can result from how people feel obligated to relate to their work in the digitalized workplace and to a digitalized society at work, as well as from internalizing the "ideal worker" image. Digital well-being is achieved through the more mindful use of technology, the development of digital and remote work skills, and the design of organizational practices aimed at solving paradoxical situations where information and communication technologies can simultaneously promote and hinder employee well-being and productivity. Most importantly, technostress can be lessened by establishing norms governing technology in work and home contexts.

7.1. Introduction

Technological advancements and digitalization have been profoundly reshaping our work and lifestyle, business models, and operations, bringing tremendous benefits to the economy and society but also posing many challenges and threats (i.e., automating jobs means certain skills will be of less demand, and those without the right capacities, knowledge, and skills risk falling further behind) (Eurofound, 2021; ILO, 2021). Companies are facing increasing pressure to digitalize their functions and adopt data-driven technologies to keep up with the competition (Ponkala *et al.*, 2022), and the growth of advanced technologies is changing the types of skills and competencies needed in the workplace (Trenerry *et al.*, 2021).

Work is still a major field of digitalization, and digitalization affects companies regardless of venture size (Eurofound & Cedefop, 2020). Altogether, 44% of establishments in Europe report that at least 60% of employees use computers for their daily tasks, 54% use software specifically developed or customized to their needs, 46% use data analytics to improve production or service delivery, and 28% are involved in e-commerce (Eurofound & Cedefop, 2020). Concerning small- and medium-sized enterprises (SMEs), it appears that 71% of SMEs in Europa have a website for their business, 55% use Internet-connected "smart" devices, 39% use online ordering and payment systems and cloud computing or storage, 32% have a company intranet, and 31% use an Internet-based video or voice calling service (European Commission, 2022).

At the same time, societies are witnessing an increase in mental health problems worldwide, and the World Health Organization (WHO) has dubbed "stress" as the "Health Epidemic of the 21st Century" (*HCA Healthcare Today*, 2019). During the COVID-19 pandemic, stress levels increased significantly in the general population, rising from 16% before February 2020 to 29% in March–April 2020 (Mahmud *et al.*, 2022).

Work plays an important part in many people's lives. Although employment in a good working environment is beneficial to physical and mental well-being, work-related stress is a leading cause of employee burnout and low job satisfaction (McDaid, 2013). A good work environment is not a reality for all employees: For example, in 2022, 27% of working people in the EU reported stress, depression, or anxiety as important work-related health problems (OSH Pulse, 2022). As the nature of work continues to change, with high levels of demand and work intensity as well as blurring boundaries between home life and work, vulnerabilities to psychosocial stress, burnout, and mental health problems are becoming more challenging (McDaid, 2013).

Technology has been recognized as a source of stress for some decades already, and a wealth of research shows that technostress (TS) impacts employee performance, productivity, and engagement (Ragu-Nathan *et al.*, 2008; Tarafdar *et al.*, 2015). Issues related to the overuse of technology, such as constant connectivity, accessibility, and information overload, can also contribute to a variety of mental health problems, including stress, anxiety, and depression (Scott *et al.*, 2017). Considering that, to a greater or lesser degree, a hybrid model of remote and office work is here to stay (Marsh *et al.*, 2022) and that technological developments continue at a fast pace, it is important to understand what can be done to mitigate the effects of technology-related stress and promote digital well-being at work. The objectives of this chapter are twofold: (1) to provide an overview of the implications of technology on work-related stress at contemporary, increasingly virtual workplaces (combining office and remote work) and (2) to delineate ways of enhancing digital well-being at work. It is suggested that technology-induced stress can be decreased (and digital well-being at work increased) by developing the competences for remote work.

The chapter proceeds as follows. First, the main work-related stressors brought about by the increasing use of digital technologies and virtual work will be discussed. Second, the causes of TS and related terms coupled with a broader approach that sees TS resulting from social norms and felt obligations are introduced. The third part defines digital well-being and lists the competences employees need to be more efficacious when working remotely.

7.2. Work-Related Stress in the Digital Age

Digitalized communication forms, digital platforms, and social media have provided opportunities to organize and complete work in fundamentally different ways (Christensen *et al.*, 2020). The COVID-19 pandemic accelerated digitalization trends by necessitating remote working arrangements (mainly working from home) worldwide. Despite the gradual return to the workplace for the majority of workers, the preference to work from home remains very strong in the European Union: 22% of workers would like to work from home daily, 27% several times per week, about 15% several times a month, and 26% prefer to work at their employer's place (Eurofound, 2022). Benefits of remote work for workers generally result from greater time and place flexibility, enhanced job autonomy, improved work–life balance, and reduced commuting time when enabling conditions, such as childcare facilities and services, digital skills training, and access to adequate and affordable broadband and information communication technology (ICT) equipment, are provided (Lodovici *et al.*, 2021).

Stress is a complex process, initiated and regulated by the central nervous system, which provides information and then interprets and acts on this information. Stressors are environmental characteristics that can have a negative impact on a person, and strains are the cognitive, behavioral, emotional, or physiological responses to these stressors (Cooper *et al.*, 2001). If coping is ineffective, stress is apt to be substantial and may have damaging consequences for health and social functioning; if coping is effective, stress is likely to remain under control (Lazarus, 2006). Work-related stress is the response people may have when presented with work demands and pressures that do not match their knowledge and abilities and which challenge their ability to cope (Leka *et al.*, 2003).

The adoption and usage of digital technologies has reshaped humans' perceptions, actions, work, and social environments, but it also has a dark side (Turel *et al.*, 2021), as it brings new risks (stresses). Virtual workplaces (i.e., remote work, telecommuting) impact employee well-being, i.e., cause stress, in two main ways (Tarafdar & Stich, 2021). First, they increase work-related stressors by adversely affecting work relationships and work–life balance and by increasing workload. Second, they increase TS by intensifying TS-creating conditions. Also, virtual work has opened up new risks by transforming traditional work stressors, such as when bullying becomes *cyberbullying* or when 24/7 information overload worsens the feelings of work overload (Tarafdar & Stich, 2021).

Numerous studies show that with the ability to work virtually from anywhere (most employees do so from their homes), the boundary between work and private life becomes blurred, and workers often work longer hours, have difficulties disengaging from work, and feel physically and emotionally exhausted, especially where there is a lack of experience in virtual work and a lack of support (ILO, 2020). Many people may

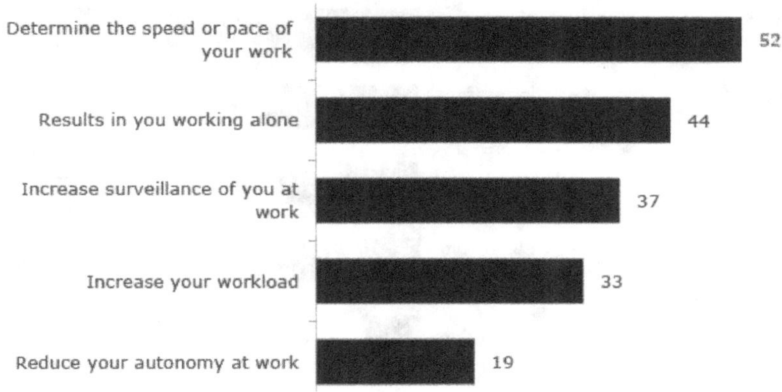

Fig. 7.1. Implications of using digital technologies at work, % (OSH Pulse, 2022).

exhibit online addiction, and the use of performance-enhancing drugs might increase, especially in cases of addiction, longer working hours, and strict performance monitoring (EU-OSHA, 2018). Figure 7.1 shows the implications of using digital technologies at work in the EU (OSH Pulse, 2022).

In spring 2022, more than four in ten respondents across the EU agreed that their work stress has increased as a result of the COVID-19 pandemic (16% "strongly agree" and 28% "agree"), 37% listed overall fatigue and 27% stress, depression, or anxiety as work-related health problems (OSHA, 2022). Stress can originate from pressures at home or at work, and good management and work organization are the best forms of work stress prevention (Leka *et al.*, 2003). Typically, work stress results from factors related to the content of work or contextual factors (Cooper *et al.*, 2001). Stress related to the work content results from the work itself (unpleasant or uninteresting tasks), workload and pace of work, working hours (long hours, inflexible schedules, or shift work), and a lack of participation and control (no opportunity to decide how to work or no control over the work environment). Work context factors that cause stress are job insecurity, unclear or conflicting work roles, poor relationships (including bullying and isolated or solitary work), organizational culture when there is poor communication and leadership, and home–work imbalance (conflicting demands or lack of support) (Cooper *et al.*, 2001). Poor work organization (i.e., how jobs and work systems are designed) and how work is managed also contribute to stress (Leka *et al.*, 2003). Survey results of over 25,000 employed workers in EU Member

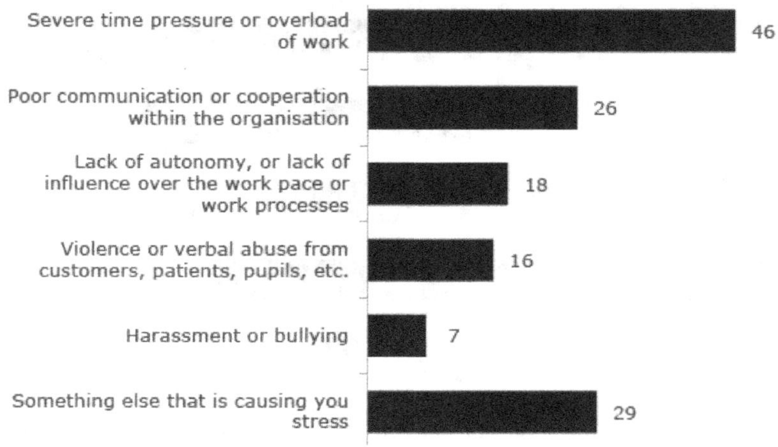

Fig. 7.2. Risk factors associated with work-related stress and mental health issues at work, % of respondents reporting that problem (OSH Pulse, 2022).

States, Iceland and Norway regarding risk factors associated with work related stress and mental health issues at work are depicted in Figure 7.2. It appears that almost half of respondents (46%) are exposed to severe time pressure or overload at work, and about a quarter (26%) agrees that there's poor communication or cooperation in organization. Also, lack of autonomy over the work pace or work processes, and violence or verbal abuse are experienced by a significant amount of workers.

Backed by research literature and empirical data, the International Labor Organization and the European Agency for Occupational Safety and Health point to the following stressors in increasingly virtual work environments (the first four issues may result in a rise in mental ill-health problems, such as anxiety and depression) (ILO, 2020; EU-OSHA, 2018). First, psychosocial risks and work-related stress will increase since the pace of work will be faster and employees might have less control over their work (especially if this is machine-dictated). Second, changes in technology will bring about frequent changes in work processes, job insecurity will increase, and there may be more frequent job changes. Third, remote virtual work from home may increase feelings of isolation and loneliness, and a lack of social interaction and support might emerge despite technological advancements supporting better communication. Fourth, challenges in communication might also arise from the use of bots and avatars, and cyberbullying may increase in virtual work since more workers will work in virtual teams, often having little opportunity to get to know their fellow workers, who might be living in other countries or might be hired only to complete that task or project. Fifth, working from home poses ergonomic risks related to the suitability of workstations and equipment, and the amount of sedentary work is increasing.

The potential effects of ICTs on well-being and functioning are paradoxical, i.e., they can have both positive and negative effects on workers and employers, as described by Day *et al.* (2019). The *autonomy paradox* concerns situations when ICTs can provide flexibility for employees and employers in terms of time and place of work and give opportunity to balance work and family roles, but at the same time, it may contribute to a perceived lack of control in the form of continuous interruptions inhibiting workflow or create the felt pressure to be constantly available. The *social connectivity paradox* refers to the issues on an isolation-to-intrusion continuum where ICTs can be used to reduce social isolation, improve communication and positive relationships between coworkers and in teams, and stay connected to the workplace but can also create feelings of intrusion, such as being overwhelmed by interruptions by colleagues (e.g., chat notifications, email requests). The *productivity paradox* stems from the possibility of ICTs to boost efficiency by providing flexibility in communication regardless of time zones and geographical locations as well as increased access to information. At the same time, ICTs can also interfere with work completion by increasing the number of task disruptions during the workday due to switching between tasks more frequently, which delays completing tasks, and more time is needed to process the increased amount of information.

7.3. Technostress

When implementing digital technologies, stress can result. Technology-induced stress also creates somatic stress responses (e.g., Riedl *et al.*, 2012), and it adds to overall work stress even when job demands, demographics, and job variables are controlled (Ayyagari *et al.*, 2011). While the relationship between stress and performance is complex, it is clear that stress and poor mental health are related to lower levels of work performance (Tenney *et al.*, 2016). The topicality of TS is evidenced by an American Psychological Association's survey (2022), which shows that 79% of employees reported technology-related stress and burnout during the COVID-19 period (Wang *et al.*, 2022).

The term *technostress* originates from 1984, when Craig Brod described it as a modern disease caused by one's inability to cope or deal with ICTs in a healthy manner (Ayyagari *et al.*, 2011). Weil and Rosen (1997) expanded the concept of TS as "any negative impact on attitudes, thoughts, behaviors, or body physiology that is caused either directly or indirectly by technology" (p. 36). Salanova *et al.* (2007, p. 1) defined TS as "a negative psychological state associated with the use or the threat of ICT use in the future" and suggested that TS is an umbrella term encompassing two different but related experiences: *techno-strain* and *techno-addiction* (Salanova *et al.*, 2013). Techno-strain refers to feelings of anxiety, mental fatigue, skepticism, and inefficacy beliefs regarding technology, and techno-addiction means feeling bad due to the excessive and compulsive use of technology.

In one of the most frequently cited articles on TS, Tarafdar *et al.* (2007) defined TS as "stress created by ICT use," explaining that it is "one of the fallouts of an individual's attempts and struggles to deal with constantly evolving ICTs and the changing cognitive and social requirements related to their use" (p. 303). Ragu-Nathan *et al.* (2008) attribute TS at workplaces to three factors. First, work is increasingly dependent on ICTs, and software and hardware are constantly updated and changing. Second, workers lack the knowledge and skills needed for specific tasks, and third, changes in the work environment and culture due to ICTs cause TS.

Tied in with the concept of TS is *digital stress*, or stress resulting from strong and perhaps almost permanent use of ICTs that is triggered by permanent access to an inconceivable amount and diversity of (social) content (Hefner & Vorderer, 2016). Digital stress, analogous to TS, includes tension, fatigue, excessive demands, and the concern that an individual is not able to handle modern digital technologies adequately (Salanova *et al.*, 2013). Digital stress is thought to play a crucial role in explaining the varied associations between mobile and social media use and its outcomes (Hall *et al.*, 2021). As smartphone users in developed nations are often described as living in a permanently online, permanently connected world, wherein the online self is inextricably linked to offline mental health, relationships, and well-being (Vorderer *et al.*, 2017), digital stress can contribute to employees' work stress by increasing their vulnerability (receptivity to stress). According to Steele *et al.* (2020), digital stress comprises four related constructs: availability stress (beliefs about the need to be constantly available online), approval anxiety (fears concerning how others react to one's digital self-presentation), fear of missing out (being afraid of missing rewarding experiences that others are having), and connection overload (excessive input from digital sources).

The construct most frequently confused with TS is *technophobia* (also described as computer anxiety or cyberphobia), which involves two related components: fear of using technology and worries concerning technology's effects on society (Nimrod, 2018). By contrast, TS is a problem of adaptation that individuals experience when they are unable to cope with or become accustomed to ICTs.

Tarafdar *et al.* (2019) differentiate between *techno-eustress* and *techno-distress*. Distress, or negative stress, is the outcome of appraising environmental demand as a *threat* (disturbing factor), and eustress, or positive stress, results from appraising demand as a *challenge* (motivating factor). People estimate environmental demands as challenges that they are motivated to tackle when they feel they have enough resources to cope with those demands, and it will result in positive outcomes, such as improved efficiency, productivity, innovation, performance, or enjoyment, and flow when using technology during work engagement. Challenging techno-stressors are thus those demands that present opportunities to use technology for learning, skill development, accomplishing tasks more efficiently, fulfilling career ambitions, or getting other rewards (Tarafdar *et al.*, 2019).

When the technology environment situation is evaluated as threatening, it may result in *techno-distress* that can lead to negative consequences for both the employee and the organization, such as decreasing job satisfaction, work performance, and organizational commitment, as well as burnout and turnover intentions (Marsh *et al.*, 2022; Tarafdar *et al.*, 2019). According to Marsh *et al.* (2022), environmental demands with the potential to induce techno-distress at workplaces arise from four main sources:

(1) the technology environment, in general, due to its ubiquity, constant connectivity, and fast-paced changes;
(2) specific technological occurrences, such as the arrival of new technologies, ICT hassles, smartphone failures, work monitoring, system breakdowns, technical errors, and low usability of specific technologies;
(3) specific characteristics of the technology (message quality and quantity, interruptive nature, usability, inadequacy, and unreliability);
(4) norms or expectations around how the technology is used both in work and home contexts, such as norms regarding availability beyond usual work hours to monitor and respond to emails or how quickly emails should be answered.

Table 7.1. Techno-stressors as conceptualized by Tarafdar *et al.* (2007).

Techno-overload	Increased work amount and speed due to ICTs and IT-enabled multitasking.
Techno-complexity	ICT-related complexity resulting in feeling of inadequate skills and the need to spend time as well as effort to understand the different aspects of respective technologies.
Techno-invasion	Being always connected to work, blurred line between work and personal life due to technology, and never feeling "free" of IT.
Techno-insecurity	Fear of losing job to other employees with better technological skills or of being replaced by an ICT.
Techno-uncertainty	Feeling insecure because of ongoing ICT changes, and the need to constantly adapt, learn, and educate themselves about new technologies.

Table 7.1 lists five stressors that generally cause TS: *techno-overload, techno-invasion*, *techno-complexity*, *techno-insecurity*, and *techno-uncertainty* (Tarafdar *et al.*, 2007; Ragu-Nathan *et al.*, 2008). Essentially, those techno-stressors can be put into a wider context of work stress, as they link technology characteristics (e.g., unreliability) to popular work stressors, such as work overload (i.e., work overload becomes techno-overload) (Fischer *et al.*, 2021). TS can also result from close monitoring of work performance, location, and working times, which can provoke distrust and loss of control in the monitored workers; unpredictability of robot or machine behavior or unspecific anxiety toward robots can be a stressor for a worker (Dragano & Lunau, 2020).

Prolonged and inappropriate use of videoconferencing or *Zoom fatigue* (a synonym for videoconference fatigue that applies to other similar tools) may also have an enormous stress potential (Riedl, 2022). Six main reasons why videoconferencing can cause stress, according to Riedl (2022), are: asynchrony of communication, lack of body language and eye contact, self-awareness, interaction with multiple faces, and multitasking. Compared to face-to-face interactions, during videoconferencing, the human brain has to work harder to overcome the issues of communication ambiguity, rapid and accurate emotion perception based only on facial expressions, and maintaining shared attention supported by eye contact in ordinary interactive dialogue. Looking at screens during videoconferencing is similar to looking into a mirror, leading to increased self-awareness, which disrupts the automatic communication processes that are typical for effective communications, accompanied by a switch to more controlled mental processes that may result in cognitive exhaustion and fatigue due to increased attentional and working memory demands. Unnatural interaction with multiple faces during videoconferencing, including the feeling of being stared at, comes along with increased stress (Riedl, 2022). As elaborated by Riedl (2022), engaging in multiple unrelated activities while in a video session, along with switching between the various software and tools and the processing of instant messages, constitutes a root cause of the fatigue and stress felt as a consequence of videoconferencing.

It must be reminded that TS describes the point at which the objective environmental demands related to technology are translated into negative outcomes via *perceptual stress*, meaning that an individual has to perceive those demands as taxing his or her resources (Marsh *et al.*, 2022; Tarafdar *et al.*, 2019). In other words, the individual appraisal is of critical importance to whether a technology-related event is perceived as a stressor or not, as individuals attribute different meanings to their environments (Biggs *et al.*, 2017). It is by changing the way a potentially stress-inducing environment or situation is evaluated that workers can experience less stress. Put differently, learning to appraise situations differently (changing cognitions or constructing new, different meanings) helps reduce stress.

According to Tarafdar *et al.* (2019), low technology self-efficacy of employees, a surveillance-prone culture, organizational expectations of availability for work outside of business, and the extent individuals are in control over their own use of technology inflict appraising aspects of the technological environment as stressors. To overcome or deal with TS, one can either alter the task in the context of which the stressor is experienced, change how the stress-inducing technology is used, change one's cognition, and/or engage in social behaviors, such as asking for help or support (Tarafdar *et al.*, 2019).

7.3.1. *An alternative approach to TS*

A sociological perspective on stress research allows us to understand how the broader social forces are at play and contribute to stress (e.g., Peterson, 2018). Stana (2021; Stana & Nicolajsen, 2022) shows how TS results from how workers *feel obligated* to relate to their work in a digitalized workplace or a digitalized society. Obligation is the feeling that we owe something to ourselves, others, organizations, or the society, and when obligations clash, people find themselves in stressful situations (Clark, 1990). According to Ross (1970), obligations are co-constructed in a society: Some of them are covert (felt but not easily explained or made visible), and some are overt; and they can be divided into social, personal, normative, and continuance obligations (Stana, 2021). Social obligations are concerns like how many hours one should work in a week or what is the most common working time (e.g., nine-to-five). Personal obligations refer to feelings where one freely and voluntarily agrees to something and regards oneself obligated to keep that promise (e.g., being a good parent means being able to guide one's child in how to relate to technology in a healthy way). Normative obligations are moral obligations toward an organization involving the belief that one has to serve the collective interests (*ibid.*).

TS, according to Stana and Nicolajsen (2022), arises in technology-related workplace situations where employees feel the obligation to take responsibility for acting in certain ways. TS in this account is constructed on workplace practices where employees feel obligated to be available (online), productive (via sophisticated use of technologies), manage work–home balance, be on time and not waste others' time due to problems with ICTs, and so on. Also, there are felt obligations for ICTs to work as expected, and TS arises due to the feeling of irritation caused by the perception of employees that troubleshooting is not part of the work. Employees may also feel obligated to learn new skills constantly, adjust to agile transformations in organizations, etc. All those felt obligations emerge from the co-construction of a social reality that is deeply rooted in our cultural, familial, and societal heritages (Stana, 2021).

I suggest the "ideal worker image" internalized by people (employees, entrepreneurs, and managers alike) as another societal level factor contributing to TS. "Ideal worker image" is a normative expectation prescribing that people are expected to be wholly devoted to work such that they attend to their jobs ahead of all else, including family, personal needs, and even their health (Reid, 2015). The personified ideal worker image is a definition of the most desirable worker as one who is totally committed to, and always available for, his or her work (Acker, 1990). Many employees may encounter a conflict between employer expectations that they be ideal workers and the sort of workers that they believe and prefer themselves to be (Reid, 2015), and it can also apply to the technology-related aspects of work. In other words, employees may also have an idealized image of how they should relate to and use technology at work (be eager to learn and adapt to new technologies, master different applications, be able to solve problems quickly, etc.), and TS results from the feeling that an individual does not measure up to that image.

Similar to organizational norms concerning work–non-work separation or employee availability after work hours, wider social norms and practices regulate our behavior and remain mostly unquestioned. Social norms are rooted in broader cultural values and widespread beliefs in society, and people internalize work identities they believe are righteous or beneficial/required for a career. Those identities shape employee behavior and perceptions of work-related obligations and responsibilities, as well as managerial expectations. Work-related stress (including TS) results when workers feel they do not match the ideal or get negative feedback from superiors or colleagues.

7.4. A Road to Digital Well-being at Work

Mäkiniemi *et al.* (2020) argue that a more balanced picture of both the negative and positive effects of intensive digitalization of work on well-being at work is needed, as technological developments also have many positive effects, such as safer and more rewarding jobs if different technologies take care of the demanding, monotonous, and dangerous tasks (e.g., industrial robots assisting workers). They propose a new concept — *techno-work engagement* — rooted in the concept of work engagement to emphasize the positive side of individual–technology–work interactions. Techno-work engagement, according to Mäkiniemi *et al.* (2020), is a positive and fulfilling well-being state or experience characterized by vigor, dedication, and absorption with respect to the use of technology at work.

Obtaining a healthy balance between constant connectivity and technology-free time can challenge both employees and employers, as studies show people rarely disconnect, spending hours per day on their smartphones or tablets (Vanden Abeele, 2021). Hoehe and Thibault (2020) refer to a UK survey showing that the average person spends 24 hours a week online, with 20% of all adults spending as much as 40 hours a week. Digital well-being can be defined as "a subjective individual experience of optimal balance between the benefits and drawbacks obtained from mobile connectivity" (Vanden Abeele, 2021). The growing interest in workplace well-being suggests a potential paradigm shift in how society thinks about and treats employee health (Bennett *et al.*, 2017).

Employers can contribute to lowering technology-induced stress and supporting employees' digital well-being in several ways.

First, as suggested by Colbert *et al.* (2016), organizations can further "the mindful use of technology" by practicing technology-free meetings and encouraging more face-to-face communication, as well as promoting smartphone-free nights to encourage employees to connect more with their family members and truly recover from the daily stresses. Programs, such as "digital minimalism" (Newport, 2019) and "deep work" (Newport, 2016), apply the belief that people should identify and define tools and technologies that support what they value and declutter their life(style). Removing all unnecessary and creating a distraction-free environment for themselves to practice deep work or intense concentration on cognitively demanding tasks are examples of how to use technology in a more mindful way.

Second, technological change also requires new skills, and both digital and soft skills are increasingly relevant to navigate the technological revolution effectively (González Vázquez, 2019). Digital skills refer to the individual competencies required to use technology to learn and work, and soft skills refer to a broad range of competencies related to effective communication, emotional regulation, and self-management. Soft skills become increasingly important because they can't be replaced by technology; they also enable employees to deal with dynamic and unpredictable environments, increasing their resilience or ability to bounce back from stresses (Tramontano *et al.*, 2021). Leader-managers and decision makers in smaller firms have to monitor and assess employees on both types of skills while providing support and development opportunities. Tramontano *et al.* (2021) delineated the skills needed for remote work that supports employee well-being, productivity, and engagement. Five sets of skills needed to be effective in remote work are presented in Table 7.2.

Third, organizational practices can be designed to solve the paradoxical situations where ICTs can simultaneously promote and hinder employee well-being and productivity. Day *et al.* (2019) suggested the following five practices. First, developing supportive culture and norms in organizations regarding (1) individual preferences for integration of work and family roles, also known as boundary management profiles; and (2) recovery from work, emphasizing the importance of recovery time and encouraging explicit recovery norms. Second, clear organizational and group norms pertaining to respectful social etiquette (including after-work rules) around the use of ICTs help ensure that workers' boundary and

Table 7.2. Remote work skills.

E-skills for managing the workload and work tasks using digital technologies. Understanding remote work practices; using digital tools effectively, and individual self-management (self-motivation, working independently, avoiding distractions and procrastination).
Trust building skills to develop and promote trustful relationships between employees and managers (overcoming the fear of losing control over employees that managers may have).
Self-care skills or capability to effectively manage work–life boundaries. Organizing working time, monitoring and maintaining healthy boundaries between work and personal life, and avoiding "always on" mentality.
Remote social skills for remotely managing and promoting social relationships. Capability to initiate, promote, and sustain formal and informal social interactions. Knowing how to combine remote and office work to maintain productivity, engagement, and a sense of belonging.
Remote emotional skills or capability to manage one's emotions and emotional demands related to remote work. Coping with potential feelings of isolation and loneliness induced by remote work as well as with the guilt and anxiety deriving from the pressure to be constantly "switched on".

interruption preferences are respected and foster control over social connectivity. Third, providing professional development, team-building, and connection opportunities for remote workers addresses concerns of social isolation and lack of support. Fourth, individual differences can be accommodated in ICT needs (fitting ICTs with job needs and the current abilities of the worker). Fifth, sufficient training and a reasonable technology adoption pace boost employee competence, and effective ICT support (staff assistance) may increase the techno-engagement of workers.

Fourth, the Digital Competence Framework for Citizens (*DigComp*) provides a common language to identify and describe the key areas of digital competence in the European Union (Vuorikari *et al.*, 2022). Accessible to everyone via the Internet, it can be used as a starting point for understanding and developing the digital competences of employees. Developing digital skills of employees is important, as a study by Arnold and colleagues (2016) demonstrated that over two-thirds of the interviewed workers indicated that they constantly needed to further develop their competencies at work because of technical innovations (Oberländer *et al.*, 2020).

The efficiency of digital transformation in organizations does not depend only on technological solutions but how motivated and skillful employees are in using the new technologies. In other words, technology acceptance and perceptions and attitudes toward technological change matter, as users' decisions to adopt a new technology or system depend on how much one believes that a technology will be useful and how easily it can be used (Davis, 1989). Also, social influence and facilitating conditions (i.e., the degree to which an individual perceives that important others believe she or he should use the technology and there is an organizational and technological infrastructure that supports users), as well as the user's experience and voluntariness predict technology adoption (Venkatesh *et al.*, 2003; Venkatesh & Zhang, 2010).

7.5. Conclusions

It is a given now that digital skills are essential for life and work as jobs are increasingly intertwined with ICTs. Hybrid workplaces combining onsite and virtual (remote) work are a new reality that many workers welcome. ICTs can simultaneously improve and impair work–life balance: It gives workers more autonomy and flexibility, opportunities for social connections regardless of time zones and geographical boundaries, and quick access to information that enables increase productivity, but it can also cause stress by blurring work and personal life, felt pressure to be constantly available, interruptions in workflow, information overload, and social isolation. Digital technologies at workplaces influence the pace of work, increase workload and surveillance, and leave people in social isolation, as reported by a significant number of EU studies. The severe time pressure of work overload causes stress for almost half of workers in Europe, and 26% report poor communication or cooperation in organizations as a source of stress. Although remote work has several shortcomings, such as working longer hours, having difficulties disengaging from work, and feeling physically and emotionally exhausted, especially where there is a lack of experience in virtual work and a lack of support, 22% of workers in Europe say they would like to work from home daily, and 27% prefer working from home several times per week. Good management and well-organized work are the best forms of work stress prevention in organizations. How motivated and skillful employees are in using the new technologies at workplaces depends on their perceptions and attitudes toward technology. Virtual workplaces increase several work-related stressors as well as intensify TS-creating conditions. TS at workplaces arises from (1) technology environment in general; (2) specific technological occurrences (the arrival of new technologies, ICT hassles, smartphone failures, and technical errors); (3) specific characteristics of the technology (message quality and quantity, usability, inadequacy, and unreliability); (4) norms or expectations around how the technology is used at work or at home. The main techno-stressors are techno-overload, techno-invasion, techno-complexity, techno-insecurity, and techno-uncertainty. Also, monitoring employees at work (surveillance), unpredictability of robot or machine behavior, and prolonged use of videoconferencing cause TS.

Techno-work engagement and techno-eustress refer to the positive side of technology's impact on workers. TS can also result from the felt obligations at work or internalizing the ideal worker image. Digital well-being refers to the individual's experience of an optimal balance between the benefits and drawbacks obtained from mobile connectivity. Organizations can support the digital well-being of employees by promoting more mindful usage of technology, developing employee skills for remote work, and managerial practices to solve the paradoxes of using ICTs.

References

Acker, J. (1990). Hierarchies, jobs, bodies: A theory of gendered organizations. *Gender & Society* 4(2), 139–158.

Ayyagari, R., Grover, V., & Purvis, R. (2011). Technostress: Technological antecedents and implications. *MIS Q* 35, 831–858.

Bennett, J., Weaver, J., Senft, M., Neeper, M. (2017). Creating workplace well-being. In *The Handbook of Stress and Health: A Guide to Research and Practice*, ed. by C. L. Cooper & J. C. Quick. John Wiley & Sons Ltd. DOI:10.1002/9781118993811.

Biggs, A., Brough, P., & Drummond, S. (2017). Lazarus and Folkman's psychological stress and coping theory. In *The Handbook of Stress and Health: A Guide to Research and Practice*, Cooper C. L. and Quick J. C. (Eds.), (pp. 351–364). Wiley Blackwell.

Christensen, J. O., Finne, L. B., Garde, A. H., Nielsen, M. B., Sørensen, K., & Vleeshouwes, J. (2020). The influence of digitalization and new technologies on psychosocial work environment and employee health: A literature review. *STAMI-rapport*.

Clark, C. (1990). Emotions and micropolitics in everyday life: Some patterns and paradoxes of "place." In T. D. Kemper (ed.), *Research Agendas in the Sociology of Emotions*, pp. 305–333. State University of New York Press, Albany, NY.

Colbert, A., Yee, N., & George, G. (2016). The digital workforce and the workplace of the future. *Academy of Management Journal* 59(3), 731–739.

Cooper, C. L., Dewe, P. J., Dewe, P. J., O'Driscoll, M. P., & O'Driscoll, M. P. (2001). *Organizational Stress: A Review and Critique of Theory, Research, and Applications*. Sage Publications, Inc. Thousand Oaks, London, New Delhi.

D'Arcy, J., Herath, T., & Shoss, M. K. (2014). Understanding employee responses to stressful information security requirements: A coping perspective. *Journal of Management Information Systems* 31, 285–318. Doi: 10.2753/MIS0742-1222310210.

Davis, F. D. (1989). Perceived usefulness, perceived ease of use, and user acceptance of information technology. *MIS Quarterly* 13(3), 319–340. https://doi.org/10.2307/249008

Day, A., Barber, L., & Tonet, J. (2019). Information communication technology and employee well-being: Understanding the "iParadox Triad" at work. *The Cambridge Handbook of Technology and Employee Behavior*, pp. 580–607.

Dragano, N. & Lunau, T. (2020). Technostress at work and mental health: Concepts and research results. *Current Opinion Psychiatry* 33(4), 407–413.

Eurofound (2021). *Digitization in the workplace*. Publications Office of the European Union, Luxembourg.

Eurofound & Cedefop (2020). *European Company Survey 2019: Workplace Practices Unlocking Employee Potential*. European Company Survey 2019 series, Publications Office of the European Union, Luxembourg.

European Commission (2022). *Directorate-general for migration and home affairs, SMEs and cybercrime: Summary*. Publications Office of the European Union, 2022, https://data.europa.eu/doi/10.2837/89101.

Fischer, T., Reuter, M., & Riedl, R. (2021). The digital stressors scale: Development and validation of a new survey instrument to measure digital stress perceptions in the workplace context. *Frontiers in Psychology* 12, 607598.

Gonzalez Vazquez, I. *et al.* (2019), *The Changing Nature of Work and Skills in the Digital Age*, Publications Office of the European Union, Luxembourg, http://dx.doi.org/10.2760/679150.

Hall, J. A., Steele, R. G., Christofferson, J. L., & Mihailova, T. (2021). Development and initial evaluation of a multidimensional digital stress scale. *Psychological Assessment* 33(3), 230.

HCA Healthcare Today (2019). Stress, the "health epidemic of the 21st century". In https://hcahealthcaretoday.com/2019/04/30/stress-the-health-epidemic-of-the-21st-century/.

Hefner, D. & Vorderer, P. (2016). Digital stress: Permanent connectedness and multitasking. In *The Routledge Handbook of Media Use and Well-being*, pp. 237–249. Routledge.

Hoehe, M. R. & Florence Thibaut (2020). Going digital: How technology use may influence human brains and behavior. *Dialogues in Clinical Neuroscience* 22(2), 93–97. Doi: 10.31887/DCNS.2020.22.2/mhoehe.

ILO (International Labour Organization) (2020). *Managing work-related psychosocial risks during the COVID-19 pandemic*. Available at: https://www.ilo.org/global/topics/safety-and-health-at-work/resources-library/publications/WCMS_748638/lang--en/index.ht.

ILO (2021). Changing demand for skills in digital economies and societies Literature review and case studies from low- and middle-income countries. International Labour Organization.

Lazarus, R. (2006). Emotions and interpersonal relationships: Towards a person-centered conceptualization of emotions and coping. *Journal of Personality* 74, 9–46.

Leka, S., Griffiths, A., Cox, T., & World Health Organization. (2003). *Work Organization and Stress: Systematic Problem Approaches for Employers, Managers and Trade Union Representatives*. World Health Organization.

Lodovici, S. M. *et al*. (2021). *The Impact of Teleworking and Digital Work on Workers and Society*. Publication for the committee on Employment and Social Affairs, Policy Department for Economic, Scientific and Quality of Life Policies, European Parliament, Luxembourg.

McDaid, D. (2013). Mental health: A key challenge for Europe in the 21st century. *Eurohealth Observer* 19(3), 20.

Mahmud, S., Mohsin, M., Dewan, M.N. *et al*. (2023). The Global prevalence of depression, anxiety, stress, and insomnia among general population during COVID-19 pandemic: A systematic review and meta-analysis. *Trends in Psychology* 31, 143–170.

Marsh, E., Vallejos, E. P., & Spence, A. (2022). The digital workplace and its dark side: An integrative review. *Computers in Human Behavior* 128, 107118.

Mäkiniemi, J. P., Ahola, S., & Joensuu, J. (2020). A novel construct to measure employees' technology-related experiences of well-being: Empirical validation of the Techno-Work Engagement Scale (TechnoWES).

Nimrod, G. (2018). Technostress: Measuring a new threat to well-being in later life. *Aging & Mental Health* 22(8), 1086–1093.

Newport, C. (2016). *Deep Work: Rules for Focused Success in a Distracted World*. Piatkus, London.

Newport, C. (2019). *Digital Minimalism: Choosing a Focused Life in a Noisy World*. Portfolio/Penguin, New York.

Oberländer, M., Beinicke, A., & Bipp, T. (2020). Digital competencies: A review of the literature and applications in the workplace. *Computers & Education* 146, 103752.

OSH Pulse (2022). Occupational safety and health in post-pandemic workplaces: Flash Eurobarometer Report 2022. European Agency for Safety and Health at Work.

EU-OSHA (European Agency for Safety and Health at Work) (2018). *Foresight on new and emerging occupational safety and health risks associated with digitalization by 2025*. European Risk Observatory report. Publications Office of the European Union, Luxembourg. https://osha.europa.eu/en/publications/foresight-new-and-emerging-occupational-safety-and-health-risks-assoc.

Peterson, C. L. (2018). *Stress at Work: A Sociological Perspective*. CRC Press/Taylor & Francis Group, Florida.

Ponkala, S., Koskinen, J., Lähteenmäki, C., & Tuomisto, A. (2022). Promoting worker wellbeing in the era of data economy. In *IFIP International Conference on Human Choice and Computers*, pp. 3–17. Springer, Cham.

Ragu-Nathan, T. S., Tarafdar, M., Ragu-Nathan, B. S., & Tu, Q. (2008). The consequences of technostress for end users in organizations: Conceptual development and empirical validation. *Information System Research* 19, 417–433.

Reid, E. (2015). Embracing, passing, revealing, and the ideal worker image: How people navigate expected and experienced professional identities. *Organization Science* 26(4), 997–1017.

Riedl, R., Kindermann, H., Auinger, A., & Javor, A. (2012). Technostress from a neurobiological perspective — System breakdown increases the stress hormone cortisol in computer users. *Business & Information Systems Engineering* 4, 61–69.

Riedl, R. (2022). On the stress potential of videoconferencing: Definition and root causes of Zoom fatigue. *Electronic Markets* 32(1), 153–177.

Ross, R. (1970). *Obligation: A Social Theory*. University of Michigan Press, Ann Arbor, MI.

Salanova, M. Llorens, S., Cifre, E., & Nogareda, C. (2007). *El tecnoestrés: Concepto, medida y prevención [Technostress: Concept, measurement and prevention]. Nota Técnica de Prevención*, 730. INSHT, Madrid, Spain.

Salanova, M., Llorens, S., & Cifre, E. (2013). The dark side of technologies: Technostress among users of information and communication technologies. *International Journal of Psychology* 48(3), 422–436.

Scott, D. A., Valley, B., & Simecka, B. A. (2017). Mental health concerns in the digital age. *International Journal of Mental Health and Addiction* 15(3), 604–613.

Stana, R. & Nicolajsen, H. W. (2021). Sociological mechanisms behind ICT-related technostress in the workplace. *Information Technology in*

Organizations and Societies: Multidisciplinary Perspectives from AI to Technostress 85–110. Doi: 10.1108/978-1-83909-812-320211004.

Stana, R. A. (2021). *Revealing the Obligations that lead to ICT-related Technostress in the Digital Workplace*. PhD dissertation, IT University of Copenhagen. Copenhagen, Denmark. https://pure.itu.dk/ws/portalfiles/portal/86482604/PhD_Thesis_Final_Version_Raluca_Alexandra_Stana.pdf.

Steele, R. G., Hall, J. A., & Christofferson, J. L. (2020). Conceptualizing digital stress in adolescents and young adults: Toward the development of an empirically based model. *Clinical Child and Family Psychology Review* 23(1), 15–26.

Turel, O., Qahri-Saremi, H., & Vaghefi, I. (2021). Dark sides of digitalization. *International Journal of Electronic Commerce* 25(2), 127–135.

Tarafdar, M., Tu, Q., Ragu-Nathan, B. S., & Ragu-Nathan, T. (2007). The impact of technostress on role stress and productivity. *Journal of Management Information Systems* 24(1), 301–328.

Tarafdar, M., Pullins, E. B., & Ragu-Nathan, T. S. (2015). Technostress: Negative effect on performance and possible mitigations. *Information Systems Journal* 25, 103–132.

Tarafdar, M., Cooper, C. L., & Stich, J. F. (2019). The technostress trifecta-techno eustress, techno distress and design: Theoretical directions and an agenda for research. *Information Systems Journal* 29(1), 6–42.

Tarafdar, M. & Stich, J. F. (2021). Virtual work, technology and wellbeing. *The SAGE Handbook of Organizational Wellbeing*, SAGE, London, pp. 159–169.

Tenney, E. R., Poole, J. M., & Diener, E. (2016). Does positivity enhance work performance? Why, when, and what we don't know. *Research in Organizational Behavior* 36, 27–46.

Tramontano, C., Grant, C., & Clarke, C. (2021). Development and validation of the e-Work Self-Efficacy Scale to assess digital competencies in remote working. *Computers in Human Behavior Reports* 4, 100129.

Trenerry, B., Chng, S., Wang, Y., Suhaila, Z. S., Lim, S. S., Lu, H. Y., & Oh, P. H. (2021). Preparing workplaces for digital transformation: An integrative review and framework of multi-level factors. *Frontiers in Psychology* 12, 620766.

Vanden Abeele, M. M. (2021). Digital wellbeing as a dynamic construct. *Communication Theory* 31(4), 932–955.

Venkatesh, V., Morris, M. G., Davis, G. B., & Davis, F. D. (2003). User acceptance of information technology: Toward a unified view. *MIS Quarterly* 27(3), 425–478.

Venkatesh, V. & Zhang, X. (2010). Unified theory of acceptance and use of technology: U.S. Vs. China. *Journal of Global Information Technology Management* 13(1), 5–27. Doi: 10.1080/1097198X.2010.10856507.

Vorderer, P., Hefner, D., Reinecke, L., & Klimmt, C. (eds.) (2017). *Permanently Online, Permanently Connected*. Routledge, Taylor & Francis Group.

Vuorikari, R., Kluzer, S., & Punie, Y. (2022). DigComp 2.2: The Digital Competence Framework for Citizens, EUR 31006 EN, Publications Office of the European Union, Luxembourg. Doi: 10.2760/115376, JRC128415.

Wang, H., Ding, H., & Kong, X. (2022). Understanding technostress and employee well-being in digital work: The roles of work exhaustion and workplace knowledge diversity. *International Journal of Manpower* ahead-of-print(ahead-of-print). Doi: 10.1108/IJM-08-2021-0480.

Weil, M. M. & Rosen, L. D. (1997). *Technostress: Coping with Technology @work @home @play*, Vol. 13, p. 240. J. Wiley, New York.

https://doi.org/10.1142/9789811270178_0008

Chapter 8

We Want to Work Smart Now! How Digitalization Challenges Entrepreneurial Leadership

Velli Parts

Department of Business Administration, Tallinn University of Technology, Ehitajate tee 5, Tallinn 19086, Estonia

velli.parts@taltech.ee

Abstract

Digital platforms and the increasing pursuit of becoming more effective and flexible have affected many traditional work structures within and across organizations. This chapter introduces the concepts of smart working and smart leadership and delineates the challenges digital transformation poses for entrepreneurial leaders. It is argued that digital workplaces do not only mean the extensive use of digital technologies at work but new and complex configurations of human and technology relationships that reshape the very nature of work. Effective leadership requires a broad behavioral repertoire, mastering new roles and mindsets. Smart leadership, as a facilitative behavior that inspires change and produces innovation in the ways of thinking about work, emerges as a response to smart working practices. Entrepreneurial leaders fostering collaborative and open relationships, empowering employees, and facilitating knowledge sharing and trust help employees to perceive their work as significant and boost employee work engagement. To be an effective leader in a virtual environment, one needs to be skillful in using information and communication technologies for communication, creating and maintaining relationships and a sense of trust. The leaders of the digitalizing companies must be able to challenge how their organizations operate, engage their personnel in the process of redefining their work roles, and keep their minds open to the possibility that their own roles will change as well.

8.1. Introduction

It is widely agreed that digitalization has significantly transformed several industries and revolutionized the way industries and organizations operate (Vaska *et al.*, 2021). The rapid development of innovative digital technologies and the associated digital transformation have changed the way in which we live, communicate, and work (Leimeister & Blohm, 2022). Digital transformation in organizations is depicted as a process of deep, structural change that occurs through the integration of multiple technologies, resulting in the fundamental redefinition of organizational value and identity (Trenerry *et al.*, 2021). Digital transformation has to be understood as a "holistic socio-technical challenge" (Schnasse *et al.*, 2021, p. 160) because its effectiveness does not depend only on integrating the latest technologies but how successful companies are (both small and big ones) in terms of adjusting their organizational routines and creating an appropriate work culture. As digitalization brings forth complex changes, effective leadership is required to transform the organization and capture the real value of digitalization (Cortellazzo *et al.*, 2019).

The COVID-19 global pandemic accelerated the pace of digital transformation within organizations of all types and sizes, and the shift to home-based telework gave new impetus to discuss what all this means for leadership (e.g., Contreras *et al.*, 2020; Iannotta *et al.*, 2020; Banks *et al.*, 2022; Trenerry *et al.*, 2021). The question of effective leadership in the context of widespread calls for smart working (SW) is thus timely and relevant, as digital platforms and the increasing pursuit of becoming more effective and flexible have affected many traditional work structures within and across organizations (Leimeister & Blohm, 2022). What "smart working" is and which challenges digital transformation poses for leaders when workplaces are increasingly becoming digital are the focus of this chapter. The objective of this chapter is to delineate how digitalization changes workplaces and what it means for entrepreneurial leadership.

The chapter proceeds as follows. First, it discusses briefly how digitalization changes workplaces. Second, the concept of SW is introduced, followed by a discussion of what kind of entrepreneurial leadership is needed in the context of SW. Third, leading digital transformation in smaller organizations is discussed, delineating the effective leadership behaviors and roles leaders have to master to tackle the challenges of digital transformation.

8.2. Digitalization at Workplaces

Advancements in the domains of electronics and information and communication technologies (ICTs) have created terms such as ambient intelligence, smart environments, cyber-physical systems, ubiquitous computing, and the Internet of Things, which is currently conquering all sectors and domains of life and human activities (Podgórski *et al.*, 2017). Companies across different sectors — both small and bigger ones — are converting their workplaces to become more digital, with many jobs involving extensive use of technology and an ability to exploit it at a fast pace (Cortellazzo *et al.*, 2019). It is agreed upon that digitalization shapes the future of work via: (1) digital tools and platforms used to improve communication, collaboration, and the organization and execution of work; (2) agile and digital work practices expected to deliver increasing effectiveness of resource utilization and overall work processes; and (3) the automation of work (Leimeister & Blohm, 2022).

Digital technologies do not simply create and destroy jobs but change what people do on the job and when, where, and how they work (Larsson-Lund, 2018). The digital workplace is foremost characterized by the set of technologies provided to execute one's work effectively, irrespective of the location and whether the tasks are performed alone or with others (Becker *et al.*, 2020). Digital technologies include devices such as smartphones or tablets but also applications that can facilitate business processes by providing tools for inter- and intra-organizational communication and collaboration (Zuppo, 2012). Messaging and video-conferencing tools, intranets, groupware systems, enterprise social networks, emails, blogs, social media, smart apps, self-service portals, calendars, and other enterprise processes or tools assisting the general or day-to-day functioning are the digital technologies widely used in contemporary organizations (Köffer, 2015; Marsh *et al.*, 2022; Roman *et al.*, 2019).

The implementation of new ICTs in the working environment leads to significant changes by modifying the methods of work and introducing new objects and complex systems that may have functions that are not fully recognized or that may not function according to users' expectations, resulting in unforeseen failures and consequences (Podgórski *et al.*, 2017). Digitalized work brings forth many new aspects of working life, such as working in virtual teams and mobile working, which can blur the boundary between leisure and work and result in constant availability and the frequent need to adapt and learn new digital tools (Bregenzer & Jimenez, 2021). Organizations and management practices may also become more digital such that new jobs, roles, and skill profiles as well as innovative modes of management and leadership emerge (Leimeister & Blohm, 2022).

Introducing and capitalizing on digital work(places) requires a shift in thinking about how organizations and employees define work (Dittes *et al.*, 2019). Devices with sophisticated capabilities, multiple functionalities, and portability have significantly changed the way we work, as ICTs that used to be primarily associated with work-related use at workplaces now enable the performance of non-work tasks at equal intensity as well as the cross-domain use of ICTs for work tasks during non-work time and vice versa (Tennakoon *et al.*, 2013). Therefore, the meaning of "digital workplace" is much broader than just using ICTs at work: It blends physical, cultural, and digital elements in the work environment, leading to fundamentally new and complex configurations of human and technology relationships that reshape the very nature of work practices (Marsh *et al.*, 2022).

To sum up, facilitating digital work requires more than just making ICTs available. Although the core component of a digital workplace is the technology platform that provides tools for collaboration and communication between employees, supports knowledge and information sharing, document management, and coordination of work and group activities, it is rooted in future-oriented organizational strategy and designed considering the specific needs of corporate culture (Williams & Schubert, 2018). To get the most out of turning workplaces digital, a different — smart — approach to work design and entrepreneurial leadership is required.

8.3. Smart Working and Smart Leadership

Since the turn of the century, there has been a growth of alternative work arrangements characterized by flexibility in the employment relationship, the scheduling of work, and where work gets done (Spreitzer *et al.*, 2017). Often referred to as "new ways of working" or "smart working," such practices are expected to lead to more efficient work processes and higher employee engagement and performance (Bregenzer & Jimenez, 2021), especially when supported by a new "philosophy of management" that promotes a more democratic governance through the deployment of a participatory and collaborative management (Taskin *et al.*, 2017).

The "smart working" term became popular among practitioners and consultation companies in the first years of the 2000s as a new way to define what is considered an innovative approach to work organization challenging the conventional models of work design and redesign, the traditional organizational hierarchy, and the classic managerial style mainly focused on control (Torre & Sarti, 2020). Most often, SW refers to the new ways of working based on flexible work arrangements and an extensive use of ICTs that support employees to work potentially anytime and anywhere (McEwan, 2016). In addition to the absence of time or space restrictions, SW is characterized by an organization of work by phases, cycles, and objectives and a managerial philosophy that grants autonomy and greater responsibility for results to the worker (CIPD, 2008). Such factors are believed to favor better performance and foster competitiveness, and the recent quick acceleration in the development and diffusion of new technologies supporting communication, collaboration, and social networking, together with the pervasive dissemination of powerful and easy-to-use mobile devices, makes it possible (Torre & Sarti, 2020). The dynamic nature of SW makes it different from more "static" forms of remote e-working, as it includes both face-to-face and virtual interactions (Iannotta *et al.*, 2020). Essentially, within a SW context, workers choose (according to specific individual agreements) the on-site and off-site mode schedules for the work week (Binci & Scafarto, 2022).

What kind of leadership is required in the SW context for smaller organizations? Iannotta *et al.* (2020) define "smart leadership behavior" as facilitative behavior in SW contexts that inspires change and produces innovation in the ways of thinking about work, which uses advanced technologies to improve organizational effectiveness and sets people at the center of all processes organized around the principles of agility, autonomy, trust, and responsibility. Iannotta *et al.* (2020) argue that leading SW evolves around: (1) changing behaviors, (2) creating shared meanings in the change management process, and (3) integrating physical and technology-mediated interactions between workers and leaders. Becoming a "smart worker" requires autonomy and empowerment, outcome-focused management, flexible time and space to work, trust and collaboration, and perceiving significance in their work. Those managerial practices result in employees developing self-determined work behaviors and strong intrinsic motivation (Iannotta *et al.*, 2020). For that to happen, leaders must (1) foster collaborative and open relationships; (2) empower employees through delegation, education, and training; (3) facilitate knowledge sharing; (4) meet employee expectations; (5) work ethically; and (6) lead virtual teams and overcome obsolete command and control styles. Figure 8.1 depicts the antecedents and outcomes of SW and smart leader attributes, as described by Iannotta *et al.* (2020).

Iannotta *et al.* (2020) summarize the smart leader attributes as follows. Smart leaders outline an inspiring vision of the future that serves as the ground to create a shared meaning of change. Self-awareness refers to the leader's ability to be conscious of one's character and feelings. Creating a climate of trust and transparent communication is based on the ability to create and cultivate good relationships. A predisposition for lifelong learning is needed to continuously enhance employees' digital and soft skills, as this motivates continuous improvement and supports effective work across the team. Execution is important for ensuring the effectiveness of business actions, and being an innovation ambassador refers to the need for smart leaders to not only manage change but create

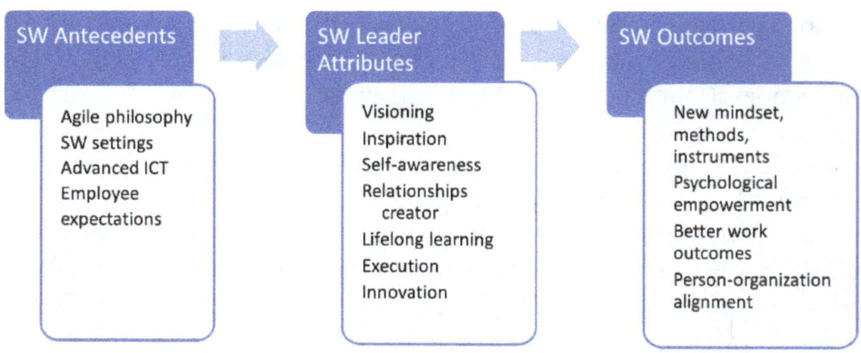

Fig. 8.1. Antecedents and outcomes of SW and attributes of smart leader.

it by supporting strong innovation in thinking about work. Agile philosophy and its principles are the starting point of SW, which, when combined with transformed employee expectations (desiring not simply extrinsic rewards but intrinsic motivation, professional growth, creativity, and better work–life balance), advanced ICTs, and time and space flexibilities lead to radical change in workplaces (Iannotta *et al.*, 2020).

Being a smart leader is rooted in positive leadership styles, such as ethical, emphatic, and transformational leadership, which aim to touch the "hearts and minds" of followers and inspire employees to go the extra mile (Iannotta *et al.*, 2020). Decuypere and Schaufeli (2022) argue that, for now, there is enough research evidence demonstrating that various positive leadership styles overlap quite a lot, as they contain engaging in similar behaviors that altogether stimulate employee work engagement. Research shows that work engagement is related to several important organizational outcomes, such as employee performance, turnover intentions, and customer loyalty, which makes it an important factor driving business success (Decuypere & Schaufeli, 2022). In other words, smart leadership, which can be described as consisting of various positive leadership behaviors, is foremost about achieving the work engagement of employees.

Leaders can enhance employee work engagement by: (1) satisfying employees' psychological needs for autonomy, relatedness, and competence (Deci & Ryan, 2008); (2) establishing an exchange relationship where favors, work, attention, resources, and support are reciprocated; (3) acting as role models (Bandura, 1986); (4) developing an emotional contagion where leader behavior infused with positive emotions is contagious (Decuypere & Schaufeli, 2022).

Steger (2016) emphasizes the importance of meaningful work for employees and leaders as it results in motivation and engagement of employees. He proposes the clarity, authenticity, respect, mattering, and autonomy (CARMA) model, which incorporates the most important leadership- and organizational-level predictors and correlates of meaningful work (see Figure 8.2). C = clarity means that organizations need a vision and a mission to be clearly shared across all levels; if a company lacks purpose, its employees might follow suit. A = authenticity says that organizations must follow their mission and leaders must behave ethically and honestly because phony purpose and exploitation kill meaning. R = respect means that building positive, effective relationships in an organization begins with leadership modeling respect and creating chances for

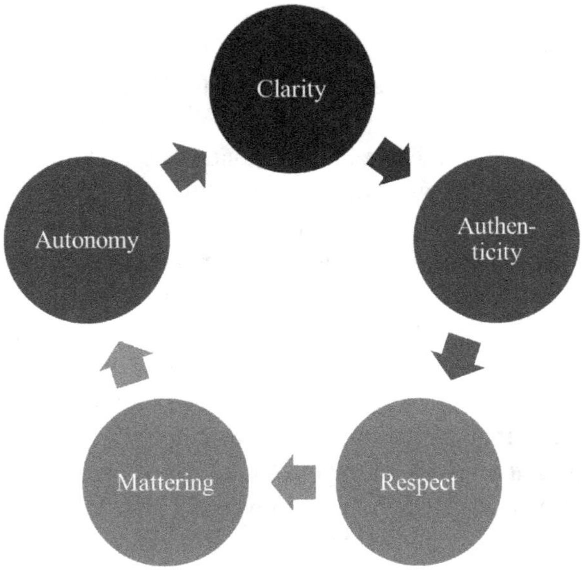

Fig. 8.2. CARMA model or predictors of meaningful work, according to Steger (2016).

beneficial interactions. M = mattering refers to leadership conveying to each employee exactly how their contribution is vital to the success and health of the organization and its mission. A = autonomy means that leaders should allow followers to express themselves by providing opportunities for self-direction, trial and error, and idea exchange.

Being a smart leader also requires a certain mindset. Mindset is a specific, recognizable, and repeatable orientation toward what a person experiences (Dweck, 1986). It functions as a mental lens through which individuals encode and organize information to make sense of their situation, and it influences also how they act and respond. Crane (2022) argues that the mindsets of high-performing individuals do not necessarily translate to the mindsets of effective leaders, as those individuals are recognized and rewarded for mindsets associated with their personal success. Effective leadership, according to Crane (2022), requires four mindsets: promotion mindset, outward mindset, learning goal mindset, and deliberative mindset. The last one means being open to new ideas or disconfirming information that may help one make a more optimal decision. The learning goal mindset reflects a focus on expanding one's abilities by mastering difficult situations (Dweck, 1986). An outward mindset promotes deep, engaging relationships that go beyond exchange and self-interest, and the promotion mindset refers to having a purpose and striving for goals, seeking opportunities, and maximizing gains.

8.4. Leading Digital Transformation in Small Entrepreneurial Organizations

Successful implementation of digital transformation in organizations is attributed to "skilled and competent leadership" (El Sawy *et al.*, 2016). Essentially, leadership is a social influence process in which someone leads and someone else follows (Bass, 1990). Leadership is related to the capacity to motivate and influence others to engage in collective activities and accomplish shared goals (Yukl, 2012). This capacity is exerted not only by formal leaders but also by those without formal authority (informal leadership). The modern approach to leadership focuses not only on the leader but also on followers, peers, supervisors, the work setting or context, and culture; it sees leadership as a dyadic, shared, relational, and complex social dynamic, not as merely an individual characteristic (Uhl-Bien *et al.*, 2007).

Organizations need and should care about effective leadership. According to Yukl (2012), effective leadership consists of various behaviors that fall into four categories:

(1) Task-oriented behaviors (clarifying, planning, and monitoring operations and problem solving) that promote accomplishing work in an efficient and reliable way.
(2) Relations-oriented behaviors (supporting, developing skills and confidence, and recognizing and empowering employees) aim for increasing the quality of human resources and relations.
(3) Change-oriented behaviors (advocating and envisioning change, encouraging innovation, and facilitating collective learning) aim for increasing innovation, collective learning, and adaptation to the external environment.
(4) External behaviors (networking, external monitoring, and representing) focus on acquiring necessary information and resources to promote and defend the interests of the team or organization.

The relevance and effect of each behavior depends on the situation; the ability to use a wide range of specific behaviors and adapt them to the situation is "behavioral flexibility," which is the cornerstone of effective leadership (Yukl, 2012). All those behaviors of leaders are as relevant today as they were before. The difference is that, nowadays, leadership is exercised both in virtual and non-virtual contexts and leveraged by various technologies (Banks *et al.*, 2022). What makes leadership in the digital context different is that communication uses more and more technological tools; information is shared through new technologies, and it develops networks that go beyond traditional organizational boundaries, creating new and unexpected relationships (Torre & Sarti, 2020).

Digital leadership refers to aiming for a customer-centered, digitally enabled, leading-edge business model by: (1) transforming the role, skills, and style of the digital leader; (2) realizing a digital organization; and (3) adjusting people management, virtual teams, knowledge, and communication and collaboration at the individual level (Eber & Drews, 2021). Successful digital transformation in organizations depends on: (1) creating a highly connected and open working environment at all levels and units, (2) engaging customers, and (3) establishing more integrated and networked relationships with partners and competitors (Berman & Korsten, 2014).

Digital Darwinism (Goodwin, 2018) describes the situation where organizations incapable of embracing digital transformation to change and reconfigure internal processes, review and develop products and services, and implement new solutions will be excluded due to natural selection. Creating a digital transformation culture is not easy (D'Este *et al.*, 2012), which is why having an entrepreneurial mindset is important for leaders (Schiuma *et al.*, 2022). Competencies that entrepreneurial leaders need to make digital transformation happen in their organizations are: (1) grasping the essence of the digital transformation, (2) envisioning digital wealth creation goodness, (3) shaping a knowledge-creating context, (4) communicating the essence of digital transformation, (5) engaging people to act with the digital transformation, and (6) making digital transformation everyone's job (Schiuma *et al.*, 2022).

It is fair to say that a broad behavioral complexity is needed to confront the emerging challenges digital transformation poses for leaders. Weber *et al.* (2022) identified seven roles that leaders have to fulfill in the context of digital transformation in organizations (see Table 8.1).

Altogether, effective leadership in contemporary organizations requires the integration of competing roles, and leaders need broad behavioral repertoire to perform all the aforementioned roles.

Table 8.1. Leader`s roles in digital transformation.

Digital pioneer understands the drivers of digital transformation, detects trends, and identifies business opportunities and risks arising from digital transformation.
Innovator drives and implements change processes based on innovative and creative ideas, shows enthusiasm, and inspires employees by inventing the new.
Enabler creates agile, flexible, and empowering work environments, encourages team members to try out new idea, and enables a culture of learning.
Mentor strives to establish strong and trusting relationships and provides individual support and feedback to encourage and motivate employees to achieve their individual goals.
Networker develops, scans, and maintains interdisciplinary networks within and outside the organization.
Manager is oriented to task and goal achievements and structures, coordinates, controls, and attends to key performance indicators.
Digital mentees seek advice from their employees on digital issues refining their digital skills.

Purvanova and Kenda (2018) argue that leadership in the virtual world means dealing with paradoxes, as the same virtuality feature (e.g., technology-mediated communication) simultaneously gives rise to opposing, yet mutually dependent, challenges and opportunities. There are three main paradoxes in virtual leadership resulting from technology dependence, geographic dispersion, and human capital. The technology dependence paradox means that: (1) technology-mediated interactions are simultaneously more impersonal (lack of nonverbal cues, loss of communication meaning, and difficulty in getting to know each other) and less biased (i.e., enabling more objective evaluations); (2) technology generates a lot of data, causing feelings of overload, but more data also enable better-informed decisions; and (3) technology-enabled 24/7 work can be stressful and exhausting, but it is also dynamic, more interesting and, therefore, has greater motivational potential. In terms of geographic dispersion, virtual work can generate social isolation, hindered bonding, and less spontaneous interactions, but it also gives workers more autonomy, sense of control, and lesser exposure to gossip and politics at workplaces. Geographic dispersion makes working across time zones challenging but enables work "around the clock"; it can create cultural and language barriers but also increase cultural diversity. The human capital paradox is rooted in tension between not prioritizing social capital (workers are highly task-oriented, virtual socialization perceived as futile) but endowing teams with great knowledge capital (high level of expertise, large extra-team knowledge network through members` personal networks).

According to Purvanova and Kenda (2018), the paradox theory holds that harnessing the power of paradox requires synergizing the opposing poles of paradoxical tensions (i.e., fully eliminating negative poles or focusing only on positive poles does not work, as each pair of opposites is part of one whole). Therefore, synergizing competing demands by simultaneously engaging in varied, even opposing, behaviors, is the right leadership action in virtual leadership. Based on that, three distinct virtual leadership styles appear. *Synergistic leaders* view virtuality through a *both–and* cognitive framework, integrate divergent forces into synergistic solutions, and engage in varied, even opposing, behaviors to leverage the power of paradox. *Selective leaders* view virtuality through an *either–or* framework, and attempt to either manage virtuality's challenges or to capitalize on its opportunities (i.e., failing to balance those tensions). *Stagnant leaders* adopt an *avoidant* framework, ignoring or avoiding virtuality's paradoxes, and fail to lead effective virtual teams.

The challenge of virtual leadership arises foremost from the lack of personal contact between the leader and employees. Also, the development of social relationships and, especially, trust is significantly influenced by the lack of personal contact (Kempner, 2022). Roman *et al.* (2019) argue that there are six critical competencies needed for effective virtual leadership (see Table 8.2). Leaders "good" at virtual leadership use a variety of advanced information technologies well to communicate effectively in one-to-one as well as team settings, create and sustain trust and a collaborative work environment, and manage change effectively.

Dery *et al.* (2017) studied how digital workplaces are created in organizations and established that focusing on employee connectedness and responsive leadership are the dimensions leaders need to address in this process. Responsive leadership refers to the extent to which management prioritizes the activities that focus on the development and continuous improvement of the employee experience in the organization (driving new behavioral norms throughout the organization).

Altogether, it can be said that digital leadership is not only about changing the types of skills and competencies needed in the workplace but demands a shift in mindset among individuals, teams, and organizations

Table 8.2. Competencies for virtual leadership.

E-communication: communicating via ICTs in a clear and organized manner, avoiding errors and miscommunication, and not being excessive or detrimental to performance.
E-social: creating positive work environment and improving communication and collaboration through a variety of virtual communication methods
E-change: managing change initiatives effectively through ICTs.
E-team: building, motivating, recognizing, and holding teams accountable in the virtual environment
E-tech: being technologically savvy and remaining current on relevant ICT developments and ICT-security-related concerns.
E-trust: creating a sense of trust when using ICTs by being perceived as honest, consistent, and fair.

(Trenerry *et al.*, 2021). Digital technologies and leadership reciprocally influence and change each other in a recursive relationship, and not only technology influences leadership but also leaders do, and it is through the interaction between information technology and organizational structures that the effect of technology on individuals, groups, and organizations emerges (Kahai *et al.*, 2017). Kahai *et al.* (2017) conclude that core leadership processes (charismatic and transformational leadership, empowerment, consideration and structure, and supervision and management) and leadership tactics (team-building, delegation and participation in decision-making, and leader–member exchange) may need to change with the greater development of IT in organizations. For example, team-building and goal alignment become more critical with IT deployment and the accompanying decentralization of decision-making. Leaders need to develop strong technical skills, be sensitive to and communicate opportunities and risks with the application of IT in order to be effective and enable successful assimilation of IT, and have to cultivate a culture of learning and development, participatory decision-making, and collaboration to succeed in the implementation of complex IT in organizations (Kahai *et al.*, 2017).

To sum up, according to Larjovuori *et al.* (2018), leaders of digitalizing companies must be able to challenge how their organizations operate, engage their personnel in the process of redefining their work roles, and keep their minds open to the possibility that their own roles will change as well.

8.5. Conclusion

This chapter tried to answer the question "What is 'smart working' and which challenges digital transformation poses for leaders when workplaces are increasingly converted digital?" It is argued that digitalization changes work through various tools and platforms used for communication, collaboration, and organizing work. Agile and digital work practices will develop, and routine work will be increasingly automated.

Digital workplace is more than using ICTs at work; to get the most of it, a shift in thinking about how work is defined is needed. By blending physical, cultural, and digital elements in the work environment, new and complex work practices emerge. Labeled as "smart working," spatially and temporally flexible work practices, drawing on the extended use of ICTs, result in specific organizational configurations of work with a concomitant change management philosophy. Smart leadership as facilitative behavior that inspires change and produces innovation in the ways of thinking about work emerges as a response. Managerial practices that foster collaborative and open relationships, empower employees through delegation, education, and training, facilitate knowledge sharing and trust, overcome obsolete command and control styles, and help employees to perceive their work as significant result in employees developing strong, intrinsic work motivation.

Agile philosophy is the starting point of SW, which when combined with satisfying employee expectations for meaningful work and work–life balance, advanced ICTs, and time and space flexibilities, leads to radical changes in workplaces. Smart leadership consists of various positive leadership behaviors aimed at increasing employee engagement at work. Leaders can enhance employee engagement by acting as role models, satisfying workers' needs for autonomy, relatedness, and competence, and by using emotional contagion as a leader behavior infused with positive emotions that will be mirrored by followers. Experiencing meaningful work results in motivation and engagement. The CARMA model incorporates the most important leadership- and organizational-level predictors and correlates of meaningful work that leaders can use.

Effective leadership presumes a mindset different from that of a high-performing individual, as leaders have to focus more on followers and how they can be supported. Effective leadership requires leaders to master four sets of behaviors related to work tasks, relationships, change management, and promoting and representing the organization outside.

Leadership in the digital context is related to new roles and paradoxical situations. Digital technologies and leadership reciprocally influence and change each other in a recursive relationship. To make digital transformation happen, leaders need to understand the essence of digital transformation and create a knowledge-creating context in organization. To be an effective leader in a virtual environment, one needs to be skillful in using ICTs for communication, creating and maintaining collaborative relationships and a sense of trust, as those skills also contribute to team leadership and change management.

References

Antonakis, J., Banks, G., Bastardoz, N., Cole, M., Day, D., Eagly, A., & Weber, R. (2019). The leadership quarterly: State of the journal. *The Leadership Quarterly* 30(1), 1–9.

Avolio, B. J., Sosik, J. J., Kahai, S. S., & Baker, B. (2014). E-leadership: Re-examining transformations in leadership source and transmission. *The Leadership Quarterly* 25(1), 105–131.

Bandura, A. (1986). *Social Foundations of Thought and Action: A Social Cognitive Theory*. Englewood Cliffs, NJ: Prentice Hall.

Banks, G. C., Dionne, S. D., Mast, M. S., & Sayama, H. (2022). Leadership in the digital era: A review of who, what, when, where, and why. *The Leadership Quarterly* 33(5), 101634.

Bass, B. M. (1990). From transactional to transformational leadership: Learning to share the vision. *Organizational Dynamics* 18(3), 19–31.

Berman, S., & Korsten, P. (2014). Leading in the connected era. *Strategy & Leadership* 42(1), 37–46.

Becker, J., Berger, M., Gimpel, H., Lanzl, J., & Regal, C. (2020). Considering characteristic profiles of technologies at the digital workplace: The influence on technostress. In *ICIS*.

Binci, D. & Scafarto, F. (2019). Leadership in safety-oriented organizations: An empirical study. *International Journal of Decision Sciences, Risk and Management* 8(4), 268–291.

Bregenzer, A. & Jimenez, P. (2021). Risk factors and leadership in a digitalized working world and their effects on employees' stress and resources: Web-based questionnaire study. *Journal of Medical Internet Research* 23(3), e24906.

Chartered Institute for Personnel and Development (CIPD). (2008). *Job Design, Research Insight*. CIPD, London.

Contreras, F., Baykal, E., & Abid, G. (2020). E-leadership and teleworking in times of COVID-19 and beyond: What we know and where do we go. *Frontiers in Psychology* 11, 590271.

Cortellazzo, L., Bruni, E., & Zampieri, R. (2019). The role of leadership in a digitalized world: A review. *Frontier Psychology* 10, 1938.

Crane, B. (2022). Leadership mindsets: Why new managers fail and what to do about it. *Business Horizons* 65(4), 447–455.

Crum, A. J., Salovey, P., & Achor, S. (2013). Rethinking stress: The role of mindsets in determining the stress response. *Journal of Personality and Social Psychology* 104(4), 716–733.

D'Este, P., Iammarino, S., Savona, M., & Von Tunzelmann, N. (2012). What Hampers Innovation? Revealed barriers versus deterring barriers. *Research Policy* 41(2), 482–488.

Decuypere, A. & Schaufeli, W. (2020). Leadership and work engagement: Exploring explanatory mechanisms. *German Journal of Human Resource Management* 34(1), 69–95.

Deci, E. L. & Ryan, R. M. (2008). Self-determination theory: A macrotheory of human motivation, development, and health. *Canadian Psychology/ Psychologie Canadienne* 49(3), 182.

Dery, K., Sebastian, I. M., & van der Meulen, N. (2017). The digital workplace is key to digital innovation. *MIS Quarterly Executive* 16(2).

Dittes, S., Richter, S., Richter, A., & Smolnik, S. (2019). Toward the workplace of the future: How organizations can facilitate digital work. *Business Horizons* 62(5), 649–661.

Dweck, C. S. (1986). Motivational processes affecting learning. *American Psychologist* 41(10), 1040.

Eberl, J. K. & Drews, P. (2021). Digital Leadership — Mountain or Molehill? A Literature Review. Internationale Konferenz Wirtschaftsinformatik 2021, March 2021, Essen, Germany.

El Sawy, O. A., Kræmmergaard, P., Amsinck, H., & Vinther, A. L. (2016). How LEGO built the foundations and enterprise capabilities for digital leadership. *MIS Quarterly Executive* 15(2), 141–166.

Goodwin, T. (2018). *Digital Darwinism: Survival of the Fittest in the Age of Business Disruption*. Kogan Page Publishers, London.

Iannotta, M., Meret, C., & Marchetti, G. (2020). Defining leadership in smart working contexts: A concept synthesis. *Frontiers in Psychology* 11, 556933.

Kahai, S., Avolio, B. J., & Sosik, J. J. (2017). E-leadership. *The Wiley Blackwell Handbook of the Psychology of the Internet at Work*, pp. 285–314.

Kempner, F. (2022). E-Leadership Competences — The Impact of Media Use and Organizational Influence. International Scientific Conference Business and Management May 12–13, 2022, Vilnius, Lithuania. 10.3846/bm.2022.865.

Korzynski, P., Kozminski, A. K., Baczynska, A., & Haenlein, M. (2021). Bounded leadership: An empirical study of leadership competencies, constraints, and effectiveness. *European Management Journal* 39(2), 226–235.

Köffer, S. (2015). Designing the digital workplace of the future–what scholars recommend to practitioners.

Larjovuori, R. L., Bordi, L., & Heikkilä-Tammi, K. (2018, October). Leadership in the digital business transformation. In *Proceedings of the 22nd International Academic Mindtrek Conference*, pp. 212–221.

Leimeister, J. M. & Blohm, I. (2022). Digitalization and the future of work. *Die Unternehmung* 76(1), 1–5.

Larsson-Lund, M. (2018). The digital society: Occupational therapists need to act proactively to meet the growing demands of digital competence. *British Journal of Occupational Therapy* 81(12), 733–735.

Marsh, E., Vallejos, E. P., & Spence, A. (2022). The digital workplace and its dark side: An integrative review. *Computers in Human Behavior* 128, 107118.

McEwan, A. M. (2016). *Smart Working: Creating the Next Wave*. Routledge, London and New York.

Podgórski, D., Majchrzycka, K., Dąbrowska, A., Gralewicz, G., & Okrasa, M. (2017). Towards a conceptual framework of OSH risk management in smart working environments based on smart PPE, ambient intelligence and the Internet of Things technologies. *International Journal of Occupational Safety and Ergonomics* 23(1), 1–20.

Purvanova, R. K. & Kenda, R. (2018). Paradoxical virtual leadership: Reconsidering virtuality through a paradox lens. *Group & Organization Management* 43(5), 752–786.

Roman, A., VanWart, M., Wang, X. H., Liu, C., Kim, S., & McCarthy, A. (2019). Defining e-leadership as competence in ICT-mediated communications: An exploratory assessment. *Public Administration Review* 79(6), 853–866.

Schiuma, G., Schettini, E., Santarsiero, F., & Carlucci, D. (2022). The transformative leadership compass: Six competencies for digital transformation entrepreneurship. *International Journal of Entrepreneurial Behavior & Research* 28(5), 1273–1291.

Schnasse, F., Menzefricke, J. S., & Dumitrescu, R. (2021, April). Identification of Socio-Technical Risks and Their Correlations in the Context of Digital Transformation for the Manufacturing Sector. In *2021 IEEE 8th International Conference on Industrial Engineering and Applications (ICIEA)*, pp. 159–166. IEEE.

Spreitzer, G. M., Cameron, L., & Garrett, L. (2017). Alternative work arrangements: Two images of the new world of work. *Annual Review of Organizational Psychology and Organizational Behavior* 4(1), 473–499.

Steger, M. F. (2016). Creating meaning and purpose at work. *Wiley Blackwell Handbook of the Psychology of Positivity and Strengths-Based Approaches at Work*, ed. by L. G. Oades, M. F. Steger, A. D. Fave, J. Passmore, pp. 60–81. Wiley-Blackwell.

Taskin, L., Ajzen, M., & Donis, C. (2017). New ways of working: From smart to shared power. In *Redefining Management*, pp. 65–79. Springer, Cham.

Tennakoon, K. U. S., Da Silveira, G. J., & Taras, D. G. (2013). Drivers of context-specific ICT use across work and nonwork domains: A boundary theory perspective. *Information and Organization* 23(2), 107–128.

Torre, T. & Sarti, D. (2020). The "way" toward e-leadership: Some evidence from the field. *Frontiers in Psychology* 11, 554253.

Trenerry, B., Chng, S., Wang, Y., Suhaila, Z. S., Lim, S. S., Lu, H. Y., & Oh, P. H. (2021). Preparing workplaces for digital transformation: An integrative review and framework of multi-level factors. *Frontiers in Psychology* 12, 620766.

Uhl-Bien, M. & Arena, M. (2017). Complexity leadership: Enabling people and organizations for adaptability. *Organizational Dynamics*.

Van Wart, M., Roman, A., Wang, X., & Liu, C. (2019). Operationalizing the definition of e-leadership: Identifying the elements of e-leadership. *International Review of Administrative Sciences* 85(1), 80–97.

Vaska, S., Massaro, M., Bagarotto, E. M., & Dal Mas, F. (2021). The digital transformation of business model innovation: A structured literature review. *Frontiers in Psychology* 3557.

Weber, E., Krehl, E. H., & Büttgen, M. (2022). The digital transformation leadership framework: Conceptual and empirical insights into leadership roles in technology-driven business environments. *Journal of Leadership Studies* 16(1), 6–22.

Williams, S. P. & Schubert, P. (2018). Designs for the digital workplace. *Procedia Computer Science* 138, 478–485.

Yukl, G. (2012). Effective leadership behavior: What we know and what questions need more attention. *Academy of Management Perspectives* 26(4), 66–85.

Zuppo, C. M. (2012). Defining ICT in a boundaryless world: The development of a working hierarchy. *International Journal of Managing Information Technology* 4(3), 13.

https://doi.org/10.1142/9789811270178_0009

Chapter 9

Disruptive Services as an Opportunity for Digital Entrepreneurs

Johann Timo Theisen

Department of Business Administration, Reykjavik University, Menntavegur 1, 102 Reykjavík, Iceland

johann23@ru.is

Abstract

Today's society is faced with rapid economic change. This change is so significant that new companies are quickly becoming the driving force of economic development around the world. It is primarily entrepreneurial companies that are shaping the global economy by challenging established standards and introducing a host of new, disruptive technologies and innovations. In the area of digital disruption, technological breakthroughs are taking entire industries and markets around the world out of their comfort zones. Against the backdrop of this change, it is no longer enough for leaders to ignore the transformative power of digitalization on business models or strategies. However, successful integration and use of new digital technologies and processes will only succeed if entrepreneurs are willing to question and, if necessary, adapt their previous strategic orientation and associated business models. The primary goal of this chapter is to demonstrate the opportunities that emerge for entrepreneurial players as a result of a shift away from innovative service or service-oriented business models. In doing so, the "Everything as a Service" approach will be examined in more detail to help entrepreneurs make the change to a service-oriented business model in a more structured way.

9.1. Introduction

Digital technologies are helping to transform large parts of our economy and society (Elia *et al.*, 2020; Sahut *et al.*, 2021; Sussan & Acs, 2017).

The new digital technologies are seen as having the potential to change even entire economic structures and societies. This becomes visible when we recognize how we live our lives, what kind of work we do, and how our consumption behavior ultimately begins to change (Pichierri *et al.*, 2018). In recent years, this trend has been driven by the introduction of new innovations, such as the Internet of Things (IoT) and artificial intelligence (AI).

Entrepreneurs face major challenges. Digital developments often lead to disruptions. Traditional business areas are increasingly being replaced by new business models. This process is typically followed by a change in the company's core business, affecting processes, goods, and services as well as organizational structures and management methods (Skog *et al.*, 2018). With profound organizational and political implications, the concepts of innovation and entrepreneurship in particular have changed dramatically. Many established organizations underestimate the dynamics, react too slowly to change, and cling to their current business models. They are struggling to adapt to this change (Matzler *et al.*, 2018).

The unstoppable convergence of entrepreneurship and digital technologies is creating a new generation of entrepreneurs who consistently make digital technologies their tool to perform most of the processes required to start a new business (Elia *et al.*, 2020). This revolution is changing the way companies do business and build relationships within and across ecosystems, bringing new opportunities and challenges for entrepreneurs (Bresciani *et al.*, 2021).

No industry or company is considered immune to the impact of emerging digital technologies, making their exploration, integration, and application among the biggest challenges facing business and society today. Whether it is a matter of goods or services, the term "digital transformation" is used to describe the transformative or disruptive impact of digital technologies on businesses (Jafari-Sadeghi *et al.*, 2021).

Digital services, in particular, are assuming an increasingly important strategic role in the actions of entrepreneurs. The greatest challenge for product-oriented companies is to consistently integrate service innovations into their business models (Rauch *et al.*, 2016). This can be justified by the fact that it is difficult to move from a product-oriented core culture to a more relationship- and customer-oriented attitude (Adrodegari *et al.*, 2015).

A very interesting approach to digital services is the idea of not selling ownership of a product but offering the consumer either the use of the product or its performance (Ranta *et al.*, 2021). For example, they enable companies to share data within their supply chains and identify and track products and materials, which improves their ability to retain value (Ranta *et al.*, 2021). This approach, also defined as an innovative combination of products and services, can be seen as a high-value and holistic response to the growing needs of today's customers. A strategic reorientation toward digital services presents entrepreneurs who have decided to transform their business models with far-reaching change processes (Heredia *et al.*, 2022). The aim of this chapter is to present a roadmap for the introduction and implementation of anything-as-a-service (XaaS) so that the transformation to a service-based business model becomes transparent.

9.2. Business Model Innovation and Digital Transformation

This section discusses the relationship between business model innovation and digital entrepreneurship opportunities. It also explains how disruptive technologies can help entrepreneurs overcome the challenges of digital transformation.

According to Hull's (2007) definition, "digital entrepreneurship" is a subtype of entrepreneurship in which all or part of the physical activities of a traditional organization have been transformed into a digital form. Digital entrepreneurship is expected to become more common in all industries given the rapid development of digital activities, so a better understanding of this phenomenon is needed. (Kostoff *et al.*, 2004; Zahra *et al.*, 2022). To this end, Liao and Hull (2007) divided digital entrepreneurship into three types:

- The first type, light digital entrepreneurship, involves entry into the digital economy as a complement to more traditional business fields.
- The second stage of digital entrepreneurship is called moderate digital entrepreneurship and focuses on digital delivery, digital products, or other digital aspects of the business. For the medium level of digital entrepreneurship, a digital infrastructure is required.
- Extreme digital entrepreneurship refers to the third stage, where all aspects of the business, including production, actual goods or services, advertising, sales, and customer care are handled digitally.

According to Naudé and Liebregts (2020), "digital entrepreneurs" can be defined as entrepreneurs who pursue opportunities to produce and trade digital value. The business model concept is one of the most crucial tools for entrepreneurs to take advantage of opportunities by developing and generating value from new technologies (Cavallo *et al.*, 2019; Massa & Tucci, 2013). Entrepreneurs can use it to outline the tasks necessary to take advantage of an opportunity, list the tasks made possible by technology, and link these tasks to a larger logic of value creation and capture (Steininger *et al.*, 2022). In essence, new technologies enable unmet customer needs or problems to be met. A notable example of how digital technologies can create new value through different business models is the development of such autonomous agents.

It cannot be assumed that newly developed digital technologies will immediately lead to economic benefits for a company (Teece, 2018). But many parts of a value chain, in particular, can combine digital technologies to create fully digital business models (Steininger *et al.*, 2019; Zahra *et al.*, 2022). This leads to changes in many areas of the value architecture and network dimensions of the business model (Steininger *et al.*, 2022). Value development for digital entrepreneurs depends on the technological infrastructure within and between companies. To successfully create new digital business models, digital entrepreneurs also require new capabilities that take the concept of digital divide into account. Agile and user-centric thinking facilitate continuous product creation, but new security and availability guarantees are required, particularly for cloud-based applications (Lehmann & Recker, 2022).

According to Christensen *et al.* (2018), the concept of disruptive innovation is widely used in practice, although its basic principles are widely misunderstood. One of the fundamental problems is the overuse of the term "disruptive innovation" or "disruption" for any new threat (or significant ongoing change) and the misunderstanding of disruptive innovation as a theoretical concept. Technology that is disruptive is not always novel or groundbreaking. Instead, it is a technology that could revolutionize an already established business or sector (Christensen, 2006; Kivimaa *et al.*, 2021). Disruptive technologies have the potential to change a particular sector of the economy. The quality, speed, and price of goods and services can be improved. In some cases, completely new markets are even created (Amshoff *et al.*, 2015; Hall & Martin, 2005).

9.3. A Practical Guide to Anything-as-a-Service

Flexible and agile models are no longer just an option but rather a prerequisite for staying ahead of the competition in the age of digital transformation, in which rapid digitization is becoming inevitable for companies. The goal of this concept, sometimes also referred to as "Anything as a Service" (XaaS), is to provide other participants in a service ecosystem with access to internal services. The Internet has enabled faster access and more capabilities in these models. Various aspects of data processing are now simply subscription-based services available on demand. These products now fall into the broad category of XaaS data processing. The digital transformation of enterprises and the future of work are also driven by this category (Duan *et al.*, 2015).

The idea of XaaS was first introduced in the computer software and services sector, where economies of scale and efficiency drove the consolidation of large network operation centers. This approach has led to the widespread use of cloud-based software solutions (Duan *et al.*, 2015). Customer loyalty can be raised through XaaS models by providing better value for their money. By fostering greater income stream growth, stability, and predictability, they can also benefit service providers.

XaaS includes utility-like offerings that can be used on a per-device or per-month basis, depending on an organization's needs. Every company's operating model is different. Basically, it is always about capturing business requirements and providing technology services to achieve specific outcomes. However, the main goal of XaaS offerings is to increase customer value. XaaS models can improve customer retention by providing better value for money. By promoting growth, stability, and predictability of revenue streams, they can also benefit service providers (Table 9.1).

Table 9.1. Benefits from XaaS.

Customer Benefits from XaaS	Business Benefits from XaaS
Increased selection and higher standards for goods and services	Expansion through new markets and revenue sources
Less expensive and more adaptable	Increased operational predictability and performance assurance
Prioritize results, experiences, and outcomes over ownership	Improved client loyalty
Easier possibilities for additional service, modifications, and upgrades	More corporate agility and competition
Risk minimization is achieved by sharing with the service provider	

Source: SAP publication about XaaS and subscription business models: How business model innovation is driving growth strategies (https://www.sap.com/insights/business-model-innovation-xaas.html).

Another significant benefit of XaaS is the inherently higher usage rate of products throughout their life cycle and better synchronization with changing market demands. This holistic XaaS perspective shifts companies' focus to the entire production process, longevity of use, maintenance, service, and disposal or recycling rather than producing products for one-off sales events. This comprehensive end-to-end perspective helps foster a "circular economy" mentality that reduces waste and increases sustainability (Chimakurthi, 2021).

9.4. Practical Steps for Implementing XaaS

In today's economy, interactions between buyers and sellers usually take place after a successful transaction. This means that buyers and sellers often have no further contact with each other after the transaction has been completed and ownership of the goods or services has been transferred, unless the customer wants to temporarily purchase new services or goods.

In an XaaS model, on the other hand, communication between providers and customers takes place continuously while the service is being used. When a product is purchased as a service, the customer enters into a contract with the producing company. In the process, the customer does not purchase the product himself. Instead, he is granted access to the entire service. Once the customer stops using the product or the subscription period ends, the product is returned to the service provider so that it can enter the next phase of its life cycle.

In XaaS models, the customer never acquires ownership of a product, so the company is interested in retaining ownership. XaaS models represent a high level of quality and continuous improvement of products and services in order to retain customers and attract new ones.

9.4.1. *Align your organization to reach your business goals*

It is important that business goals and outcomes are aligned. Only when this alignment is achieved can the business strategy be specified, including the resources and technologies required and the involvement of external service providers or the development of resources that may be needed. Alignment may include the following:

- a holistic risk assessment;
- definition and, if necessary, adjustment of existing price points;
- contracts appropriate for transitioning to a digital business model;
- analysis of market and customer segments and their potential.

Because XaaS involves a shift in the core of a company's current business model, changes may be required in organizational planning, research, development, production, marketing, sales, and service.

9.4.2. *Selecting an XaaS model that fits the business purpose*

To the extent that the core business realignment could be defined across the enterprise, the company needs to determine what type of XaaS model it wants to offer. According to Deloitte's Flexible Consumption Business Models (2020), the following examples may be considered:

- A service offering with no restrictions: For a set period of time, the service offers a subscription package with limitless calls, features, and devices.
- A service plan with predefined restrictions: Access to a set number of products or features for a set amount of time, typically requiring a minimum commitment.

- A service plan with an enhancement option: A service that provides access to a specified amount for a specified period of time, with additional charges based on actual usage.
- A service plan with basic features and additional expansion options: Basic services are accessible for free, but premium or unique features cost extra.
- A customized service offering: pay-per-use monetization, typically without a minimum purchase or commitment.
- Success-based service offering: Revenue is based on a target value set in collaboration with the customer, based on the value provided to the customer and measured as a tangible result.

9.4.3. *Drive the change from top down*

New and innovative services, not products, are the future of business. By becoming customer-centric, subscriptions can be offered that are tailored to customers' needs and satisfy their need for convenience.

To make the transition to a service- or service-oriented business, entrepreneurs must change their business models from a product to a service offering that provides the following business benefits:

- By offering a new service-based business model, the company can access recurring revenue streams.
- The expanded service offering and the flexibility of the product and service offerings suggest an engaged and committed customer base, with the opportunity to create close and, more importantly, lasting customer relationships.
- The operational transparency of the business model and the continuous interaction with the customer create iterative processes that enable the company to act with foresight and thus continuously evolve.

9.5. Potentials for Digital Entrepreneurs Shifting to XaaS

As outlined previously in this chapter, it is often necessary to take an existing corporate structure out of its comfort zone in order to drive digital transformation. This is achieved by forcing long-term strategic decisions about an unpredictable future (Nylén & Holmström, 2015). This section addresses the five recommendations for digital awareness, according to Saarikko *et al.* (2020). It is intended to further support entrepreneurs in their transition to an XaaS-oriented business model.

9.5.1. *Think from game to game and build on your insights*

The term "digital transformation" is intended to describe a company's ability to use available digital technologies as efficiently and effectively as possible to gain and improve a holistic perspective on the value chain. Since digital transformation usually involves far-reaching changes in a company, every organization should be aware that resource- and capital-intensive advance planning is necessary before significant benefits can be realized. The transformative aspect is expressed not in the technical value creation itself but in the insight required to realize the benefits that can be derived from using a digital tool to solve a business problem. Moreover, a defining characteristic of digital technology is its ability to increase the density of information and knowledge resources that can be leveraged for each data set.

9.5.2. *Leveraging brand awareness in the value chain*

Saarikko *et al.* (2020) also pointed out that it is advantageous for companies that already have high brand awareness in the market to implement innovative business models and new market offerings more easily than companies that are new to a market. This brand awareness is used as an advantage when it comes to adding connected products or disruptive service offerings to their portfolio and having an existing customer base that is convinced of their products and services. The value chain in an ecosystem considered as a whole can help mitigate risks and create benefits for all stakeholders, with incumbents gaining rapid access to technological know-how and new business models. Conversely, small technology companies with lesser-known brands can leverage the strengths of their partners within the value chain to gradually build their own credibility and expand their offerings.

9.5.3. *Drive standardization going forward*

Digital innovation relies on the ability to combine many digital technologies that are relatively mature and easy to implement on their own. When different companies pool their intellectual and material resources, they can begin to develop standards and interfaces that are widely used in an industry or market. Over time, standards can spread to other contexts and gain legitimacy and strength along the way. Given the widespread and enduring influence of standards, the digitally aware enterprise should ensure that its interests are considered in the development and implementation of standards. Otherwise, it could find itself in a technology landscape that runs counter to its strategic interests. Standardization has a significant strategic component that should attract management attention (Saarikko *et al.*, 2020).

9.5.4. *Create responsible data handling*

The generation of data in all areas is not the main feature of digital transformation, but it is an unavoidable consequence of working with digitized products and business models. With an infinite variety of connected products, companies have the opportunity not only to offer connectivity solutions but also to capture a larger share of a market that increasingly derives its revenue from services based on collected data. Because digitized products and services can be used simultaneously for business and personal purposes, companies have every opportunity to create solutions that satisfy both sides and generate multiple types of value. Increased awareness of data management responsibilities is a turning point in a company's digital maturity. Saarikko *et al.* (2020) point out that successful digital transformation requires recognition of the legal dimension, i.e., careful consideration of the legal and practical implications of owning and managing data.

9.5.5. *Independently drive change and ensure organizational commitment*

As outlined in the study by Kane *et al.* (2015), corporate culture is an important component when it comes to adopting and leveraging digital technologies as part of transformation efforts. However, such a move requires a clear vision and consideration of each company's unique characteristics, including current corporate practices, norms, and business values. It also requires leadership and support from top management. To reduce uncertainty about the outcome, digital transformation efforts must start at the top management level, be firmly embedded in the middle and lower management levels, and be able to permeate all aspects of corporate life. Raising awareness of digitalization can significantly improve the company's ability to embrace digital technologies and take ownership of the transformation (Saarikko *et al.*, 2020).

9.6. The XaaS Model and its Advantages

When companies want to implement new and innovative solutions in less time, the XaaS model offers several advantages:

- Lower, more predictable expenses: The XaaS approach, which significantly reduces running costs, allows capital expenditures to be converted into predictable monthly operational expenses. The infrastructure is purchased and maintained by the service provider. The XaaS model can therefore aid in lowering overhead, labor, and maintenance expenses. Because computing power and storage are available on demand, enterprises can enjoy additional cost reductions.
- Maximum flexibility: The XaaS model offers companies more flexibility in developing novel solutions by enabling them to adapt to changing market conditions or take advantage of new opportunities. Customers' or employees' wishes can be taken into account immediately in technological environments.
- Time-efficient use of resources: Partial or full outsourcing to a service provider can save internal resources. By outsourcing certain activities to a service provider, companies can streamline their operations and focus their efforts on higher-value projects.
- Better backup planning: Having a thorough backup and recovery plan in place is essential since the XaaS model as a digital service depends on processing and backing up enormous volumes of data. In the event of a crisis, XaaS solutions might be crucial to keeping a firm operational.
- Making data usable: Virtually unlimited storage capacity helps companies store data over a very long period of time. This allows them to continuously analyze data sets to improve customer satisfaction, make smarter business decisions, and identify trends that they can then build on to increase competitiveness.

9.7. XaaS and Innovation

The trend toward digitization offers companies more opportunities to reach consumers on the market. In addition, digitization is shaping an increasingly competitive market. Companies must constantly develop new concepts and seize these opportunities. Companies' ability to innovate is influenced by whether they need to increase their resources or can do so without long-term financial commitments.

Innovative projects can be implemented more easily with the XaaS concept. It is more likely that XaaS will become the new standard as more services are delivered via the cloud and digital technologies, such as the IoT and AI, become more integrated. XaaS models can help entrepreneurs implement novel, disruptive business models that have the potential for rapid growth while increasing productivity. It is critical to differentiate business models and adapt them to the needs of the market. There are many obvious benefits for entrepreneurs, while XaaS models also offer some unexpected advantages. Those could have a greater impact on how companies make products, how their customers use products and services, and how the useful lives of goods and services can be extended.

A circular economy can be fostered by moving to XaaS and developing services that combine products, especially in the manufacturing sector. In this sector, the focus is no longer on the one-time manufacture of a product but on its continuous use over time. This is accompanied by a greater focus on the quality, durability, use, maintenance, and disposal or recycling of the product.

9.8. Conclusion and Implications

The digital technology, set out in greater detail in this book chapter, has been specifically discussed as the concept of XaaS. It is important to understand that it would be wrong to say that XaaS is mainly limited to providing services around software solutions. Rather, the trend toward XaaS models extends far beyond the PC and is now taking the form of numerous service innovations enabled by the support of digital technology. This shift means that traditional business models, whether based on products, software, or processes, are no longer delivered in vertical, separate silos but horizontally. In a sense, they are merging into a service offering for the customer. There will be other interesting formats as the concept catches on. One thing is certain: There is a huge potential to disrupt the typical purchase and use cycle of product sales, as it will change to the point where everything is delivered as a utility.

Overall, however, XaaS as a technological concept will have an increasing impact on the entire traditional enterprise supply chain and product life cycle. "Disruption as a Service" will offer an opportunity to those entrepreneurs who are risk-tolerant enough to rethink their current business models from the ground up, and they will gradually move from resource-intensive production processes to services. In this context, the roadmap described in this chapter is intended to serve as a guide to help entrepreneurs decide whether to apply disruptive services as potential new business models and to accompany them during implementation.

References

Adrodegari, F., Alghisi, A., Ardolino, M., & Saccani, N. (2015). From ownership to service-oriented business models: A survey in capital goods companies and a PSS typology. *Procedia CIRP* 30, 245–250.

Amshoff, B., Dülme, C., Echterfeld, J., & Gausemeier, J. (2015). Business model patterns for disruptive technologies. *International Journal of Innovation Management* 19(3), 1540002.

Bresciani, S., Ferraris, A., Huarng, K. H., & Malhotra, A. (2021). Digital transformation as a springboard for product, process and business model innovation. *Journal of Business Research* 128, 204–210.

Cavallo, A., Ghezzi, A., Dell'Era, C., & Pellizzoni, E. (2019). Fostering digital entrepreneurship from startup to scaleup: The role of venture capital funds and angel groups. *Technological Forecasting and Social Change* 145, 24–35.

Chimakurthi, V. N. S. S. (2021). Strategic Growth of Everything-as-a-Service (XaaS) business model transformation. *Engineering International* 9(2), 129–140. Doi: 10.18034/ei.v9i2.589.

Christensen, C. M., McDonald, R., Altman, E. J., & Palmer, J. E. (2018). Disruptive innovation: An intellectual history and directions for future research. *Journal of Management Studies* 55(7), 1043–1078.

Christensen, C. M. (2006). The ongoing process of building a theory of disruption. *Journal of Product Innovation Management* 23(1), 39–55.

Deloitte (2022). Flexible consumption business models. Driving growth through the right pay-per-use business models. https://www2.deloitte.com/us/en/pages/technology-media-and-telecommunications/articles/flexible-consumption-business-models.html.

Duan, Y., Fu, G., Zhou, N., Sun, X., Narendra, N. C., & Hu, B. (2015, June). Everything as a service (XaaS) on the cloud: Origins, current and future trends. In 2015 IEEE 8th International Conference on Cloud Computing, pp. 621–628. IEEE.

Elia, G., Margherita, A., & Passiante, G. (2020). Digital entrepreneurship ecosystem: How digital technologies and collective intelligence are reshaping the entrepreneurial process. *Technological Forecasting and Social Change* 150, 119791.

Hall, J. K. & Martin, M. J. (2005). Disruptive technologies, stakeholders and the innovation value added chain: A framework for evaluating radical technology development. *R&D Management* 35(3), 273–284.

Heredia, J., Castillo-Vergara, M., Geldes, C., Gamarra, F. M. C., Flores, A., & Heredia, W. (2022). How do digital capabilities affect firm performance? The mediating role of technological capabilities in the "new normal". *Journal of Innovation & Knowledge* 7(2), 100171.

Hull, C. E. K., Hung, Y. T. C., Hair, N., Perotti, V., & DeMartino, R. (2007). Taking advantage of digital opportunities: A typology of digital entrepreneurship. *International Journal of Networking and Virtual Organizations* 4(3), 290–303.

Jafari-Sadeghi, V., Garcia-Perez, A., Candelo, E., & Couturier, J. (2021). Exploring the impact of digital transformation on technology entrepreneurship and technological market expansion: The role of technology readiness, exploration and exploitation. *Journal of Business Research* 124, 100–111.

Kane, G. C., Palmer, D., Phillips, A. N., Kiron, D., & Buckley, N. (2015). "Strategy, Not Technology, Drives Digital Transformation", *MIT Sloan Management Review* and Deloitte University Press.

Kivimaa, P., Laakso, S., Lonkila, A., & Kaljonen, M. (2021). Moving beyond disruptive innovation: A review of disruption in sustainability transitions. *Environmental Innovation and Societal Transitions* 38, 110–126.

Kostoff, R. N., Boylan, R., & Simons, G. R. (2004). Disruptive technology roadmaps. *Technological Forecasting and Social Change* 71(1-2), 141–159.

Lehmann, J. & Recker, J. (2022). Offerings that are "ever-in-the-making". *Business & Information Systems Engineering* 64(1), 69–89.

Liao, A., Hull, C. E., & Sriramachandramurthy, R. (2013). The six facets model of technology management: A study in the digital business industry. *International Journal of Innovation and Technology Management* 10(04), 1350019.

Massa, L. & Tucci, C. L. (2013). Business model innovation. *The Oxford Handbook of Innovation Management* 20(18), 420–441.

Matzler, K., Friedrich von den Eichen, S., Anschober, M., & Kohler, T. (2018). The crusade of digital disruption. *Journal of Business Strategy* 39(6), 13–20.

Naudé, W. & Liebregts, W. (2020). Digital entrepreneurship research: A concise introduction. IZA Discussion Paper No. 13667, Available at SSRN: https://ssrn.com/abstract=3691380 or http://dx.doi.org/10.2139/ssrn.3691380.

Nylén, D. & Holmström, J. (2015). Digital innovation strategy: A framework for diagnosing and improving digital product and service innovation. *Business Horizons* 58(1), 57–67.

Pichierri, M., Pizzi, G., & Scarpi, D. (2018). To buy or to rent?: an experimental study on the antecedents of consumers' acquisition-mode decisions. *MERCATI & COMPETITIVIT?* 1(1), 63–92.

Ranta, V., Aarikka-Stenroos, L., & Väisänen, J. M. (2021). Digital technologies catalyzing business model innovation for circular economy — Multiple case study. *Resources, Conservation and Recycling* 164, 105155.

Rauch, M., Wenzel, M., & Wagner, H. T. (2016). The digital disruption of strategic paths: an experimental study. Thirty Seventh International Conference on Information Systems, Dublin 2016 (https://core.ac.uk/download/pdf/301370343.pdf).

Saarikko, T., Westergren, U. H., & Blomquist, T. (2020). Digital transformation: Five recommendations for the digitally conscious firm. *Business Horizons* 63(6), 825–839.

Sahut, J. M., Iandoli, L., & Teulon, F. (2021). The age of digital entrepreneurship. *Small Business Economics* 56(3), 1159–1169.

SAP: XaaS and subscription business models: How business model innovation is driving growth strategies. https://www.sap.com/insights/business-model-innovation-xaas.html.

Skog, D. A., Wimelius, H., & Sandberg, J. (2018). Digital disruption. *Business & Information Systems Engineering* 60(5), 431–437.

Steininger, D. M., Kathryn Brohman, M., & Block, J. H. (2022). Digital entrepreneurship: What is new if anything? *Business & Information Systems Engineering* 64(1), 1–14.

Sussan, F. & Acs, Z. J. (2017). The digital entrepreneurial ecosystem. *Small Business Economics* 49(1), 55–73.

Teece, D. J. (2018). Profiting from innovation in the digital economy: Enabling technologies, standards, and licensing models in the wireless world. *Research Policy* 47(8), 1367–1387.

Zahra, S. A., Liu, W., & Si, S. (2023). How digital technology promotes entrepreneurship in ecosystems. *Technovation*, 119, 102457.

https://doi.org/10.1142/9789811270178_0010

Chapter 10

Transformation of Entrepreneurial Business Finance

Fabian Zimmermann

Department of Business Administration, Reykjavik University, Menntavegur 1, 102 Reykjavik, Iceland

fabian23@ru.is

Abstract

The future of entrepreneurial business finance is strongly connected with technological developments and the manufacturing of new investment products. New technologies make it easier to collect investor money and invest it in profitable business ideas. The technological transformation makes the pooling of funds easier and reduces processing and transaction costs. For business finance, this trend means that by allowing a larger group of retail investors to invest in collective funds, more liquidity will be provided to businesses. This chapter aims to provide a condensed overview of the most common funding methods and the changes they undergo. Furthermore, this chapter seeks to shed light on new forms of funding. Entrepreneurs will get familiar with recent emerging trends in business finance and learn about the latest terminology. Each of the funding methods is described in detail, and their advantages and potential shortcomings are summarized.

10.1. Introduction

Technology changes every corner of our society. Thus, it also impacts the economy and the business players within it. In industries and sectors in which transformational processes can lead to better performance, i.e., faster processing of data, elimination of failures, and reduction of costs, companies will adopt these new technologies to have a competitive edge or to stay relevant (Prause, 2019). Especially in the business sector, transformational processes are often triggered by new technologies becoming an industry standard and revolutionizing the market (Veldhoven & Vanthienen, 2022; Maddikunta *et al.*, 2022).

On the contrary, central market participants, such as banks, regulators, and infrastructure providers, are not very keen on change and are rarely among the first adopters of new technologies. However, as they are on the brink of business interactions, they significantly impact industries' transformation (Toufaily *et al.*, 2021). Every business will, at some point, interact with at least one of these market players in one way or another. New regulations, emerging market participants, and the development of new technologies shape how these institutions interact with their clients on the market (Bradley *et al.*, 2021). For entrepreneurs, choosing the proper environment is crucial to their businesses' success and getting access to funding. The financial service sector is important for entrepreneurs, which faces a vast transformational process, thus shaping the way how entrepreneurs acquire financing for their businesses. The different financing methods for businesses are traditionally described by the life-cycle approach, which indicates which form of financing to use at each development stage of the company (Wilson, 2013). Wilson (2013), in his study, links the growth phases of a business venture with the available funding methods most likely required for each phase. However, as the business world is changing fast and new emerging companies often jump life-cycle stages, the traditional approach only holds sometimes. Furthermore, new technologies change the complexity and access to funding (Łasak, 2022). Thereby, the differences between the funding methods are blurring.

10.2. Entrepreneurial Business Finance: The Transformation of Traditional Funding Methods

Finance is one of the crucial factors for any successful business undertaking (Garg & Shivam, 2017). Without financial support, it is nearly impossible for any business to grow or sometimes even to start. Even if the entrepreneurial venture started as a hobby or side hustle, at some point, the entrepreneur would need to face the question of how to finance the production or its employees. Therefore, the overarching reason for all business financing is to obtain funds to finance or maintain a business undertaking and to grow it further to bolster profits. (Ronchini *et al.*, 2021). Especially for entrepreneurial undertakings, the appropriate analysis of the required funds is essential to provide banks and potential investors with the necessary information about the intended scope of financing (Alizadeh & Rahmati, 2022). Thereby, investors and banks can evaluate the growth of the entrepreneurial undertaking and the prospective financial return of their investments (Salomon, 2018).

The following section provides an overview of the most common business finance methods, which will be described in this chapter, as well as their specifications and the transformational processes they undergo (Rao *et al.*, 2021) (Figure 10.1).

10.2.1. *Venture capital funds*

One commonly known form of early-stage investment in the business finance context is venture capital (VC) funding. VC funds generally invest in several private companies — named portfolio companies — which are expected to grow over time (Metrick & Yasuda, 2021). The VC funds aim to develop these companies and for a successful sale or listing in an initial public offering (IPO) on a stock exchange (Metrick & Yasuda, 2021).

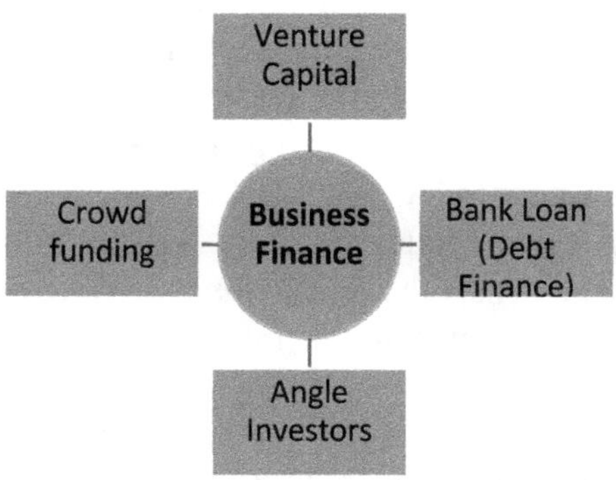

Fig. 10.1. Overview of most common funding methods (Rao *et al.*, 2021).

VC funds seldom invest in already established companies and specifically intend to profit from the business growth of an emerging venture. However, the variety of VC funds investing in entrepreneurial ventures is significant, as private and institutional investors constantly search for profitable new ventures to invest in. VC funds thereby pool the funds of cooperations or affluent individuals to generate returns for them. The VC funds are thus tasked with performing the market screening and evaluation of the entrepreneurial ventures (Bollazzi *et al.*, 2019). This form of investment used to be exclusively for more prominent investors, such as institutional investors and affluent private investors. However, recently, private investors became able to participate in joint VC investments (Lin & Nestarcova, 2019). By lowering the required investment amounts, referred to as "ticket size," the entrance barriers become smaller, allowing even more investors to participate in the funding activity (Hornuf & Schwienbacher, 2018). The pooled funds are generally provided as equity or cash investments to young, early-stage entrepreneurial ventures (Gompers & Lerner, 2001).

The reasons for this new trend of VC funding are lower entrance barriers (transaction costs) and the creation of new participation schemes with significantly lower ticket sizes (Bonini & Capizzi, 2019). The reduction of these barriers and the onboarding of numerous smaller investors result from constantly shrinking transaction and monitoring costs. Thus, lower costs directly result from the digital transformation process occurring in the financial services sector. Ongoing standardization and automation of processes also enable a significantly larger group of smaller investors (Gabison, 2019) to participate in VC activities. With an increasing platform economy and decreasing costs (Diamond *et al.*, 2019), collective investment undertakings have become more accessible. This trend will likely continue and even intensify while fostering financial inclusion (Gurumurthy *et al.*, 2018). The increasing accessibility of VC funds (Willman *et al.*, 2021) and the growing interest of retail investors will continue to enable access to VC funding.

Businesses aiming to acquire VC funding should be able to explain their business model extensively. As VC funds are interested in the growth potential, the following minimum information should be prepared beforehand:

(a) the product, its usability, and its importance for customers;
(b) potential market share, market competitors, and market growth;

(c) existing revenues and potential profits;
(d) a financial plan of required funding and its intent to be used.

Platforms such as Steableton,[1] Companisto,[2] or Titanbay[3] allow retail investors to participate in VC investments. As an entrepreneur, it is easiest to identify these platform providers, contact the investment team directly, and pitch the business idea. However, as there is no defined way to acquire VC funding, it can be difficult to get in contact with corresponding funds. Hence, VC funds often invest internationally and follow their own investment policies by identifying their investment targets directly (Devigne *et al.*, 2018). Despite the increasing number of VC funds — making it easier to access funding — entrepreneurs should carefully evaluate the VC fund as it can significantly impact the business. Entrepreneurs seeking VC funding should connect with more than just one VC firm to test the different offers. Above all, the entrepreneur should also check with which other companies the VC firm is collaborating, especially if it has connections to potential competitors.

10.2.2. *Angel investors*

In comparison to VC funding, which is an institutionalized collective financial gathering, an angel investor acts as a single person who often has significant excess funds (Edwards, 2021). That form of business financing is widely known through TV shows, such as *Shark Tank* or *Dragons Den*. The professional angel investor generally conducts a more diligent process with a deeper financial analysis and evaluation of the business model (Forrester, 2019). The advantage of angel investors is that they are often entrepreneurs and have grown an extensive network which can help push the business forward (Morrissette, 2007). In addition, their experiences and knowledge can strongly contribute to the business's success. Furthermore, their potential credibility could add a competitive edge when negotiating business deals or attracting further investors. However, as conditions for their financial involvement, angel investors often

[1] https://www.stableton.com/.
[2] https://www.companisto.com/en.
[3] https://www.titanbay.com/.

demand a large stake in the new business; some even require a considerable influence within the company (Broughman, 2018).

Compared to other business funding methods, angel investments are less prone to digital transformation, as the whole process is mainly human based (Dang, 2021). The sourcing and analysis of prospective companies might be easier for the investor as general technological advancements allow easier access. However, the process has not undergone a substantial transformational shift and is still human based. A recent development is that more and more private individuals are looking for new investment opportunities in times of negative interest rates. Therefore, more and more angel investors were introduced to the market, making it easier for the entrepreneur to find a potential investor (Sohl, 2021).

Entrepreneurs looking for angel investor funding have the possibility to approach angel investors directly via their websites, such as AngelListe[4] and Enterprise-Ireland,[5] or the more global angel investor platforms such as 500Global[6] or SFC Capital.[7] The traditional networking events and investor panel discussions are still the go-to approach to engaging directly with angel investors. However, on a local level, regional business associations or chambers of commerce often offer services to find investors (Ratinho & Mitsopoulos, 2021). Some industry organizations, such as the German Chamber of Commerce (DIHK), have even set up platforms, such as INVEST[8] and Investor Networks,[9] similar to the French Chambre de Commerce et d'Industrie (CCI), where entrepreneurs can interact with each other and have the opportunity to match with investors.

10.2.3. *Crowdfunding*

Crowdfunding plays a crucial role in collective financing, as it pools the funds of various investors (Paoloni *et al.*, 2019). Enabled through online funding pages, this form of business financing is steadily growing. Compared to VC funds and angel investors, the crowdfunding investor does not necessarily receive ownership rights in the company. Thus, this

[4]https://www.angellist.com/.

[5]https://www.enterprise-ireland.com/en/.

[6]https://500.co/.

[7]https://sfccapital.com/.

[8]https://www.bmwk.de/Navigation/DE/InvestDB/INVEST-DB_Liste/investdb.html.

[9]https://www.ccifrance-international.org/notre-reseau/les-cci-fi.html.

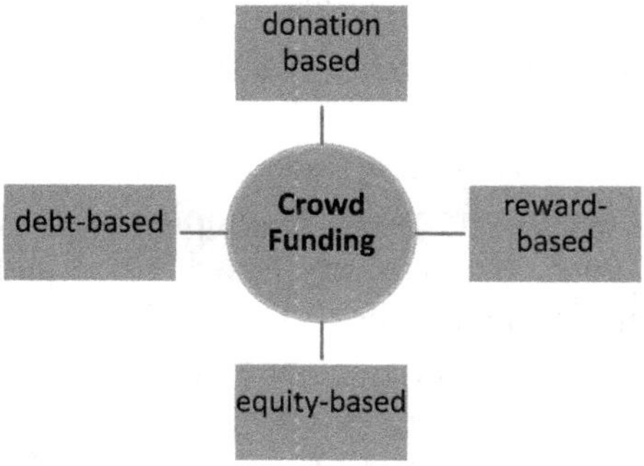

Fig. 10.2. Forms of crowdfunding (adapted and reproduced from Gabison, 2019 and Salido-Andres *et al.*, 2021).

form of funding can be used when bank financing becomes difficult and a bank loan might not be an option (Miglo, 2022).

In fact, crowdfunding can occur in different ways, such as those based on donation, reward, debt, or equity (Figure 10.2).

In the *donation-based* crowdfunding process, the altruistic approach is at the center of the funding process and is not intended to be an immediate financial investment. This is particularly interesting for emerging business ventures with a kind of altruistic business model (Nakagawa *et al.*, 2022). This method of funding can be found among social entrepreneurs (Salido-Andres *et al.*, 2021), whereby the business activity follows a greater good. Furthermore, businesses with a lack of a profit profile, a difficult-to-understand business model, or just an insufficient credit score could profit from that kind of funding. In the *reward-based* approach, investors typically receive goods or services from the company and are mentioned as "first-funders" of the business but don't necessarily receive paybacks for their financial contributions (Sewaid *et al.*, 2021).

The *debt-based* one is similar to a bank loan. However, to make the investment lucrative for an investor, the interest being paid is usually required to be higher than the interest on a savings account (Gabison, 2019). Furthermore, considering the risk of never receiving the initial investment, an investor would require a significantly higher interest rate than a "risk-free interest rate" on their bank account. This requires the entrepreneur to achieve the required interest payments through his business activities (Miglo, 2021). Entrepreneurs are therefore required to carefully assess the duration, amount, and interest required to be paid compared to other funding methods. These forms of crowdfunding are for businesses that need some financial backing but are unwilling to hand over ownership rights.

On the contrary, *equity-based* (Bade & Walther, 2021) crowdfunding is nearly indistinguishable from the developing venture capitalism platforms. As with VC investments, equity-based crowdfunding allows investors to obtain ownership rights. The difference is that VC funding is often “big-money” (Taboga, 2022) and collected through institutionalized collective assets (Chemmanur *et al.*, 2021).

The example of equity-based crowdfunding demonstrates that the technological transformation and reduction of barriers directly affect the liberalization of funding methods. The borders between the different forms fade away as the new platform economies liberate the market and make the funding by institutional investors indistinguishable from the one by private investors. The continuing development of the platform economy can thus be seen as a vital enabler for small businesses to obtain funds. The use of crowdfunding is still increasing (Clauss *et al.*, 2020), and the effective use of social media could further bolster its development. Thereby, social media aims to attract specifically the mass market retail investors.

For entrepreneurs, this means that the emergence of platforms such as Kickstarter,[10] Patreon,[11] GoFundMe,[12] or Indiegogo[13] makes it easier nowadays to get access to collective funding possibilities. Some platforms allow sharing a link to the funding projects directly via WhatsApp with friends and family. This trend of investments from accredited and nonaccredited private investors (Bonini & Capizz, 2019) will become more common and provide easier funding access for the entrepreneurs. Despite crowdfunding platforms being an easy form of funding, the amount that can be raised is often low. This makes it an unsuitable form for more mature companies with higher funding needs. However, entrepreneurs should carefully evaluate from whom they are obtaining funding and what they need to offer in return.

[10]https://www.kickstarter.com/?ref=nav.

[11]https://www.patreon.com/.

[12]https://www.gofundme.com/.

[13]https://www.indiegogo.com/.

10.2.4. *Bank loans*

Regarding the classical financing methods, bank loans are considered the traditional financing method for entrepreneurs (Zhang *et al.*, 2020). Depending on the amount, it can get increasingly challenging to acquire the intended amount of funding. As banks require substantial documentation, an assessment of the company, and business development (Witzen, 2022), higher amounts above the standard consumer credit limit might take up some significant evaluation time. All the necessary information, from deposited securities to the business plan and cash flow statement, needs to be available and checked.

In the future, the development of collaborative data sharing will intensify among market players and significantly increase the processing time while minimizing the evaluation costs per loan (Temelkov, 2022). As banks, insurance companies, regulators, and other financial institutions work closer together, sharing client data (Eybers & Setsabi, 2021) will lead to a more transparent client profile and allow financial institutions to process data and loans faster. However, banks are not the only player in the market of loans anymore; new fintech firms have already entered the market and started to provide loans to smaller businesses (Berg & Puri, 2021) or act as a liaison by providing loan broker services (Knewtson & Rosenbaum, 2020). With increasing competition within European countries, it is possible to receive bank loans from financial institutions in other EU countries with potentially more favorable rates and fewer requirements (Duijm & Schoenmaker, 2021). The online accessibility of these loans, paired with comparably easy proof of creditworthiness, allows European entrepreneurs to size funding opportunities in other EU countries (Baba *et al.*, 2020). However, the transformation from a single jurisdiction approach and loan acquiring toward a multi-jurisdictional approach is suitable for more developed businesses or business models with a decentralized focus.

The rise of neo-banks specializing in different fields of finance allows businesses to receive loans through these new market players (Temelkov, 2022). Some neo-banks offering business loans are Aoin-Bank,[14] Novo Bank,[15] and Bluevine.[16] As these loans are only available up to a certain

---

[14]https://www.aion.eu/be-en/business.

[15]https://www.bluevine.com/.

[16]https://www.novo.co.

amount, they are not suitable for financing large investments. However, businesses will profit from more accessible loans and potentially better rates than at their local bank.

With neo-banks on the rise and often operating internationally, entrepreneurs can expect faster access to smaller loans. As an additional option to get the best rates and suitable conditions, loan brokers are an excellent go-to option. Their commissions are usually paid by the banks or financial institutions; the entrepreneur making the request typically need not pay for the request. These brokers provide easy-to-compare offerings from financial institutions, saving the entrepreneur's time.

10.3. New Ways of Entrepreneurial Business Finance

The emergence of financial technology (fintech) has led to a tremendous shift in how banks and companies conduct business. The Financial Stability Board defines fintech as "technology-enabled innovation in financial services that could result in new business models, applications, processes or products with an associated material effect on the provision of financial services" (Rupeika & Thalassionos, 2020). Thereby, it has led to more accessible capital and financing for private persons and companies alike (Dorfleitner & Braun, 2019). In addition, fintech connects clients with access funds to clients with financial needs and substantially reduces transactional barriers. The following provides a condensed overview of the emerging trends in business financing and the transformational shift it will undergo in the future (Stulz, 2019). One of the main trends, which is extensively developed and fostered by financial institutions, is to improve the validation time of client data (Elghaish *et al.*, 2020). Thus, blockchain technology plays a crucial role by significantly changing the financing market for banks and businesses alike.

10.3.1. *Tokenization of business value*

Blockchain technology, widely known through cryptocurrencies, has been around for nearly a decade (Rao *et al.*, 2022). However, their use cases for business activities have become more apparent and mature in recent years. The use of blockchain has grown increasingly important for validating transactions and contracts (Serrano, 2022). In comparison to initial coin offerings (ICOs), often created for tech products (Cai & Gomaa, 2019), the token sale represents a financial product. This development aims to significantly speed up the processing of funds through more accessible securities validation. This also reduces human labor spent on the extensive evaluation of client data, as the technical validation of a blockchain replaces this.

10.3.1.1. *Tokenization*

The source of business funding which is starting to become increasingly important for financial institutions is to make non-bankable assets bankable. This means that traditionally illiquid assets (collectables, art, etc. and company values) are made bankable, i.e., making them tradable and therefore building the foundation to raise liquidity (Barbereau *et al.*, 2022).

The tokenization of assets can thereby be seen as a new form of collateralization and financing (Harvey *et al.*, 2021). The practical process works as follows and is summarized in Figure 10.3:

(1) A company or an entrepreneur possesses a valuable asset which is not easy to liquidate.
(2) A tokenization provider:
    (a) evaluates the authenticity of the assets,

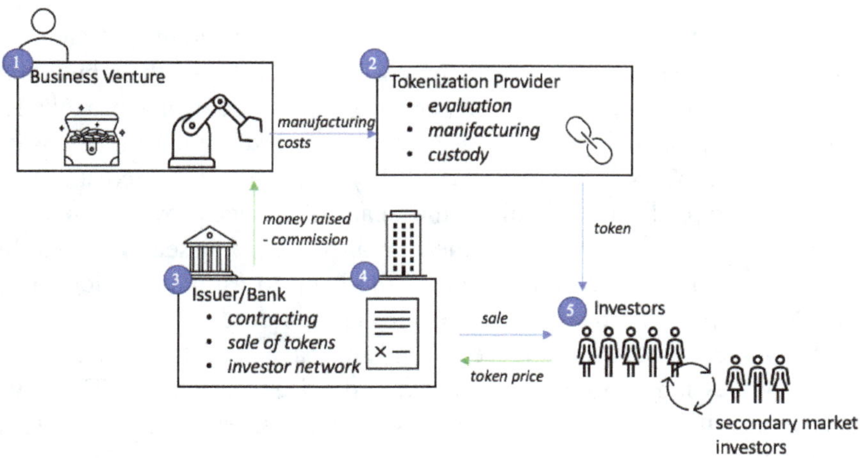

Fig. 10.3. Process of tokenizing business value (adapted and reproduced from Lacity and Treiblmaier, 2022 and Momtaz *et al.*, 2019).

   (b) decides on how much money should be raised for the asset,
   (c) manufactures blockchain-based ownership tokens.
(3) An issuer, offering ownership or profit tokens to potential buyers via the banks or financial institutions network:
   (a) tokens or ownership rights are usually insured by either the bank or another third party.
(4) A financial service provider (traditionally a bank) allows the trading of the tokens via their platform among their clients or openly for everyone.
(5) A client buying the tokens can freely sell them to other eligible buyers.

Lately, the focus in financing has shifted toward asset classes that can have significant value but are not easily tradable (Romero-Catro *et al.*, 2022). Examples of these kinds of assets are collectibles, such as art, cars, and wine, or even intellectual properties, such as patents or copyrights (Heines *et al.*, 2021). These assets might already exist in the possession of the entrepreneur or the company itself but are hard to assess, as the banks would require specific expertise to evaluate these assets. This new form of collateralizing assets and using them for financial purposes would also allow retail investors to participate in funding activities. Thereby, collateralization through tokenization contributes to the democratization of entrepreneurial finance (Fisch *et al.*, 2022).

For banks, it is risky to provide loans based on collateral with a not-easily-assessable value. In order to overcome this uncertainty, financial institutions will start by tokenizing these assets and offering them bundled with other asset classes to investors. By providing these ownership tokens to clients, the financial institution can observe how much money was raised in the process (Hargrave *et al.*, 2019). This observed interest in the token and the paid price will allow the financial service provider, such as a bank, to assess how much these non-bankable assets are worth (Ackermann *et al.*, 2020). This allows the bank to estimate which loan offering they could provide to the venture in the future.

However, for business finance, this means that assets already in a company's possession can be collateralized and priced reasonably. Thereby, companies will be able to raise business funding easier in the future. The largest tokenization providers offering their services are *tZERO*,[17] based in

[17] https://www.tzero.com/.

the United States, Polymath,[18] operating out of Canada, and Berlin-based Bitbond.[19] As this form of funding has emerged more recently, businesses should not only rely on this form of funding alone but rather make use of a mixed funding approach.

10.3.2. *Employee equity participation*

Compared to traditional business financing methods, such as bank loans and VC funding, a new business financing trend is emerging. New emerging entrepreneurial ventures increasingly provide the possibility for their employees to participate directly or indirectly in the company (Sun & Xiaolan, 2019).

In the **direct process**, the new emerging venture collects investment capital from its employees and participates directly in the company's success. This so-called contribution capital is similar to a loan, which is granted to the company and can be individually agreed upon. There is usually a minimum duration, and the maximum duration is limited to the employee's exit but can vary from contract to contract. Depending on the agreement, contribution capital can receive either interest payments (Khatavkar, 2018), direct profit participation, or no payments at all. This form of funding can traditionally be found in law firms or consultancy firms, whereby newly appointed partners must provide a financial contribution to obtain their partner status. This new funding trend is especially used in companies where the C-level employees are more senior or have sufficient financial backing to provide such loans.

In the **indirect process**, the company provides the possibility of deducting a certain amount from the salary or even as part of the compensation package, which will be transferred into ownership rights (Morales, 2021). Thereby, the company does not need to pay a full salary and can use the freed up resources for their business finance. Ownership participation plans retain cash outflow (Turner, 2018) as ownership rights and, therefore, delayed cash outflow. The money which would have been traditionally paid to the employees can be reinvested. Thereby, not only the company might profit from it but also the employees. As the company

[18]https://polymath.network/.

[19]https://www.bitbond.com/.

continues to grow and expand, so do its participation shares (Arbaugh *et al.*, 2004).

This transformation from pure "work-for-money" employment toward a "work-and-participate" development helps companies increase the ownership feeling of their workforce and thereby increase productivity (Jones, 2018). The process of engaging employees financially at the company can be complicated. New ventures, in particular, face the difficulty of reasonably pricing the participation rights of the company (Le Guyader & Meyer, 2021). The ownership rights or profit rights at the company need to have a certain value in order to make employees buy into them. However, some start-ups demonstrated that even sole participation possibilities are accepted by employees (Menke & Buxton, 2010). Thus, for some companies, the promise of a prosperous future with potentially lucrative growth might sometimes be the only form of compensation they can offer, which is often the case for start-up companies (Menke & Buxton, 2010). This is often due to their low liquidity within the company and the difficulty of competing with regular market salaries. In some jurisdictions, this form of compensation needs significant legal clarification.

Therefore, this form of compensation is made easier through third-party providers who take care of the appropriate amount of participation, the legal and regulatory limits, and the custody of the employees' participation rights. For established companies, the more professional providers, such as EquatePlus[20] from Computershare, Global Shares,[21] or Shareworks,[22] are used to make employees participate in stock purchase programs. But also, for smaller ventures, there are affordable employee participation plan providers, such as Equiniti.[23]

10.4. Conditions and Implications for Future Business Finance

For entrepreneurs, the developments in the field of financing can be a blessing but also a burden when dealing with it. The new emerging

[20]https://www.computershare.com.

[21]https://www.globalshares.com/uk/all-employee-share-plans/.

[22]https://www.shareworks.com/.

[23]https://equiniti.com/us/services/equity-compensation-services/.

financing trends require the necessary legal recognition. In the case of employee participation schemes and loan grants, the process is generally very simple, and third-party companies make participation easier and deal with the necessary paperwork and legal implications. However, in terms of the tokenization of assets, it becomes increasingly complex, as, in many jurisdictions, the transfer of digital ownership is not fully recognized by law. In jurisdictions such as Germany and France, a notary would still be required in order to confirm the transfer of ownership rights. Thereby, the process is not much different from acquiring traditional ownership participation in a company. As the technology becomes more recognized, the processes become leaner and more accessible.

10.4.1. *Regulatory constraints*

All the above requirements for businesses to engage in new forms of business finance are dependent on regulatory reliability (Hendrikse *et al.*, 2020). Without the regulatory and legal recognition of new funding methods, the entrepreneur not only risks losing business funding but also faces the risk of being held liable for damages (Kramer & Meier, 2019). Especially, blockchain used to be a gray field for ownership rights and enforcement of such. However, more countries have passed new laws and regulations connected with blockchain. The European Union[24,25] published several frameworks for the use of blockchain by businesses, providing the latest technology with legal backing (Boreiko *et al.*, 2019). However, an innovative funding method should only be used if the entrepreneur or one of the employees has sufficient knowledge about it or can at least make use of a knowledgeable third party.

10.4.2. *Cybersecurity*

Despite the benefits the new platform economy and technological novelties hold for businesses, it also has security implications for them (Cutolo & Kenney, 2021). Traditional business finance methods are getting more and more digitalized and platform based. While blockchain technology is

---

[24] https://www.europarl.europa.eu/news/en/search?searchQuery=blockchain.

[25] https://blogs.ec.europa.eu/eupolicylab/files/2017/04/Blockchain4EU_Kickoff-announcement.pdf.

considered relatively safe from cybersecurity threats, continuing news about hacked platform providers regularly leads to uncertainty in the market. The entire platform economy, with client data sharing and several entrance points, bears a significant cybersecurity risk. Businesses should be aware that these risks can substantially threaten their businesses (Corallo *et al.*, 2020). New entrepreneurial ventures should consider that these threats can occur and take precautions to circumvent them wherever possible. The use of new financing channels should be assessed carefully, and potential risks should be anticipated. However, collaborating only with legitimate business partners that have the required security measures and insurance policies in place if such threats occur can eliminate the risk for businesses already significantly.

10.4.3. *Legal recognition*

Like regulatory constraints, legal recognition is crucial for new technologies. Despite the recognition from supranational authorities, such as the European Commission, legal uncertainty remains (Boreiko & Navroop, 2018). As of now, the judicial experience regarding ownership or profit rights, which are token based, is relatively low (Fairfield, 2022). Thus, not many courts have yet the rulings that could show how token rights are enforced in the case of legal proceedings. This becomes even more apparent when dealing across borders. Businesses seeking business finance possibilities through these new channels are advised to get professional support and perform their funding activities in countries where the intended form of financing has legal backing.

10.5. Conclusion

Despite traditional business financing methods remaining in place, technological advancements will significantly transform how fast and efficiently entrepreneurial ventures can obtain their funding. The business finance market constantly transforms from a single stand-alone financial provider market to a more collaborative and data-driven environment. As funding providers increasingly interact with other financial service providers (e.g., insurance, banks) as well as other data providers (e.g., rating agencies and regulators), the market will become more transparent.

Table 10.1. Suitability of funding methods by company size (adapted and reproduced from Wilson, 2013).

Funding type (company type)	**Venture capital**	**Angle investor**	**Crowd funding**	**Bank loan**	**Business token**	**Employee participation**
Small/start-up (general)			X	X		
Small/start-up (tech)		X			X	X
Medium size (general)	X	X		X		
Medium size (tech)					X	X
Large size (general)	(X)			X		X
Large size (tech)	(X)			X		X

Thus, it will make it easier to single out bad business practices and favor well-thought-out business ideas. The shift to a holistic platform economy will allow the faster processing of entrepreneurial funding for the most promising ventures. The blockchain and its use for data validation will additionally lead to more instantaneous information processing and cost reduction due to the elimination of labor-intensive processes, such as notary and certification services. While the new platform-based services hold enormous potential for business finance, they also pose a cybersecurity risk as well as the risk of being too dependent on third-party providers.

Table 10.1 summarizes the discussed funding methods. It provides a subjective view of which funding might be most suitable for which company. The table considers the life-cycle funding approach from Wilson (2013). As the business models of companies can differ substantially and some companies might be more traditional while others are more technologically advanced, the company types are further divided into "general" and "tech." Thus, aiming to provide an indication of which funding methods could be suitable while taking into consideration the technological stage of the company.

With the current developments and advantages emerging for business finance, it is up to the entrepreneurs to carefully evaluate which form of funding is most beneficial for their businesses. While access to funding became easier, sourcing the right option became more difficult because of the abundance of new possibilities.

References

Ackermann, E., Bock, C., & Bürger, R. (2020). They are democratizing entrepreneurial finance: The impact of crowdfunding and initial coin offerings (ICOs). In *Contemporary Developments in Entrepreneurial Finance*, pp. 277–308. Springer, Cham.

Alizadeh, P. & Rahmati, M. (2022). The role of capital market in innovation finance. In *Innovative Finance for Technological Progress*, pp. 233–256. Routledge, London.

Arbaugh, J. B., Cox, L. W., & Camp, S. M. (2004). Employee equity, incentive compensation, and growth in entrepreneurial firms. *New England Journal of Entrepreneurship*, London.

Baba, C., Batog, C., Flores, E., Gracia, B., Karpowicz, I., Kopyrski, P., Roaf, J., Shabunina, A., Elkan, R. V., & Xu, X. C. (2020). Fintech in Europe: Promises and Threats. Available at SSRN 3758074.

Bade, M. & Walther, M. (2021). Local preferences and the allocation of attention in equity-based crowdfunding. *Review of Managerial Science* 15(8), 2501–2533.

Barbereau, T. J., Smethurst, R., Sedlmeir, J., Fridgen, G., & Rieger, A. (2022). Tokenization and regulatory compliance for art and collectible markets: From regulators' demands for transparency to investors' demands for privacy. *Blockchains and the Token Economy: Studies in Theory and Practice.*

Fuster, A., Berg, T., & Puri, M. (2021). FinTech lending. *Annual Review of Financial Economics* 14.

Bollazzi, F., Risalvato, G., & Venezia, C. (2019). Asymmetric information and deal selection: Evidence from the Italian venture capital market. *International Entrepreneurship and Management Journal* 15(3), 721–732.

Bonini, S. & Capizzi, V. (2019). The role of venture capital in the emerging entrepreneurial finance ecosystem: Future threats and opportunities. *Venture Capital* 21(2-3), 137–175.

Boreiko, D., Ferrarini, G., & Giudici, P. (2019). Blockchain startups and prospectus regulation. *European Business Organization Law Review* 20(4), 665–694.

Boreiko, D. & Sahdev, N. K. (2018). To ICO or not to ICO–Empirical analysis of initial coin offerings and token sales. Available at SSRN 3209180.

Bradley, S. W., Kim, P. H., Klein, P. G., McMullen, J. S., & Wennberg, K. (2021). Policy for innovative entrepreneurship: Institutions, interventions, and societal challenges. *Strategic Entrepreneurship Journal* 15(2), 167–184.

Broughman, B. J. & Fried, J. M. (2018). Do founders control start-up firms that Go Public. *European Corporate Governance Institute (ECGI)-Law Working Paper* (405), 18–23.

Cai, J. & Gomaa, A. (2019). Initial coin offering to finance venture capital: A behavioral perspective. *The Journal of Private Equity* 22(3), 93–101.

Chemmanur, T. J., Hu, G., & Wei, K. J. (2021). The role of institutional investors in corporate and entrepreneurial finance. *Journal of Corporate Finance* 66, 101833.

Clauss, T., Niemand, T., Kraus, S., Schnetzer, P., & Brem, A. (2020). Increasing crowdfunding success through social media: The importance of reach and utilization in reward-based crowdfunding. *International Journal of Innovation Management* 24(3), 2050026.

Corallo, A., Lazoi, M., & Lezzi, M. (2020). Cybersecurity in the context of industry 4.0: A structured classification of critical assets and business impacts. *Computers in Industry* 114, 103165.

Cusmano, L., Koreen, M., & Pissareva, L. (2018). 2018 OECD ministerial conference on SMEs: Key issues paper.

Cutolo, D. & Kenney, M. (2021). Platform-dependent entrepreneurs: Power asymmetries, risks, and strategies in the platform economy. *Academy of Management Perspectives* 35(4), 584–605.

Dang, T. (2021, December). Investment selection criteria of foreign angel investors in startups in Vietnam. In *International Conference on Emerging Challenges: Business Transformation and Circular Economy (ICECH 2021)*, pp. 312–319. Atlantis Press. Doi: 10.2991/aebmr.k.211119.030.

Derek C. J. (2018). The economics of Participation and Employee Ownership (PEO): An assessment. *Journal of Participation and Employee Ownership*, 1(1), pp. 4–37, https://doi.org/10.1108/JPEO-02-2018-0004.

Devigne, D., Manigart, S., Vanacker, T., & Mulier, K. (2018). Venture capital internationalization: Synthesis and future research directions. *Journal of Economic Surveys* 32(5), 1414–1445.

Dorfleitner, G. & Braun, D. (2019). Fintech, digitalization and blockchain: Possible applications for green finance. In *The Rise of Green Finance in Europe*, pp. 207–237. Palgrave Macmillan, Cham.

Duijm, P. & Schoenmaker, D. (2021). European banks straddling borders: Risky or rewarding? *Finance Research Letters* 38, 101525.

Edwards, C. (2021). How wealth fuels growth: The role of angel investment. *Cato Institute, Policy Analysis*, no. 921, Cato Institute, Washington, DC, September 29, 2021.

Elghaish, F., Abrishami, S., & Hosseini, M. R. (2020). Integrated project delivery with blockchain: An automated financial system. *Automation in Construction* 114, 103182.

Eybers, S. & Setsabi, N. (2021). Responsible data sharing in the digital economy: Big Data governance adoption in bancassurance. In *Inventive Computation and Information Technologies*, pp. 379–394. Springer, Singapore.

Fairfield, J. A. (2022). Tokenized: The law of non-fungible tokens and unique digital property. *Indiana Law Journal* 97(4), 1261.

Fisch, C., Meoli, M., & Vismara, S. (2022). Does blockchain technology democratize entrepreneurial finance? An empirical comparison of ICOs, venture capital, and REITs. *Economics of Innovation and New Technology* 31(1–2), 70–89.

Forrester, R. C., Williams, R. I., Manley, S. C., Martinez, J. E., & Hair, J. F. (2019). Behavioral finance: Factors influencing angel investor due diligence. *American Journal of Entrepreneurship* 12(1), 6–30.

Garg, A. & Shivam, A. K. (2017). Funding to growing start-ups. *Research Journal of Social Sciences* 10(2), 22–31.

Gabison, G. A. (2019). Understanding crowdfunding and its regulations. *European Commission*, JRC Science and Policy Report.

Gompers, P. & Lerner, J. (2001). The venture capital revolution. *Journal of Economic Perspectives* 15(2), 145–168.

Gurumurthy, A., Bharthur, D., & Chami, N. (2018)., Policies for the Platform Economy: Current Trends and Future Directions (September 1, 2018). IT For Change, 2018, Available at SSRN: https://ssrn.com/abstract=3876146 p:36ff.

Hahn, C. & Frey, P. (2021). Forto (Michael Wax). In *Venture Capital*, pp. 347–351. Springer Gabler, Wiesbaden.

Hargrave, J., Sahdev, N., & Feldmeier, O. (2019). How value is created in tokenized assets. *Blockchain Economics: Implications of Distributed Ledgers-Markets, Communications Networks, and Algorithmic Reality* 1. Available at SSRN: https://ssrn.com/abstract=3146191 or http://dx.doi.org/10.2139/ssrn.3146191.

Harvey, C. R., Ramachandran, A., & Santoro, J. (2021). *DeFi and the Future of Finance*. John Wiley & Sons. Available at SSRN: https://ssrn.com/abstract=3711777 or http://dx.doi.org/10.2139/ssrn.3711777

Hendrikse, R., Van Meeteren, M., & Bassens, D. (2020). Strategic coupling between finance, technology and the state: Cultivating a Fintech ecosystem for incumbent finance. *Environment and Planning A: Economy and Space* 52(8), 1516–1538.

Heines, R., Dick, C., Pohle, C., & Jung, R. (2021). The tokenization of everything: Towards a framework for understanding the potentials of tokenized assets. In *PACIS* (p. 40).

Hornuf, L. & Schwienbacher, A. (2018). Internet-based entrepreneurial finance: Lessons from Germany. *California Management Review* 60(2), 150–175.

Janeway, W. H., Nanda, R., & Rhodes-Kropf, M. (2021). Venture capital booms and start-up financing. *Annual Review of Financial Economics* 13, 111–127.

Jones, D. C. (2018). The economics of Participation and Employee Ownership (PEO): An assessment. *Journal of Participation and Employee Ownership.*

Khatavkar, Y. (2018). Benefits of employee stock option plan to multinational corporations: A comprehensive review. *Asian Journal of Research in Banking and Finance* 8(5), 58–67.

Knewtson, H. S. & Rosenbaum, Z. A. (2020). Toward understanding FinTech and its industry. *Managerial Finance* 46(8), 1043–1060.

Kramer, S. & Meier, U. (2019). Switzerland's framework for cryptoassets. *International Financial Law Review* 45, 90. https://heinonline.org/HOL/Page?handle=hein.journals/intfinr38&id=3&collection=journals&index=.

Lacity, M. C. & Treiblmaier, H. (eds.). (2022). *Blockchains and the Token Economy: Theory and Practice (Technology, Work and Globalization),* 1st edn, Springer Nature.

Łasak, P. (2022). The role of financial technology and in entrepreneurial funding small and finance medium-sized. *Financial Determinants of SME Activity in Developing Countries* 18(1), 7.

Le Guyader, L. P. & Meyer, T. O. (2021). Employee stock options and the flawed use of the Black–Scholes option pricing model. *Journal of Corporate Accounting & Finance* 32(1), 7–12.

Lin, L. & Nestarcova, D. (2019). Venture capital in the rise of crypto economy: Problems and prospects. *Berkeley Business Law Journal* 16, 533.

Maddikunta, P. K. R., Pham, Q. V., Prabadevi, B., Deepa, N., Dev, K., Gadekallu, T. R., Ruby, R., & Liyanage, M. (2022). Industry 5.0: A survey on enabling technologies and potential applications. *Journal of Industrial Information Integration* 26, 100257.

Menke, J. D. & Buxton, D. C. (2010). The origin and history of the ESOP and its future role as a business succession tool. *Journal of Financial Service Professionals* 64(3), 58–67.

Metrick, A., & Yasuda, A. (2021). *Venture Capital and the Finance of Innovation.* John Wiley & Sons.

Morales-Lemieux, K. (2021). How compensation is determined and potential pitfalls for pay equity. In *Closing the Gender Pay Gap in Medicine* (pp. 17–28). Springer, Cham.

Morrissette, S. G. (2007). A profile of angel investors. *The Journal of Private Equity* 10(3), 52–66.

Miglo, A. (2021). Crowdfunding: Definitions, foundations and framework. In *Crowdfunding in the Public Sector* (pp. 1–19). Springer, Cham.

Miglo, A. (2022). Crowdfunding and bank financing: Substitutes or complements? *Small Business Economics* 59, 1115–1142. https://doi.org/10.1007/s11187-021-00571-9.

Momtaz, P. P., Rennertseder, K., & Schroeder, H. (2019). Token Offerings: A Revolution in Corporate Finance? Available at SSRN 3346964.

Mygind, N. & Poulsen, T. (2021). Employee ownership–pros and cons–a review. *Journal of Participation and Employee Ownership* 4.

Nakagawa, K. & Kosaka, G. (2022). What social issues do people invest in? An examination based on the empathy–altruism hypothesis of prosocial crowdfunding platforms. *Technovation*, Elsevier, Vol. 114(C).

Neubert, M. (2019). Funding innovations for sustainable growth in emerging markets. *International Journal of Economics and Finance* 11(4). ISSN 1916-971X E-ISSN 1916-9728.

Paoloni, P., Paoloni, N., & Modaffari, G. (2019). Crowdfunding as a new collaborative process in the knowledge economy: A literature review. *VINE Journal of Information and Knowledge Management Systems* 49(2).

Rao, P., Kumar, S., Chavan, M., & Lim, W. M. (2021). A systematic literature review on SME financing: Trends and future directions. *Journal of Small Business Management* 1–31. DOI: 10.1080/00472778.2021. 1955123.

Rao, T. V. N., Likhar, P. P., Kurni, M., & Saritha, K. (2022). Blockchain: A new perspective in cyber technology. In *Blockchain Technology for Emerging Applications*, pp. 33–66. Academic Press. https://doi.org/10.1016/C2020-0-03280-9

Ratinho, T. & Mitsopoulos, M. (2021). New forms of entrepreneurship support in a growing entrepreneurial ecosystem: The case of business incubation in Greece. In *Handbook of Research on Business and Technology Incubation and Acceleration*, pp. 299–315. Edward Elgar Publishing. https://www.elgaronline.com/display/edcoll/9781788974776/9781788974776.xml

Romero-Castro, N., Pérez-Pico, A. M., & Ulrich, K. (2022). ICOs, IEOs and STOs: Token sales as innovative formulas for financing start-ups. In *Financing Startups*, pp. 117–147. Springer, Cham.

Ronchini, A., Moretto, A., & Caniato, F. (2021). A decision framework for inventory-and equipment-based supply chain finance solutions. *Journal of Purchasing and Supply Management* 27(4), 100712.

Rupeika-Apoga, R. & Thalassinos, E. I. (2020). Ideas for a regulatory definition of FinTech.

Prause, M. (2019). Challenges of industry 4.0 technology adoption for SMEs: The case of Japan. *Sustainability* 11(20), 5807.

Salido-Andres, N., Rey-Garcia, M., Alvarez-Gonzalez, L. I., & Vazquez-Casielles, R. (2021). Mapping the field of donation-based crowdfunding for charitable causes: Systematic review and conceptual framework. *VOLUNTAS: International Journal of Voluntary and Nonprofit Organizations* 32(2), 288–302.

Salomon, V. (2018). Strategies of startup evaluation on crowd investing platforms: The case of Switzerland. *Journal of Innovation Economics Management* 26(2), 63–88.

Serrano, W. (2022). Verification and validation for data marketplaces via a blockchain and smart contracts. *Blockchain: Research and Applications* 3(4), 100.

Sewaid, A., Garcia-Cestona, M., & Silaghi, F. (2021). Resolving information asymmetries in financing new product development: The case of reward-based crowdfunding. *Research Policy* 50(10), 104345.

Sohl, J. (2021). The Angel Market in 2020: Return of the Seed and Start-Up Stage Market for Angels. Center for Venture Research.

Stulz, R. M. (2019). Fintech, bigtech, and the future of banks. *Journal of Applied Corporate Finance* 31(4), 86–97.

Sun, Q. & Xiaolan, M. Z. (2019). Financing intangible capital. *Journal of Financial Economics* 133(3), 564–588.

Taboga, M. (2022). Cross-country differences in the size of venture capital financing rounds: A machine learning approach. *Empirical Economics* 62(3), 991–1012.

Taghizadeh-Hesary, F., Yoshino, N., & Aboojafari, R. (2022). *Innovative Finance for Technological Progress: Roles of Fintech, Financial Instruments, and Institutions*. Routledge.

Temelkov, Z. (2022). Factors affecting neobanks sustainability and development. *Journal of Economics* 7(1), 1–10.

Toufaily, E., Zalan, T., & Dhaou, S. B. (2021). A framework of blockchain technology adoption: An investigation of challenges and expected value. *Information & Management* 58(3), 103444.

Turner, E. (2018). Survey of accountancy in generally accepted accounting principles and financial statement analysis.

Van Veldhoven, Z. & Vanthienen, J. (2022). Digital transformation as an interaction-driven perspective between business, society, and technology. *Electronic Markets* 32(2), 629–644.

Wilson, K. (2013). Policies for seed and early stage finance. In *OECD Science, Technology and Industry Policy Papers*. Organization for Economic Co-Operation and Development (OECD).

Witzen, B. H. (2022). Small business credit demand and application costs. *Consumer Financial Protection Bureau Office of Research Working Paper*, (5).

Zhang, Y., Xing, C., & Guo, X. (2022). The shielding effect of access to finance on small and medium-sized enterprises during the COVID-19 crisis: Comparing fintech and traditional finance. *Emerging Markets Finance and Trade* 1–15. Doi: 10.1080/1540496X.2022.2072201.

https://doi.org/10.1142/9789811270178_0011

Chapter 11

Moving to New Digital Platforms: A Case Study of Kazakhstani Small- and Medium-Sized Enterprises

Talshyn Tokyzhanova

Department of Business Administration,
Tallinn University of Technology, Ehitajate tee 5,
Tallinn 19086, Estonia

talshyn.tokyzhanova@taltech.ee

Abstract

This chapter explores the motivations of small- and medium-sized enterprises (SMEs) to move to third-party digital platforms and the early-stage challenges in transforming their offline businesses into these online marketplaces. According to the findings of in-depth interviews with seven SMEs in Kazakhstan, online marketplaces enabled SMEs to scale their businesses by helping them overcome resource limitations and facilitating access to networks. Businesses are developing platform utilization capabilities by working with online reviews, digital representations of their products, and basic data science skills.

11.1. Introduction

Between 50% and 60% of the value added in the OECD is produced by small- and medium-sized enterprises (SMEs), which make up 99% of all firms. Nearly one in three people work for micro-businesses with fewer than 10 employees, and two in three work for SMEs (OECD, 2019). When the COVID-19 crisis hit, many SMEs benefited from digitalization and online sales; e-commerce enabled businesses of all sizes to advertise their offers, was crucial in helping users connect to markets, suppliers, and resources during the pandemic, and helped lessen the crisis's economic impact on SMEs (Papadopoulos *et al.*, 2020; Belitski *et al.*, 2022; Giotopoulos *et al.*, 2022).

E-commerce retail sales amounted to approximately USD 5.2 trillion worldwide in 2021, and it is forecast to grow by 56% over the following years, reaching about USD 8.1 trillion by 2026. In 2021, over 2.14 billion people purchased goods online globally (Statista, 2022). E-commerce is an effective instrument for emerging SMEs to increase productivity, improve firm performance, and survive in a competitive market. It can increase SMEs' internal capacity and economies of scale without considerable investment (MacGregor & Vrazalic, 2005; Hossain *et al.*, 2021). By facilitating better and quicker information access and integrating SME personnel, suppliers, and networks, e-commerce helps to lower communication and transaction costs. It offers a direct channel and easy access to information for customers, which will inevitably enhance awareness, brand recognition, and customers' exposure to products (Qizhi Dai, 2002; Kumar & Petersen, 2006; Wirdiyanti *et al.*, 2022). The costs of search, replication, distribution, tracking, and verification can all be significantly reduced by e-commerce platforms (Goldfarb & Tucker, 2019).

Large businesses can create and use their own e-commerce digital platforms. With abundant resources and capabilities, they may coordinate their internal resources to build crucial skills that let them innovate and scale up (Zhu *et al.*, 2006; Cui & Pan, 2015). Unlike larger firms, the ability of SMEs to create internal e-commerce infrastructures is hampered by a lack of finance and/or skills; thus, most SMEs rely on third-party digital platforms (Banerjee & Ma, 2012; Li *et al.*, 2018; OECD, 2021). Numerous studies (e.g., Hamed & El-Deeb, 2020; Oliveira *et al.*, 2017; Malak *et al.*, 2021) demonstrate a consistent growth tendency in the use of e-commerce platforms by SMEs in developed and developing nations.

The adoption of third-party digital platforms by SMEs has attracted research over the past few years (e.g., Li *et al.*, 2018; Jin & Hurd, 2018;

Cenamor *et al.*, 2019; Witek-Hajduk *et al.*, 2021); much of it, however, has tended to focus on the benefits of particular technological functionalities provided by the platforms and, among other factors, organizational readiness, information system (IS) characteristics, external influences, and strategic commitment to e-commerce (Grandón *et al.*, 2011; Cui & Pan, 2015; Li *et al.*, 2018; Matarazzo *et al.*, 2021).

However, besides the liability of smallness, many SME entrepreneurs display cognitive inertia that prevents them from fully engaging with online marketplaces (Cenamor *et al.*, 2019). Yet, SMEs will need to develop various capabilities to overcome these obstacles. Academics have paid little attention to the construction of capabilities beneficial for successful competition on digital platforms (Li *et al.*, 2018; Warner & Wäger, 2019; Matarazzo *et al.*, 2021). It is necessary to balance the usage of current capabilities with the development of new digital capabilities (Cenamor *et al.*, 2019). Moreover, specific insights into entrepreneurial SMEs' digital platform experiences are relatively scarce (Jin & Hurd, 2018; Cenamor *et al.*, 2019), not to mention the scant empirical research on online marketplace participation from the perspective of small sellers in developing countries (Hossain *et al.*, 2021; Misra *et al.*, 2022).

Considering this context, we raised the following research questions: Why are SMEs moving to online marketplaces? How are SMEs transforming their businesses to operate on online marketplaces? In order to answer those questions, first, we analyze the academic literature on third-party online marketplaces and SME participation. Then, we discuss the initial experiences of Kazakhstan SMEs with using third-party e-commerce platforms. Finally, we recommend strategies for SMEs to succeed in their initial years on online marketplace platforms.

11.2. Online Marketplace and SME Participation

In general, three types of e-commerce can be distinguished: e-procurement driven by buyers, e-distribution driven by sellers, and online marketplaces (e-marketplaces) driven by third parties (Son *et al.*, 2006; Chang & Wong, 2010). Online marketplaces (e.g., Amazon, Taobao) facilitate trading activities between partners who have not previously interacted, involving buyers, sellers, and a marketplace provider. They are Internet-based e-commerce platforms that provide transaction opportunities to multiple buyers and suppliers (Tan *et al.*, 2016). E-marketplaces can be horizontal or vertical (Issa *et al.*, 2003) and serve as an innovative model that enables interfirm online transactions worldwide (Fu *et al.*, 2008).

Third-party online marketplaces can help businesses avoid the difficulties and expenses of building their internal digital infrastructures, but they impose both direct and indirect costs. SMEs in a marketplace pay fees, share business-related sensitive data, and operate according to the algorithms imposed by the platform; thus, they have weak negotiating power (Duch-Brown, 2017; Di Porto & Zuppetta, 2021).

Many research projects have examined what factors affect the adoption of online marketplaces by SMEs over the past few decades. Gengatharen and Standing (2005) discovered that the innovativeness of SME owners, regional electronic marketplace ownership structures, and trust-based governance encourage SMEs to adopt e-commerce marketplaces. Hossain *et al.* (2021) found the factors and variables involved in Bangladeshi small firms' e-marketplace entry decisions, which included relative advantages, compatibility, complexity, security, firm size, organizational e-readiness, owners' innovativeness, firm characteristics, top management's support, industry and government support, customer readiness, and cultural influences. Misra *et al.* (2022) observed that performance expectancy, effort expectancy, social impact, and perceived vulnerability are significant determinants of behavioral intention toward the adoption of e-marketplaces.

Previous research on small companies has looked at the benefits and barriers of SMEs' participation in online marketplaces; for example, online marketplaces help SMEs by offering the tools, expertise, and frameworks necessary to aid them in the creation of new ideas and speed up the commercialization process (Walsh *et al.*, 2017). The average time for international penetration has decreased from multiple years to a few weeks, as more and more companies enter global online marketplaces (Shaheer & Li, 2020).

However, managing digital transformation is more of a managerial than a technological task (Besson & Rowe, 2012; Li *et al.*, 2018; Tortora *et al.*, 2021). Organizations must develop organizational capabilities and e-commerce human resources and must redesign business processes, training, and technical resources (Markus, 2004; Cha *et al.*, 2015). However, few studies have examined how SMEs use third-party digital platforms to address managerial difficulties in the digital transition (Li *et al.*, 2018). Li *et al.* (2018) did an inductive research study on SMEs undergoing digital transformation to examine how business owners with limited resources and capabilities could use third-party digital platform services and functionalities to transform their organizations digitally. Based on the research of 230 entrepreneurial SMEs, Cenamor *et al.* (2019) showed that digital platforms capability, positively, and indirectly affect SMEs' performance via network capability. Digital platform capability is the ability to deploy ICT-based resources in conjunction with other internal and external resources (Mikalef & Pateli, 2017). Due to the complexity of digitalization, however, digital platform capability may not directly improve firm performance but could do so indirectly through dynamic capabilities (Ravichandran, 2018; Cenamor *et al.*, 2019).

11.3. Study Context

Central Asia, a dynamic market with a young population, is of great interest to e-commerce players. The region-wide retail turnover in 2021 amounted to more than USD 60 billion (KPMG, 2022).

Kazakhstan is a leader in the development of e-commerce in the region, where the share of e-commerce in the country's total retail sales is 10% (Bureau of National Statistics in Kazakhstan, 2022). It has been growing dramatically in the past three years; the sales volume in 2021 is 75% more than the market volume in 2020 and three times more than in 2019. The number of transactions also increased by 45% compared to that in 2020 and amounted to more than 37 million transactions. The share of online marketplaces in e-commerce is about 82% of the total sales in the country (PwC, 2022). The compound annual growth rate for 2022–2026 is expected to be 40% (KPMG, 2022).

Kaspi.kz is the largest B2C online marketplace in Kazakhstan. It maintains a remarkable rate of business unit growth. At the end of 2021, the number of sellers on the platform increased by 130% (60 thousand sellers) and the number of active customers increased by 35% (3.7 million active customers) compared to the previous year. The marketplace's revenue for 2021 is USD 1,690 million, which is 85% more than that in 2020 (*Forbes Kazakhstan*, 2022).

11.4. Methodology

For this investigation, a qualitative study was used. This helps identify key commonalities in the participants' experiences and allows them to develop a clear and comprehensive understanding of a phenomenon (Bowen, 2008). Moreover, as our research focuses on how SME entrepreneurs in Kazakhstan are using third-party digital platforms, a qualitative approach is ideal for answering the question of how and uncovering the why underlying the observed occurrences (Yin, 2009).

In this study, semi-structured interviews were used to gather empirical data. In addition, secondary sources were used, including literature, governmental reports, news articles, and websites. The research protocol had two components. The first part includes questions related to the backgrounds of the interviewees and SMEs. The second part of the questionnaire has questions about the SMEs' experiences with using the online marketplace "Kaspi" and their difficulties.

The participating companies were chosen using a snowball sampling strategy. The criteria of participants' selection comprised the (1) SMEs already using the platform and (2) those who had been operating in this business before joining the marketplace. Access to the first two interviewees was arranged through the researcher's personal connections with the companies, and the remaining SMEs were contacted based on recommendations. A total of 13 potential informants were contacted, and five agreed to participate in this research. In each SME, the owners or owner-directors were interviewed.

The firms' ages ranged from two to eight. Their businesses included home textiles, clothing, furniture, and the resale of beauty products and home appliances. More information regarding those selected participants is shown in Table 11.1.

Table 11.1. Profile of participating firms.

SME ID	Nature of business	Number of employees	Firm age	Online marketplace age	Current position
I1	Home textile	5	7	2	Owner
I2	Beauty appliances (reselling)	3	5	1	Owner-director
I3	Home appliances (reselling)	4	4	3	Owner-director
I4	Home appliances (reselling)	3	5	2	Owner-director
I5	Clothing	20	8	2	Owner-director
I6	Furniture	11	5	3.5	Owner-director
I7	Furniture	4	2	1	Owner-director

This study used a qualitative thematic analytical strategy as it provides rich, extremely detailed, and yet multifaceted, accounts of data (Braun & Clarke, 2006), allowing for the interpretation of many research themes. All the themes in this study were formulated using MAXQDA software by first identifying and coding "basic themes" and then interpreting their similarities or "organizing themes" to identify "global themes" that represent a higher level.

11.5. Results and Discussion

The results of our exploratory research are presented according to the identified themes: background, motivation, and challenges to transforming an offline business into a marketplace-based online merchant. First, the key business model attributes of marketplaces are given to better understand the experience of interviewees (Section 11.5.1). Then, the motivations to join a marketplace (Section 11.5.2), and the initial challenges related to the operation in the marketplace (Section 11.5.3) are presented.

11.5.1. *The marketplace description*

Based on Täuscher and Laudien's work (2018), the interviewees were asked to describe the Kaspi marketplace, where they are currently operating. Also, publicly available sources of information were searched online. Table 11.2 summarizes the key business model attributes of the Kaspi marketplace. The first four characteristics are a part of the value creation model (key resources and activities), the following six characteristics are a part of the value delivery dimension (value proposition, product or service, and target customers), and the last four characteristics represent the value capture dimension (revenue and pricing models). The marketplace first opened up a web-based e-commerce platform in 2014; later, in 2017, it launched a mobile app. It analyzes and visualizes transactional data for sellers and actively co-designs product listings. The sellers in the marketplace set the prices for their products, and the merchants with the lowest prices appear first on the product page. The platform creates value for buyers through the ease of use of the platform, the availability of a large selection of the most popular products, and price competitiveness. The sellers can take advantage of scale-related savings through platform

Table 11.2. Key business model attributes of the Kaspi marketplace.

Value creation dimension	Value delivery dimension	Value capture dimension
Platform type: web-based platform and mobile app	**Key value proposition:** price/cost/efficiency	**Key revenue stream:** commissions, advertising
Key activity: data services, community-building, content creation	**Transaction content:** product	**Pricing mechanism:** differentiated pricing
Price discovery: set by sellers	**Industry scope:** horizontal	**Price discrimination:** feature-based
Review system: user reviews	**Marketplace participants:** B2C	**Revenue source:** seller
	Geographic scope: local (Kazakhstan)	

Source: Compiled by the author based on the information available at www.kaspi.kz and in-depth interviews with the SMEs.

investments in product technology, marketing, customer acquisition, and brand-building. Kaspi provides its merchants with fulfillment through delivery services and payment options, such as "buy-now, pay-later." The company cooperates with 20 logistics companies, owns four sorting warehouses, and offers mostly free shipping for goods, with 54% of positions delivered in less than two days. The most common products sold are electronics; however, Kaspi is shifting toward other categories such as clothing, jewelry, furniture, and groceries. The company earns through commission from each successful transaction, amounting to 5–11% for different product categories, and advertising inside the platform.

11.5.2. *Motivation for moving to online marketplaces*

For most SMEs, the main reasons for moving to online marketplaces were to expand their scope and attract more customers. The sellers enjoy a large customer base, low marketing costs, ready-made technological platform, customer trust toward the marketplace, and low logistics costs. The main reasons for utilizing online marketplaces indicated by the interviewed SMEs are shown in Table 11.3.

Table 11.3. Motivation for moving to Kaspi marketplace.

Benefits	Examples of excerpts (SME ID)
Customer base: large base of active consumers: 5.7 million.	"We saw an increased demand in the Kazakhstani market for using such digital platforms. We decided to test how it can be suitable to acquire more customers, so, then we registered, put our products and began to analyse sales." (Interviewee 1) "Kaspi has the largest audience among marketplaces in Kazakhstan." (Interviewee 4)
Trust: Customers and sellers trust the advertised trading platform and are not afraid to pay for an order.	"I didn't even consider other platforms. We all know this brand and trust this platform." (Interviewee 2) "There is no analogue of this in the entire European part, and it is no wonder how Kaspi Bank did a successful IPO in London a couple of years ago." (Interviewee 7) "Kaspi has established itself as a high-tech platform with excellent support service. Customers trust it, and they are very loyal." (Interviewee 3)
Ready-made platform: The website and mobile versions of the marketplace work very well. The seller does not need to worry about the technical issues related to the logic and design of the site, connecting payment systems, maintaining the portal, and developing its application.	"You need business registration proof, bank account, and company name to register on the platform. You will send these documents by email and go to the bank branch to sign the agreement. That's it. You are ready to go." (Interviewee 6) "Almost all Kazakhstan chain stores and small shops are represented in this marketplace. You can see the prices and product information from many Kazakhstan stores and compare your offer. And then you can immediately, in a couple of clicks, place your product in the store." (Interviewee 4)
Logistics: The marketplace works with delivery companies, and currently, the platform subsidizes 60–100% of the logistics costs, so the delivery cost is negligible. The delivery cost is covered 100% if an order is returned.	"The marketplace has contracts with various delivery companies, and thanks to this, delivery prices throughout Kazakhstan costs less than if I did the delivery by myself." (Interviewee 5)

(*Continued*)

Table 11.3. (*Continued*)

Benefits	Examples of excerpts (SME ID)
Financing the purchases: The marketplace allows customers to buy goods on credit without prepayment and additional interest. Customers can also pay for a product in installments for up to three months.	"… you will get customers who are not ready to pay the full cost immediately. They are ready to take the goods in installments or on credit, or they might be attracted to cash bonuses from the marketplace. I even myself ordered goods many times through the Kaspi store. An installment plan is a fantastic tool because you know the income level of the average Kazakhstani. Besides other benefits, this option already makes Kaspi marketplace attractive." (Interviewee 7) "Here, the payment system is convenient. There are a lot of cash bonuses which attract buyers, and as a result, it's very attractive for sellers as well." (Interviewee 1)

11.5.3. *Early-stage digital transformation of a business in moving to the online marketplace*

Most of the firms that participated in the study mentioned how they are improving their platform utilization skills to get the most out of the marketplace. Platform utilization capability is an organization's ability to benefit from its technological features and adapt to its ongoing upgrades and adjustments (Li *et al.*, 2017).

In an online marketplace, vendors frequently sell the same products, change prices based on demand, and engage in ongoing competition within the platform. Therefore, the interviewees faced, for the first time, creating visual product information, making dynamic price adjustments, working with online customer reviews, and constantly adjusting to platform rules.

11.5.3.1. *Creating visual representation in the marketplace*

Businesses create product pages to showcase their products in the marketplace. Colorfully designed, informative, and easy-to-view product pages attract a site visitor's attention, turning him into a potential client. Interviewee 6, from a furniture manufacturer, said:

> Descriptions, characteristics of goods, photos, and videos are essential to differentiate ourselves from competitors. If you have an extensive catalogue of products, you need a product content management system to organize all product details.

Interviewee 2 said:

> Technically, creating a product without a photo is impossible, so I upload the photos. My cousins are good at this. They came and helped me. But for me, the product descriptions are more important. You can tell how to use the product and the advantages and benefits of a particular product.

Another furniture firm has outsourced work to a freelancer to create new product pages with photos and descriptions:

> We found someone who can take photos and process them slightly. Then he prepares a description page, and I pay him for every product page. I don't have time for that, and his service is not very expensive. (Interviewee 7)

11.5.3.2. *Working with reviews*

Online reviews are essential to making the company stand out from competitors in the marketplace. These reviews could be used for online word-of-mouth promotion (Ha *et al.*, 2019; Jansen *et al.*, 2009). Reviews provide details that reduce customers' risks and uncertainties about the products and services, which makes it simpler for customers to make purchases (Zhu & Zhang, 2010). However, it needs intentional communication with customers:

> In the beginning, we waited for reviews after purchases. We thought that it would be gathered naturally if customers liked our products. Unfortunately, it didn't happen, and it took a long time. Therefore, now we try to motivate users to leave reviews — for example, offer some discounts or free goodies. Sometimes we call to ask whether they liked our product and ask a favour to write a review. (Interviewee 1)

Interviewee 3 calls the customers after deliveries to avoid potentially negative customer reviews about the company:

> Kaspi is very strict. If we receive too many negative customer reviews, it might remove us immediately or reduce our rank in the system. Therefore, before a client writes a review, I want to know their thoughts. If they don't like our product or service, I will try to find a way to make them satisfied.

Interviewee 3 also mentioned that she is against faking consumer reviews. However, she has experienced unethical situations:

> Sometimes competitors write negative reviews to reduce your ranking on the marketplace. In this case, you should ask for proof and contact the support team to remove the fake review.

11.5.3.3. *Analyzing data to identify market trends*

The online marketplace offers internal sales analytics and explores current marketplace trends. Interviewees 4 and 7 expressed satisfaction with the data analytic tools provided by the platform:

> As I'm reselling different home appliances, I always need to be updated, and the platform allows me to analyse sales dynamics, products and prices. (Interviewee 4)

> Kaspi has a free service where you can view sales statistics, which allows you to generate a report that shows how quickly the product is being sold. This helps me respond to product shortages and fill them quickly. (Interviewee 7)

However, interviewee 2 thinks that the data analytics offered by the platform doesn't give a complete understanding of the market trends. The owner-director of the beauty appliances shop says:

> I'm using an external automatization program. it creates comprehensive sales data by city, and also, I can download my competitors' prices in one sheet. This program can also automatically set prices based on competitors' positions. In the end, I offer the best price, and my company is shown first on the product page.

11.5.3.4. *Keeping pace with the platform's ever-changing service and rules*

The marketplace can unilaterally change the terms of handling disputes, returns, content design, and customer response times. It can refuse registration, block the supplier's account without giving reasons, or limit the number of firms in a particular category.

> One day, Kaspi organized a big campaign. The next morning, I went to the office and discovered that we had received many orders. Unfortunately, we didn't have many products, and we couldn't ship these products to customers immediately. My business partner cancelled the orders. Later Kaspi blocked our store because the volume of cancelled transactions exceeded 5%. I was very disappointed with my partner and getting the store back into the system took some time. (Interviewee 4)

The marketplace creates campaigns and offers increased cashback for buyers on particular products. All businesses automatically become participants in the promotional offer. The merchants must remove all goods in the store before the start of the promotion if they do not want to participate:

> Now you must look at everything, read the news the marketplace sends and decide in advance. I make only a 20 per cent margin on some products, so if I give half of it as a commission and half as a bonus to the client, I will have nothing left. (Interviewee 6)

11.6. Conclusion

SMEs are currently pressured to pursue sophisticated growth strategies to increase their competitiveness and keep up with changing social and technical environments (Denicolai *et al.*, 2021). They are now looking for new methods to adapt their business models to a connected digital environment (Veile *et al.*, 2022). Online platforms — institutions developed via digital innovations that link buyers and sellers — are one of the ways to access the markets, which help overcome resource limitations and facilitate access to networks. They successfully implement platform-based features, such as working with reviews, creating a visual representation of the products, and using simple data analytics. They are also learning to communicate with the platform providers and operate within the marketplace regulations.

The notion of competition changes dramatically with platforms. Reviews are very critical in the online marketplace. By purchasing products on the platform, the buyer gets an opportunity to share his impressions about the quality of the goods, the ordering process, and other transaction details. SMEs can get additional tools for brand development and promotion within the platform by engaging with customers online and getting positive reviews. A virtual marketplace, however, does not allow potential buyers to see a product live and evaluate its size and quality. Therefore, it is essential to create comprehensive descriptions and demonstrate the advantages of products by posting high-quality multimedia content.

As a result, competitor analysis becomes more voluminous and complex. For example, a store had to compete only with enterprises in its city earlier. Now, due to the large customer base and logistics capabilities of marketplaces, companies from all over the country are "fighting" for customers in one marketplace. Developing capabilities to collect data, analyze it, and form recommendations for further development will assist SMEs in staying competitive.

11.6.1. *Recommendations*

Based on the experiences of SMEs at their initial digital transformation stage, the following recommendations for an entrepreneur of a smaller company have been compiled:

- When choosing a marketplace, it is essential to consider the marketplace conditions for each product: financial (commission size), logistics (delivery and return policies, geography, and coverage), and trade rules.
- Each third-party marketplace has its own requirements for selling goods there and regulations for paperwork. If the seller fails to fulfill the requirements or makes several mistakes, the goods will most likely not be accepted, and the merchandise account might be blocked. Therefore, SMEs need to familiarize themselves with the regulations in detail.

- To understand the rules and regulations and utilize all available opportunities in the system, it's essential to keep up with the marketplace's platform resources and knowledge base.
- Marketplace sellers compete for the top positions in customers' search results. The quality of the digital product page is one of the most important factors influencing the promotion of the product on marketplaces. To increase conversion and sales, SMEs need to optimize the page constantly: test photos, edit product descriptions, and work with platform features.
- Third-party marketplaces usually have detailed analytics features; SMEs can estimate sales, compare monthly data, and track sales forecasts.

References

Banerjee, P. K. & Ma, L. C. (2012). Routinization of B2B E-commerce by small firms: A process perspective. *Information Systems Frontiers* 14(5), 1033–1046.

Belitski, M., Guenther, C., Kritikos, A. S., & Thurik, R. (2022). Economic effects of the COVID-19 pandemic on entrepreneurship and small businesses. *Small Business Economics* 58(2), 593–609.

Besson, P. & Rowe, F. (2012). Strategizing information systems-enabled organizational transformation: A transdisciplinary review and new directions. *The Journal of Strategic Information Systems* 21(2), 103–124.

Bowen, G. A. (2008). Naturalistic inquiry and the saturation concept: A research note. *Qualitative Research* 8(1), 137–152.

Boyatzis, R. E. (1998). *Transforming Qualitative Information: Thematic Analysis and Code Development*. Thousand Oaks: SAGE.

Braun, V. & Clarke, V. (2006). Using thematic analysis in psychology. *Qualitative Research in Psychology* 3(2), 77–101.

Bureau of National Statistics in Kazakhstan (2022). Business Statistics.

Cenamor, J., Parida, V., & Wincent, J. (2019). How entrepreneurial SMEs compete through digital platforms: The roles of digital platform capability, network capability and ambidexterity. *Journal of Business Research* 100, 196–206.

Cha, K. J., Hwang, T., & Gregor, S. (2015). An integrative model of IT-enabled organizational transformation: A multiple case study. *Management Decision* [Preprint].

Chang, H. H. & Wong, K. H. (2010). Adoption of e-procurement and participation of e-marketplace on firm performance: Trust as a moderator. *Information & Management* 47(5–6), 262–270.

Cui, M. & Pan, S. L. (2015). Developing focal capabilities for e-commerce adoption: A resource orchestration perspective. *Information & Management* 52(2), 200–209.

Danziger, P. (2018). Thinking of selling on Amazon marketplace? Here are the pros and cons.

Denicolai, S., Zucchella, A., & Magnani, G. (2021). Internationalization, digitalization, and sustainability: Are SMEs ready? A survey on synergies and substituting effects among growth paths. *Technological Forecasting and Social Change* 166, 120650.

Di Porto, F. & Zuppetta, M. (2021). Co-regulating algorithmic disclosure for digital platforms. *Policy and Society* 40(2), 272–293.

Digital Kazakhstan State Program (2022). Available at: https://egov.kz/cms/en/digital-kazakhstan (accessed 23 May 2023).

Duch-Brown, N. (2017). The competitive landscape of online platforms, (No. 2017-04). JRC Digital Economy Working Paper.

Forbes Kazakhstan. (2022). 40 krupneyshikh torgovykh internet-ploshchadok Kazakhstana. Available at: https://forbes.kz/ranking/40_krupneyshih_torgovyih_internet-ploschadok_-_2022 (accessed 23 May 2023).

Fu, H. P., Chao, P., Chang, T. H., & Chang, Y. S. (2008). The impact of market freedom on the adoption of third-party electronic marketplaces: A fuzzy AHP analysis. *Industrial Marketing Management* 37(6), 698–712.

Gengatharen, D. E. & Standing, C. (2005). A framework to assess the factors affecting success or failure of the implementation of government-supported regional e-marketplaces for SMEs. *European Journal of Information Systems* 14(4), 417–433.

Gielens, K. & Steenkamp, J.-B. E. M. (2019). Branding in the era of digital (dis) intermediation. *International Journal of Research in Marketing* 36(3), 367–384.

Giotopoulos, I., Kontolaimou, A., & Tsakanikas, A. (2022). Digital responses of SMEs to the COVID-19 crisis. *International Journal of Entrepreneurial Behavior & Research* 28(7), 1751–1772.

Goldfarb, A. & Tucker, C. (2019). Digital economics. *Journal of Economic Literature* 57(1), 3–43.

Grandón, E. E., Nasco, S. A., & Mykytyn Jr, P. P. (2011). Comparing theories to explain e-commerce adoption. *Journal of Business Research* 64(3), 292–298.

Ha, S., Kankanhalli, A., Kishan, J. S., & Huang, K. W. (2016). Does social media marketing really work for online SMEs? An empirical study. *Thirty Seventh International Conference on Information Systems*, Dublin, Ireland.

Hamed, S. & El-Deeb, S. (2020). Cash on delivery as a determinant of E-commerce growth in emerging markets. *Journal of Global Marketing* 33(4), 242–265.

Herhausen, D., Miočević, D., Morgan, R. E., & Kleijnen, M. H. (2020). The digital marketing capabilities gap. *Industrial Marketing Management* 90, 276–290.

Homburg, C. & Wielgos, D. M. (2022). The value relevance of digital marketing capabilities to firm performance. *Journal of the Academy of Marketing Science* 50(4), 666–688.

Hossain, M., Azam, M. S., & Quaddus, M. (2021). Small firm entry to e-marketplace for market expansion and internationalization: A theoretical perspective. *Journal of International Entrepreneurship* 19(4), 560–590.

International Telecommunication Union (2021). Digital Development, ITU.

Issa, R. R., Flood, I., & Caglasin, G. (2003). A survey of e-business implementation in the US construction industry. *Journal of Information Technology in Construction (ITcon)* 8(2), 15–28.

Jansen, B. J., Zhang, M., Sobel, K., & Chowdury, A. (2009). Twitter power: Tweets as electronic word of mouth. *Journal of the American Society for Information Science and Technology* 60(11), 2169–2188.

Jin, H. & Hurd, F. (2018). Exploring the impact of digital platforms on SME internationalization: New Zealand SMEs use of the Alibaba platform for Chinese market entry. *Journal of Asia-Pacific Business* 19(2), 72–95.

KPMG (2022). Is there a future for e-commerce development in Central Asia? KPMG Kazakhstan, KPMG.

Kumar, D. (2018). Five reasons why selling on your own brand E-commerce website is better than selling on marketplaces.

Kumar, S. & Petersen, P. (2006). Impact of e-commerce in lowering operational costs and raising customer satisfaction. *Journal of Manufacturing Technology Management* 17(3), 283–302.

Li, L., Su, F., Zhang, W., & Mao, J. Y. (2018). Digital transformation by SME entrepreneurs: A capability perspective. *Information Systems Journal* 28(6), 1129–1157.

MacGregor, R. C. & Vrazalic, L. (2005). A basic model of electronic commerce adoption barriers: A study of regional small businesses in Sweden and Australia. *Journal of Small Business and Enterprise Development* 12(4), 510–527.

Malak, F., Ferreira, J. B., Pessoa de Queiroz Falcão, R., & Giovannini, C. J. (2021). Seller reputation within the B2C e-marketplace and impacts on purchase intention. *Latin American Business Review* 22(3), 287–307.

Maier, E. & Wieringa, J. (2021). Acquiring customers through online marketplaces? The effect of marketplace sales on sales in a retailer's own channels. *International Journal of Research in Marketing* 38(2), 311–328.

Markus, M. L. (2004). Technochange management: Using IT to drive organizational change. *Journal of Information Technology* 19(1), 4–20.

Masiello, P. (2017). Using Amazon to build an ecommerce brand. *Practical Ecommerce*, 27 January.

Matarazzo, M., Penco, L., Profumo, G., & Quaglia, R. (2021). Digital transformation and customer value creation in Made in Italy SMEs: A dynamic capabilities perspective. *Journal of Business Research* 123, 642–656.

Mikalef, P. & Pateli, A. (2017). Information technology-enabled dynamic capabilities and their indirect effect on competitive performance: Findings from PLS-SEM and fsQCA. *Journal of Business Research* 70, 1–16.

Misra, R., Mahajan, R., Singh, N., Khorana, S., & Rana, N. P. (2022). Factors impacting behavioral intentions to adopt the electronic marketplace: Findings from small businesses in India. *Electronic Markets* 32, 1639–1660.

Moorman, C. & Day, G. S. (2016). Organizing for marketing excellence. *Journal of Marketing* 80(6), 6–35.

OECD (2019). *OECD SME and Entrepreneurship Outlook 2019*. Organization for Economic Co-operation and Development, Paris.

OECD (2021). *OECD SME and Entrepreneurship Outlook 2021*. Organization for Economic Co-operation and Development, Paris.

Oliveira, T., Alhinho, M., Rita, P., & Dhillon, G. (2017). Modelling and testing consumer trust dimensions in e-commerce. *Computers in Human Behavior* 71, 153–164.

Palmié, M., Miehé, L., Oghazi, P., Parida, V., & Wincent, J. (2022). The evolution of the digital service ecosystem and digital business model innovation in retail: The emergence of meta-ecosystems and the value of physical interactions. *Technological Forecasting and Social Change* 177, 121496.

Papadopoulos, T., Baltas, K. N., & Balta, M. E. (2020). The use of digital technologies by small and medium enterprises during COVID-19: Implications for theory and practice. *International Journal of Information Management* 55, 102192.

Peter, M. K. & Dalla Vecchia, M. (2021). The digital marketing toolkit: A literature review for the identification of digital marketing channels and platforms. *New Trends in Business Information Systems and Technology* 291, 251–265.

Phiri, M. (2020). Impact of digital marketing capabilities on market performance of small to medium enterprise agro-processors in Harare, Zimbabwe. *Verslas: Teorija ir praktika/Business: Theory and Practice* 21(2), 746–757.

PwC (2022). Analysis of the retail e-commerce market in Kazakhstan, PwC. Available at: https://www.pwc.com/kz/en/publications/e-commerce-analysis/e-commerce-12m-2021.html (accessed 23 May 2023).

Qizhi Dai, R. J. K. (2002). Business models for internet-based B2B electronic markets. *International Journal of Electronic Commerce* 6(4), 41–72.

Ravichandran, T. (2018). Exploring the relationships between IT competence, innovation capacity and organizational agility. *The Journal of Strategic Information Systems* 27(1), 22–42.

Shaheer, N. A. & Li, S. (2020). The CAGE around cyberspace? How digital innovations internationalize in a virtual world. *Journal of Business Venturing* 35(1), 105892.

Son, J.-Y., Tu, L., & Benbasat, I. (2006). A descriptive content analysis of trust-building measures in B2B electronic marketplaces. *Communications of the Association for Information Systems* 18(1), 6.

Singh, J., Flaherty, K., Sohi, R. S., Deeter-Schmelz, D., Habel, J., Le Meunier-FitzHugh, K., Malshe, A., Mullins, R., & Onyemah, V. (2019). Sales profession and professionals in the age of digitization and artificial intelligence technologies: Concepts, priorities, and questions. *Journal of Personal Selling & Sales Management* 39(1), 2–22.

Sridhar, S. & Fang, E. (2019). New vistas for marketing strategy: Digital, data-rich, and developing market (D3) environments. *Journal of the Academy of Marketing Science*. Springer. 47, 977–985.

Statista (2022). Global e-commerce share of retail sales 2026, Statista.

Taiminen, H. M. & Karjaluoto, H. (2015). The usage of digital marketing channels in SMEs. *Journal of Small Business and Enterprise Development* [Preprint].

Tan, F. T. C., Tan, B., & Pan, S. L. (2016). Developing a leading digital multi-sided platform: Examining IT affordances and competitive actions in Alibaba. com. *Communications of the Association for Information Systems* 38(1), 36.

Täuscher, K. & Laudien, S. M. (2018). Understanding platform business models: A mixed methods study of marketplaces. *European Management Journal* 36(3), 319–329.

The Generalist (2022). Kaspi: The Shapeshifter | The Generalist.

Tortora, D., Chierici, R., Briamonte, M. F., & Tiscini, R. (2021). 'I digitize so I exist'. Searching for critical capabilities affecting firms' digital innovation. *Journal of Business Research* 129, 193–204.

Trainor, K. J., Krush, M. T., & Agnihotri, R. (2013). Effects of relational proclivity and marketing intelligence on new product development. *Marketing Intelligence & Planning* 31, 788–806.

Veile, J. W., Schmidt, M.-C., & Voigt, K.-I. (2022). Toward a new era of cooperation: How industrial digital platforms transform business models in Industry 4.0. *Journal of Business Research* 143, 387–405.

Verhoef, P. C. & Bijmolt, T. H. (2019). Marketing perspectives on digital business models: A framework and overview of the special issue. *International Journal of Research in Marketing*. Elsevier. 36(3), 341–349.

Walsh, G. S., Przychodzen, J., & Przychodzen, W. (2017). Supporting the SME commercialization process: The case of 3D printing platforms. *Small Enterprise Research* 24(3), 257–273.

Warner, K. S. & Wäger, M. (2019). Building dynamic capabilities for digital transformation: An ongoing process of strategic renewal. *Long range planning* 52(3), 326–349.

Witek-Hajduk, M. K., Grudecka, A. M., & Napiórkowska, A. (2021). E-commerce in the internet-enabled foreign expansion of Polish fashion brands owned by

SMEs. *Journal of Fashion Marketing and Management: An International Journal* 26(1), 51–66.

Wirdiyanti, R., Yusgiantoro, I., Sugiarto, A., Harjanti, A. D., Mambea, I. Y., Soekarno, S., & Damayanti, S. M. (2022). How does e-commerce adoption impact micro, small, and medium enterprises' performance and financial inclusion? Evidence from Indonesia. *Electronic Commerce Research.*

Yin, R. K. (2009). *Case Study Research: Design and Methods*. Thousand Oaks: SAGE.

Zhu, K., Xu, S., Kraemer, K. L., & Dedrick, J. (2006). Global convergence and local divergence in e-commerce: Cross-country analyses. In *Global e-commerce: Impacts of National Environment and Policy*. Cambridge University Press, pp. 345–384.

Zhu, F. & Zhang, X. (2010). Impact of online consumer reviews on sales: The moderating role of product and consumer characteristics. *Journal of Marketing* 74(2), 133–148.

https://doi.org/10.1142/9789811270178_0012

Chapter 12

Digitalizing Micro-Business in Times of Disruption: Insight into Innovative Strategies in the Kazakh Economy

Tommaso Aguzzi

Department of Business Administration, Tallinn University of Technology, Ehitajate tee 5, Tallinn 19086, Estonia

tommaso.aguzzi@taltech.ee

Abstract

The aim of this chapter is to provide an account of the innovative strategies devised by microentrepreneurs as a consequence of the COVID-19 crisis in Kazakhstan. To do so, the chapter initially introduces the most recent developments of digital transformation and micro-entrepreneurship in the Kazakh context, and building on this overview, it closely examines the innovative practices implemented by a number of micro-entrepreneurs over the past two years. The outcome is a timely analysis of the country's digitalization process, the recent approaches to dealing with the disruptive consequences of the global pandemic, and an insight into the present and future ways of doing business by micro-entrepreneurs in Kazakhstan.

12.1. Introduction

The advancement of informational and digital sciences allowed the development of sophisticated technologies at a high rate, which is made available to business organizations, enabling them to undergo organizational transformation (Vial, 2019). Digital transformation (DT) is changing the way of doing business: new ways of communication, interaction, operation, and value creation are being introduced (OECD, 2021). The adoption of these new media and practices is not straightforward and requires the unity of intent and collaboration of different actors. Their adoption and use have immensely increased over the past decade, and the unforeseen impact of the COVID-19 global pandemic accelerated the process of DT in emerging economies (Adam & Alarifi, 2021; Caballero-Morales, 2021; Priyono *et al.*, 2020). According to Berman (2012), the business transformation process involves creating new business models, improving operational processes, and enhancing customer experiences. Developing and implementing strategies to better use digital technologies has become essential for every entrepreneur and business, regardless of its size (OECD, 2021). The disruptive effects of lockdowns and restrictions had made apparent once and for all the necessity to embed IT strategies into business models. The increasing importance of digital transformation for small and micro businesses is also reflected in the greater attention given to the topic in the academic literature (Fernández-Esquinas *et al.*, 2019; Pelletier & Coultier, 2019). However, the existing literature is overwhelmingly focused on the economies of the Global North, while the developments taking place in the emerging economies are understudied (Ramdani *et al.*, 2022). The primary aim of this chapter is to illustrate the current transformational process in the field of digital innovation for small and micro entrepreneurship in Kazakhstan while providing a concrete analysis of the practical innovations implemented by a number of micro-entrepreneurs since the global pandemic outbreak. Finally, this chapter offers hands-on insights into the most recent developments in the ways of operating a small business in the country while suggesting critical avenues for future research.

This chapter looks at the practice of DT in Kazakhstan, a country where micro, small, and medium enterprises make up 96.7% of all businesses and employ 37.5% of the total employed population (OECD, 2020). MSMEs contributed to 34.7% of the country's GDP in 2021, and the total number of employed citizens in SMEs grew by 10.6% and reached 3.5 million people in the same year (Satubaldina, 2022). To facilitate the DT of small businesses, the country's authorities have promoted a digitalization process by launching a national program named "Digital Kazakhstan" in 2018. Digitalization is indeed a chance for micro-businesses to improve efficiency while implementing new business models that are less costly, and governmental initiatives, such as "Digital Kazakhstan," have the potential to accelerate the digital transition. However, the process of DT requires a shift in mindset and business culture that does not occur without costs and risks (Oney *et al.*, 2018). In addition, the unexpected and sudden breakout of the global pandemic in December 2019 posed a major threat to small- and micro-businesses as retail spaces and markets had to temporarily shut down, service providers could not physically interact with customers, and most industries experienced a significant reduction in product demand as well as supply chain disruptions. Unlike medium and large businesses, small and micro businesses are not endowed with crisis management resources, as well as economic, social, and organizational capital to counter the unforeseen hurdles posed by the pandemic.

Given the above-mentioned premises, this book chapter aims at analyzing how micro-business owners operating in Kazakhstan coped with the COVID-19 crisis and how they transformed their businesses through digitalization processes in these challenging times. In the following sections, the extant literature on DT, small and micro entrepreneurship in emerging economies, and the global pandemic impact on SMEs operations are outlined before turning our attention to the findings of the semi-structured interviews with the micro-entrepreneurs participating in this study.

12.2. Literature Review

12.2.1. *Digital transformation in SMEs*

Recently, an extensive body of literature on digital innovation in SMEs has emerged (e.g., Crupi *et al.*, 2020; Garzoni *et al.*, 2020; Li *et al.*, 2018; Pelletier & Cloutier, 2019; Vial, 2021). SMEs globally represent the vast majority of enterprises and substantially contribute to income and employment in both developed and developing economies (OECD, 2020). The DT of a small business entails the rearrangement of technology, business models, and processes to secure new values for customers and employees in developing the digital economy.

The DT of small firms has increased rapidly over the past decade, and digital innovation has changed the way companies conduct business, interact with consumers, suppliers, and other stakeholders, and support business models and customer value creation (Matarazzo *et al.*, 2021). An increasing number of consumers have access to multiple media channels through which they can communicate, purchase, and deal with small firms and other customers in a faster way. Digitalization thus reshapes the conventional relationships between consumers and businesses, as well as the business processes, organizational capabilities, and operational routines (Li *et al.*, 2018).

SMEs are likely to digitize marketing and administrative operations first. The newest digital technologies that SMEs are employing in their operations support different functions, namely marketing (e.g., social media applications, e-commerce platforms), accounting and finance (e.g., mobile secure payment solutions), and human resources (e.g., collaborative platforms and tools). The digital gap between SMEs and large firms decreases by way of e-government interactions, electronic invoicing, and using e-commerce platforms and social media. In contrast, the gap widens for the use of more sophisticated technologies, such as data analytics or cloud computing (OECD, 2021; Pelletier & Coultier, 2019). SMEs tend to outsource solutions to offset costs and internal capabilities. Small and micro businesses increasingly rely on digital platforms to advertise and sell their products and services while optimizing their operations at lower costs.

Westerman *et al.* (2014) suggest that DT occurs in three different business domains: operational processes, business models, and customer experience. Consequently, the impact of this transformation is manifesting itself in these three areas. In addition to these manifestations, Vial (2019) proposes four different paths to value proposition, namely: new value propositions (e.g., shifting from physical goods to services), new value networks (e.g., disintermediation), use of digital distribution and sale channels (e.g., e-commerce through digital platforms), and optimization of organizational agility and ambidexterity (e.g., improving the opportunity identification process). Despite the shared consideration of digital technologies as beneficial and necessary for business development and the assumption that each company should embrace DT in today's business environment, SMEs are still facing challenges when it comes to assessing the actual IT needs, the alignment of strategies and objectives, and the necessary competencies to manage the implemented digital innovations, in addition to the growing complexity of emerging technologies and the competitiveness of the business ecosystems.

12.2.2. *Micro-business metamorphosis*

The global economic reconstruction has been characterized by a replacement of market relations with contractual (legal and administrative) ones, an increasing importance of distributive channels and the intellectualization of labor, less division of labor, as well as the transformation of an enterprise into a "certain sum of contracts" between suppliers, experts, consumers, and the society (Berdykulova *et al.*, 2014). In today's economy, the micro-entrepreneur carries out both practical and intellectual work, and the distribution of its products has become as important as its production, thus requiring a broader set of skills to perform business activities. The distribution channels (e.g., online stores, Instagram, Facebook, TikTok, etc.) play an essential role, which cannot be overlooked by business owners.

Until a few years ago, academic literature offered limited empirical evidence on the role of micro-businesses in emerging economies and often relied only on data from formally registered businesses, which did not consider the large number of self-employed or microenterprises operating in the informal sector and are notoriously difficult to quantify. A micro-business is intended here in a range from start-ups, with both high and low growth potential, to family businesses, which have been operating for many years. More recently, and spurred by the increasing attention of international organizations, there has been an important recognition of the role played by microenterprises in driving employment and innovation in the emerging economies. In 2019, the International Labor Organization (ILO) published a report titled "Small Matters," which, unlike previous studies on firms, is based on data obtained through household and labor force surveys, thus including self-employed entrepreneurs and all types of enterprises from micro (2–9 employees) to medium or large (50 or more employees). The report highlights the global relevance of micro and small enterprises (MSEs) and the crucial role they play in achieving the Sustainable Development Goals (SDGs). Furthermore, the report outlines DT opportunities and barriers for MSEs in emerging economies and identifies the following ones: increased access to information and an improved ability to communicate; the ability to trade and to access markets more easily and over greater distances;

access to a variety of financial services with low barriers to entry; new pathways to enterprise formalization; DT and entrepreneurship as fundamental shifts in value creation; and synergies with the development and diffusion of green businesses and technologies. With regard to the barriers faced by MSEs, the report distinguishes digital divides and locally incomplete digital infrastructures, multifaceted digital skill shortages, low adoption readiness, risk-averse cultures, and gender barriers among others (ILO, 2021). It is also crucial to highlight the development of a critical stream of academic literature that emphasizes the necessity of exploring the informal sector entrepreneurship. This research focuses on businesses that, at the beginning of their operations, did not register their entity or did not report some or all of their production and/or sales to the tax authorities when they should have been compelled to (Ketchen *et al.*, 2014; Siqueira *et al.*, 2016), and it was found that enterprises that are starting up informally, avoid paying taxes initially, and comply with onerous regulations perform better at a later stage than those that are registered from the very beginning of their operations (Williams *et al.*, 2017). These findings lead us to reconsider some of the assumptions of the orthodox literature on informality, which sees informal entrepreneurship as underproductive and advocates for tougher policies in order to eradicate the informal sector (Oviedo *et al.*, 2009).

12.2.3. *The pandemic test*

Despite the hardships that the Kazakh economy has been enduring as a consequence of the global health crisis, SMEs operating in Kazakhstan have increased in terms of total number, productivity output, and employed citizens (Satubaldina, 2022). In this historical period and due to the shortage of work opportunities, informal entrepreneurship has most likely increased globally (ILO, 2021). The figures show an increase of 15.2% in the total number of SMEs operating in Kazakhstan, signaling an outstanding resilience of small entrepreneurs to economic shocks and the potential of entrepreneurship as a source of employment and sustainment in times of crises. The negative repercussions of the lockdowns and temporary closures on SMEs have been alleviated by a series of measures, such as the three-year moratorium on taxation, the inspections of small and micro enterprises, and the deferral of loans to SMEs in affected industries, launched by the government a few months after the COVID-19 outbreak (E-gov, 2021). As hinted at in the introduction, the national authorities have also launched an ambitious program of DT named "Digital Kazakhstan," which aims at improving society's living standards by adopting digital technologies and paving the country's path toward a digital economy. This program has been implemented in the period 2018–2022, and it foresees the "transition to the digital state and knowledge-based economy," as well as the creation of an innovative ecosystem, where technological entrepreneurship development and the evolution of human capital assets are favored (Government of the Republic of Kazakhstan, 2018). Digitalization is indeed a chance for micro-businesses to improve their efficiency by implementing new business models which are less costly. The introduction of digital technologies potentially leads to a reduction in fixed costs while creating a competitive advantage, which allows enterprises to survive and most likely grow (Melnyk & Salin, 2018; Peppard, 2016). However, the process of DT requires a shift in mindset and business culture that does not occur without costs and risks (Oney *et al.*, 2018).

The unexpected and sudden breakout of the global pandemic in December 2019 posed an unprecedented obstacle for SMEs. While their intrinsic characteristics provide them with a greater ability to adapt and change in a dynamic global economy, they are simultaneously vulnerable to external shocks due to their limited resources (Durst & Henschel, 2021). The COVID-19 crisis proved to be a critical litmus test for SMEs. The probability of failure in these disruptive times is high among small firms, while, on the other hand, such a shock may have accelerated the process of DT, which equips them with the necessary means to endure the difficulties and thrive on the long term. Thus, the disruptions caused by the COVID-19 emergency have increased the necessity and importance of DT and have functioned as an accelerator. Micro and small entrepreneurs have moved their business activities online and devised innovative solutions to keep their businesses afloat during lockdowns and to overcome supply chain ruptures. The online platforms played a major role in allowing the business owners to reach new suppliers and customers. It is likely that these transformations will be irreversible and permanent, as the small and micro firms have survived thanks to them and the market conditions have adjusted to the new reality. Given these premises, the aim of this chapter is to explore and analyze how Kazakh microentrepreneurs responded to the disruptions brought about by the global pandemic and what sort of innovative strategies and measures they have been adopting in their business operations.

12.3. The Study Context

Kazakhstan's economy has been heavily reliant on the extraction of mineral resources such as gas and crude oil. This sector used to account for over 60% of total exports and over 50% of government revenue until a decade ago, but with the steady decline of the international oil price since 2014, these figures dropped to less than 50% and 30%, respectively (Atakhanova, 2021). The national government had to start a process of economic diversification and redirect significant investment into the trade and production sectors, which led to an increase in their shares in the Kazakh economy and placed SMEs at the center of a sustainable development plan for the country's future (OECD, 2020). Despite the efforts of the central government, the approach to diversification has been imposed as a "top-down" policy, leaving the regional administrations with no say in how to use organizational, financial, and human resources locally. As a consequence of the centralized management system, this approach has not yet delivered the desirable results in areas beyond the two major cities of Almaty and Astana and more peripheral, where growth is still driven largely by resource extraction (Anderson *et al.*, 2018).

The focus on Kazakhstan is particularly interesting because of the fact that the country regained independence from the Soviet Union in 1991 and entrepreneurship has been growing since then but still represents something new for its citizens. In less than 20 years, Kazakhstan managed to establish a business environment that, compared to other emerging market economies, has been seen as being relatively supportive (Teal *et al*., 2011). In Kazakhstan, micro, small, and medium enterprises (MSMEs) make up 96.7% of all businesses and employ 37.5% of the total employed population (OECD, 2020). MSMEs contributed to 34.7% of the country's GDP in 2021, and the total number of employed citizens in SMEs grew by 10.6% and reached 3.5 million people in the same year (Satubaldina, 2022). By taking a closer look at the composition of this group of enterprises, the number of microenterprises consisting of 15 or less employees stands out with 76% of the total SMEs (see Table 12.1). Table 12.1 shows that micro-businesses constitute the very texture of the socioeconomic environment in Kazakhstan and contribute to the dynamic rendering and constant evolution of its business environment, while bolstering the national economy.

Table 12.1. Distribution of SMEs in Kazakhstan as of January 1, 2019.

Firm size	Number
Individual entrepreneurs and farms	1,188,629
Small	377,925
Medium	2,782
Total	1,569,341

Despite the increasing relevance of entrepreneurship in the regional context, scant research has been carried out on the topic in Kazakhstan. Thus, the field of entrepreneurship studies would greatly benefit from more diverse studies conducted in underrepresented regions of the globe. In the following section, the research approach, methods, and analysis of the data resulting from the semi-structured interviews with the micro-entrepreneurs are illustrated.

12.4. Methodology

12.4.1. *Research approach*

This book chapter is based on an exploratory qualitative approach to understanding how micro-entrepreneurs operating in Kazakhstan transformed their businesses as a consequence of the COVID-19 pandemic emergency. Data were collected using semi-structured interviews. This type of interview is suitable when the planned study includes an exploratory element (Saunders *et al.*, 2009). An interview guide supported the interview process. The focal topics of interest were specified at the outset of the study; that is, they were derived from the extant literature. In line with the process focus considered in this study, the interview guide had two main sections. In the first section, questions related to the ways business was affected by lockdowns and restrictions during the COVID-19 crisis. Whereas, the second one addresses the innovations introduced in the past two years of operation and how the business transformed in the same period of time. The whole guide starts with a series of demographic questions and concludes with two questions related to the allocation of a firm's resources in its current operation and the desirable measures necessary to overcome the challenges faced by the firm.

12.4.2. *Data collection*

The level of analysis was the microenterprise. To be selected, the firms, or the individual entrepreneurs, had to fulfill the following criteria, namely being a company that falls under the category of microenterprises (*micropredprinimatel, individualny predprinimatel*) and operating in the territory of the Republic of Kazakhstan. There were no limitations regarding start-ups or more mature micro-businesses. Thus, the firms were selected purposefully (Patton, 2002). Business owners and/or managers represented the unit of analysis of the study. These individuals were considered suitable participants for the current study because they possessed the necessary knowledge and experience concerning the topic under investigation within the current, real-life setting. Suitable entrepreneurs and interviewees were identified by using an advertising post on social media, to which business owners voluntarily responded either directly by getting in touch with the author or indirectly by reaching out to the author's contacts, who then forwarded the interested entrepreneurs' contact details to the author. Using these contacts, the entrepreneurs were briefly informed about the study and invited to participate in a Zoom or Skype interview.

The selection process resulted in 12 interviews that were conducted between September 4 and 20, 2022. As Eisenhardt (1989) identified a saturation degree of newly gained knowledge at approximately 12 interviews, I decided on that number of interviews. Each interview lasted between 30 and 50 minutes. The interviews were conducted in both Russian and English. Informed consent to use the interview data for the current research purposes was given by all research participants in written and/or verbal form, and confidentiality is ensured at all times. All of the firms involved in the study had fewer than 10 employees, which indicates that this study examined microenterprises. This figure reflects the most prevalent company structure found in Kazakhstan, as mentioned in the introductory section. As for the sector, different areas of the service and retail sectors were included, which increased its external validity (Gray, 2017).

12.4.3. *Data analysis*

The overall approach to data analysis followed the thematic analysis principles. Thematic analysis can be synthesized as a search for topics that appear to be important to the understanding of the phenomenon under investigation (Braun & Clarke, 2006). Thematic analysis also includes the coding of qualitative data into clusters of similar entities and the identification of consistent relationships and patterns between themes. This approach to data analysis allowed me to reduce the amount of data by segmenting, categorizing, and grouping relevant concepts within the data set under examination. The first step of the data analysis process involved transcribing the interviews' recordings, noting down the major ideas, and thus familiarizing with the data. Once the transcriptions were completed, the author generated codes to highlight "interesting features of the data in a systematic fashion" (Braun & Clarke, 2006, p. 87). The generated codes followed the two macro topics outlined in the interview guide. The codes were then analyzed and grouped into subthemes, as presented in the following section. A number of meaningful statements representing the data were extracted to illustrate the research participants' opinions, ideas, and feelings. The analysis process was completed by using the in-built tools in Dedoose, which assisted the author in capturing the most relevant data from each interview, comparing the data, finding patterns and divergences, and drawing conclusions.

12.5. Findings

12.5.1. *Shift in organizational culture*

Through the thematic analysis of the semi-structured interviews with the microentrepreneurs, two major areas can be identified as the critical avenues of DT: organizational culture and the development of human capital. The former refers to the fundamental assumptions that a given group has invented, discovered, or developed while learning to solve problems of adaptation to the ecosystem and internal integration. This dimension regards the norms and values shared by the participants of a business venture that result in ways of action or behavior. Organizational culture represents a key aspect of business innovation, and its transformation is a necessary condition for the development of a pro-innovative character. The latter avenue is intended as the knowledge, skills, and experiences that entrepreneurs invest in and accumulate throughout their lives, enabling them to recognize and exploit business opportunities. Knowledge and skills are acquired through formal and informal education and training, and their increase potentially leads to a higher probability of perceiving and achieving a greater variety of opportunities (Becker, 1964). Thus, the entrepreneur's ability to understand, identify, interpret, and apply new information, as well as to discover new opportunities, is directly influenced by the acquisition and retention of knowledge (Roberts, 1991; Venkataraman, 1997).

The most critical change in organizational culture consists of shifting to the online format as a consequence of the restricting measures implemented by the national government to tackle the COVID-19 spread. This change was generally shared by the totality of research participants while highlighting different aspects that were particularly challenging to address at the individual level. As most of the businesses were predominantly operating offline and through face-to-face interactions with their customers, the lockdown measures forced them to switch to online platforms to provide services or sell their products. A psychologist, a mental coach, and a yoga teacher participating in this study mentioned that they had to transfer all their work online within just a few hours, as one of them put it: "there was a moment where the whole environment has begun to go online." The new format required a shift in the professionals' approach to their clients. The lack of physical presence has prompted them to learn how to engage with their clients behind the computer's screen, though this shift has not occurred without difficulties. The transfer of working activities from the office to remote modalities has affected a large number of employers and employees and the content of their work. Professionals working in the mental health field, for example, witnessed a change in the problematics and challenges shared by their patients, who now had to cope with the consequences of isolation and the uncertain scenarios brought about by the global pandemic. Initially, the shift to the online format had heavily impacted their business operations, as their client base had not switched to remote sessions in its entirety. To alleviate these effects and save small businesses from closure, the Kazakh government passed a contingency plan which established a tax exemption moratorium for all micro-entrepreneurs and small-business owners from January 2020 to December 2022 (E-Gov, 2021). In most cases, the online regime was partially maintained after the easing of restrictions, with almost the totality of the businesses working on a 50/50 regime, with half of their services continuing remotely.

12.5.2. *A digital opportunity*

The advantages of the digital shift were highlighted by two business partners who have recently acquired a small business selling skin care and cosmetic products in Kazakhstan. The couple decided to take over the business and close the physical store in the city of Almaty run by the previous owner to fully operate online. During the first months of operation, they had realized that "it's not really important to have the offline store anymore, it's much faster to just open an Instagram page and establish a direct contact with the customers." This way, they could also extend their pool of customers "by focusing not only on people who live in Almaty, but all over Kazakhstan, where there is no access to certain kinds of products."

Over the past five years, online stores and social media platforms have come to dominate the local marketplace (Barykin & Smirnova, 2021), and the pandemic only accelerated this trend, which led a lot of small-business owners to invest increasing resources in digital marketing, online advertisements, and social media management (SMM). A research participant explained well the challenging equation characterizing the Kazakh small-business environment: "I think the biggest struggle for me is gaining more followers. Followers turn into clients. We can only grow if we engage with more people online." On that note, it is especially interesting to emphasize that most of the respondents stated that their company's resources were mostly reinvested in digital literacy or online learning activities aimed at acquiring the necessary tools to thrive in the current business environment. Micro-entrepreneurs shared a feeling of increasing competition due to the recent surge in digital enterprises in Kazakhstan, and in order to maintain their competitive advantage over other micro-businesses, they chose to undertake formal online learning to learn social media marketing, engage with new customers, and promote their business activities. In this context, it is relevant to mention the increasing interest of entrepreneurs toward social media, such as TikTok, which engage more and more youth worldwide. As one of the participants acknowledges, "it is a very powerful tool to reach out to a young audience and we have recently signed up for an expert consultation on how to run a business on the platform."

12.5.3. *Supply chain reshuffling*

In addition to paying increasing attention to social media engagement, microentrepreneurs have been spending a greater amount of time conducting market research. In order to stand out from the competition, business owners noted that they have to allocate more resources to researching new products in international and local markets. In some cases, a new item has the effect of drawing the attention of new customers thanks to its popularity in international markets or, as in the case of the introduction of male skin care products, because it seeks to overcome common misconceptions and stereotypes present in Kazakh society. As a consequence of the disruptions to the global supply chains amid the pandemic, as well as the decreased movement of people worldwide, another interesting phenomenon resulted from the interviews. A number of micro-entrepreneurs undertook the "localization" of their goods' supply chain and, in other cases, of their target customers. Cross-border trade and the expansion of the global supply network have been increasing over the past decade in Kazakhstan; however, socioeconomic shocks, such as the global pandemic and the Russian invasion followed by the outbreak of war in Ukraine, have led to supply chains becoming more localized, ensuring fewer disruptions in the case of limited movement of people and goods and higher shipping costs. In a world where the costs of moving goods and people have suddenly increased, micro-businesses had to prioritize resilience over efficiency. As one of the entrepreneurs describes: "While we used to import coffee from Russian suppliers, we now move our orders locally and most of the coffee is coming from Kazakh suppliers." Furthermore, the manager of a ski travel agency noted: "We switched the focus group from foreign tourists to local ones and we increasingly promoted our tours on social networks to promote domestic tourism." These changes came as a surprise to the business owners, who had to readily respond to this new challenging scenario. However, they have been able to identify opportunities in previously unexplored terrain, which may potentially bring about long-term benefits and alternatives to their firms, as well as prevent them from suffering losses in the event of another crisis of such magnitude.

12.6. Conclusion

To summarize the findings of this research on the basis of the interview study, this chapter illustrates how micro-businesses coped with the sudden and unexpected COVID-19 crisis and what kind of DTs they have been implementing over the past two years. From the analysis of the collected data set, two major areas of innovation can be discerned: The first one deals with aspects related to organizational culture, such as the increasing reliability of the platform economy for service and retail promotion and distribution, as well as the implementation of innovative digital solutions. The second one is related to the development of human capital, such as the increasing investments of resources on the acquisition of digital skills or market research, with a tendency to localize the supply chain. Furthermore, the findings suggest that the COVID-19 crisis was a challenging test for the micro-entrepreneurs' ability to adjust to the new business scenario. Thus, this chapter contributes to the field of small entrepreneurship, digital innovation, and crisis management from a novel perspective by using a data set from Kazakhstan, which expands the existing literature dominated by studies conducted in Western economies.

The main takeaways for decision-makers of small entrepreneurial firms are the following:

- The organizational culture plays a fundamental role in the DT process of a small business, and it is a prerequisite to implementing a successful innovative strategy.
- Online platforms provided a number of opportunities during the COVID-19 crisis, which could be leveraged by small entrepreneurs to reach new and diverse customers.
- Investments in internal R&D are increasingly important in a digital competitive environment, and the "localization" of supply chains and markets offers opportunities at lower costs which are also more sustainable in the long term.

As for future avenues of research, the replication of this study across different geographical areas would be useful to examine whether the cultural background and/or geographical location affect the entrepreneur's response to the COVID-19 crisis and whether similar kinds of innovative strategies have been devised to tackle it. Future research on small entrepreneurship and digital innovation may also benefit from the inclusion of additional participants (e.g., customers, online platform providers) to better assess the perception of DT from their perspectives. By focusing the lens on Kazakhstan, it is possible to note that the significant leap in the development of the digital economy over the past two decades has not always been supported by an equivalent investment and effort to provide Internet access for all, especially in rural areas outside of the major urban conglomerations. This great divide between the center and the peripheries as well as the mismatch between the magnitude of business digitalization and institutional investments suggest that a lot is yet to be done to support digital entrepreneurship and the DT of businesses in Kazakhstan.

References

Adam, N. A. & Alarifi, G. (2021). Innovation practices for survival of small and medium enterprises (SMEs) in the COVID-19 times: The role of external support. *Journal of Innovation and Entrepreneurship* 10, 15. Doi: 10.1186/s13731-021-00156-6.

Alibekova, G., Medeni, T., Panzabekova, A., & Mussayeva, D. (2020). Digital Transformation Enablers and Barriers in the Economy of Kazakhstan. *The Journal of Asian Finance, Economics and Business*, 7(7), 565–575. https://doi.org/10.13106/JAFEB.2020.VOL7.NO7.565.

Anderson, K., Capannelli, G., Ginting, E., & Taniguchi, K. (2018). Kazakhstan Accelerating Economic Diversification. Asian Development Bank. http://hdl.handle.net/11540/8759.

Atakhanova, Z. (2021). Kazakhstan's oil boom, diversification strategies, and the service sector. *Mineral Economics* 34, 399–409. Doi: 10.1007/s13563-021-00275-2.

Barykin, S. Y. & Smirnova, E. (2021). Development of the Kazakhstan digital retail chains within the EAEU E-commerce market. *Academy of Strategic Management Journal* 20(2), 1–13.

Becker, G. S. (1964). *Human Capital: A Theoretical and Empirical Analysis, with Special Reference to Education.* University of Chicago Press, Chicago.

Berdykulova, G., Sailov, A., Kaliazhdarova, S. & Berdykulov, E. (2014). The emerging digital economy: Case of Kazakhstan. *Procedia — Social and Behavioral Sciences* 109, 1287–1291. Doi: 10.1016/j.sbspro.2013.12.626.

Berman, S. J. (2012). Digital transformation: Opportunities to create new business models. *Strategy & Leadership* 40(2), 16–24. Doi: 10.1108/10878571211209314.

Besson, P. & Rowe, F. (2012). Strategizing information systems-enabled organizational transformation: A transdisciplinary review and new directions. *The Journal of Strategic Information Systems* 21, 103–124.

Braun, V. & Clarke, V. (2006). Using thematic analysis in psychology. *Qualitative Research in Psychology* 3(2), 77–101. Doi: 10.1191/1478088706qp063oa.

Caballero-Morales, S. (2021). Innovation as recovery strategy for SMEs in emerging economies during the COVID-19 pandemic. *Research in International Business and Finance*, Elsevier, vol. 57(C). Doi: 10.1016/j.ribaf.2021.101396.

Crupi, A., Del Sarto, N., Di Minin, A., Gregori, G. L., Lepore, D., Marinelli, L., & Spigarelli, F. (2020). The digital transformation of SMEs — A new knowledge broker called the digital innovation hub. *Journal of Knowledge Management* 24(6), 1263–1288. Doi: 10.1108/JKM-11-2019-0623.

Durst, S. & Henschel, T. (2021). COVID-19 as an accelerator for developing strong(er) businesses? Insights from Estonian small firms. *Journal of the International Council for Small Business* 2(1), 1–29. Doi: 10.1080/26437015.2020.1859935.

Eisenhardt, K. M. (1989). Agency Theory: An Assessment and Review. *The Academy of Management Review* 14(1), 57–74. https://doi.org/10.2307/258191

E-Gov (2021). *Who fall within a moratorium and is tax-exempt for 3 years?* Electronic government of the Republic of Kazakhstan. https://egov.kz/cms/en/articles/moratorium.

Fernández-Esquinas, M., Van Oostrom, M. & Pinto, H. (2019). *Innovation in SMEs and Micro Firms: Culture, Entrepreneurial Dynamics and Regional Development*. Routledge, London.

Garzoni, A., De Turi, I., Secundo, G., & Del Vecchio, P. (2020). Fostering digital transformation of SMEs: A four levels approach. *Management Decision* 58(8), 1543–1562. Doi: 10.1108/MD-07-2019-0939.

Gray, D. (2017). *Doing Research in the Real World* (4th ed.). SAGE Publishing.

Hess, T., Matt, C., Benlian, A., & Wiesboeck, F. (2016). Options for formulating a digital transformation strategy. *MIS Quarterly Executive* 15(2), 123–139.

Ketchen, D. J., Jr, Ireland, R. D., & Webb, J. W. (2014). Conclusion. *Strategic Entrepreneurship Journal* 8, 95–100. Doi: 10.1002/sej.1175.

Litvishko, O., Beketova, K., Akimova, B., Azhmukhamedova, A., and Islyam, G. (2020). Impact of the digital economy on the banking sector. *The 1st International Conference on Business Technology for a Sustainable Environmental System (BTSES-2020)*, Vol. 159, E3S Web Conf. doi: https://doi.org/10.1051/e3sconf/202015904033.

Matarazzo, M., Penco, L., Profumo, G., & Quaglia, R. (2021). Digital transformation and customer value creation in Made in Italy SMEs: A dynamic capabilities perspective. *Journal of Business Research, Elsevier* 123(C), 642–656. Doi: 10.1016/j.jbusres.2020.10.033.

Melnyk, M. V. & Salin, V. N. (2018). Preconditions of effective development of digital economy. *Accounting, Analysis & Auditing* 5(6), 6–16.

Morakanyane, R., Grace, A. A., & O'Reilly, P. (2017). Conceptualizing digital transformation in business organizations: A systematic review of literature. BLED 2017 Proceedings, 21. https://aisel.aisnet.org/bled2017/21.

OECD (2020). Regional Policies to Support Diversification and Productivity Growth in Kazakhstan, OECD Publishing, Paris. www.oecd.org/eurasia/competitiveness-programme/central-asia/Regional-Policies-to-Support-Diversification-and-Productivity-Growth-in-Kazakhstan-ENG.pdf.

OECD (2021). The Digital Transformation of SMEs, OECD Studies on SMEs and Entrepreneurship. OECD Publishing, Paris. Doi: 10.1787/bdb9256a-en.

Oney, C., Özdinç, G., & Çavuşyan, S. (2018). Digital transformation: A mutual understanding and strategic alignment perspective. 39th International Conference on Information Systems, San Francisco, CA, 13–16 December.

Oviedo, A. M., Thomas, M. R., & Karakurum-Ozdemir, K. (2009). Economic informality: Causes, costs, and policies — A literature survey (English). World Bank Working Paper; No. 167. World Bank Group, Washington, DC http://documents.worldbank.org/curated/en/567571468331805356/Economic-informality-causes-costs-and-policies-a-literature-survey.

Patton, M. Q. (2002). *Qualitative Research and Evaluation Methods* (3rd ed.). Sage Publications, Thousand Oaks, CA.

Pelletier, C. & Cloutier, L. M. (2019). Conceptualizing digital transformation in SMEs: An ecosystemic perspective. *Journal of Small Business and Enterprise Development* 26(6/7), 855–876. Doi: 10.1108/JSBED-05-2019-0144.

Peppard, J. (2016). A tool for balancing your company's digital investments. *Harvard Business Review*. Retrieved on November 24, 2022. http12.0s://hbr.org/2016/10/a-tool-for-balancing-your-companys-digital-investments.

Priyono, A., Moin, A., & Putri, V. N. A. O. (2020). Identifying digital transformation paths in the business model of SMEs during the COVID-19 pandemic. *Journal of Open Innovation: Technology, Market, and Complexity* 6(4), 104. Doi: 10.3390/joitmc6040104.

Ramdani, B., Raja, S., & Kayumova, M. (2022). Digital innovation in SMEs: A systematic review, synthesis and research agenda. *Information Technology for Development* 28(1), 1–25. Doi: 10.1080/02681102.2021.1893148.

Roberts, E. B. (1991). *Entrepreneurs in High Technology: Lessons from MIT and Beyond*. Oxford University Press, New York.

Samara, G. & Terzian, J. (2021). Challenges and opportunities for digital entrepreneurship in developing countries. In M. Soltanifar, M. Hughes, & L. Göcke (eds.), *Digital Entrepreneurship*. Future of Business and Finance. Springer, Cham. Doi: 10.1007/978-3-030-53914-6_14.

Satubaldina, A. (2022, April 20). Share of SMEs in Kazakhstan Reaches 34.7 Percent. *The Astana Times*. https://astanatimes.com/2022/04/share-of-smes-in-kazakhstan-reaches-34-7-percent/.

Saunders, M., Lewis, P., & Thornhill, A. (2009). *Research Methods for Business Students*. Pearson, New York.

Szczepańska-Woszczyna, K. (2014). The importance of organizational culture for innovation in the company. *Forum Scientiae Oeconomia* 2(3), 27–39. Retrieved from http://83.230.104.195/index.php/fso/article/view/121.

Siqueira, A. C. O., Webb, J. W., & Bruton, G. D. (2016). Informal entrepreneurship and industry conditions. *Entrepreneurship Theory and Practice* 40(1), 177–200. Doi: 10.1111/etap.12115.

Teal, E. J., Toxanova, A. N., & Izzo, G. M. (2011). Entrepreneurial development in Kazakhstan: A review and update. *Journal of International Business and Cultural Studies*, Academic and Business Research Institute 5, 1–10.

Venkataraman, S. (1997). The distinctive domain of entrepreneurship research: An editor's perspective. In J. Katz et R. Brockhaus (eds.), *Advances in Entrepreneurship, Firm Emergence, and Growth.* JAI Press, Greenwich, CT. Vol. 3, pp. 119–138.

Vial, G. (2019). Understanding digital transformation: A review and a research agenda. *The Journal of Strategic Information Systems* 28(2), 118–144. Doi: 10.1016/j.jsis.2019.01.003.

Westerman, G., Bonnet, D., & McAfee, A. (2014). *Leading Digital: Turning Technology into Business Transformation.* Harvard Business Press, pp. 26–96.

Williams, C. C., Martinez-Perez, A., & Kedir, A. M. (2017). Informal entrepreneurship in developing economies: The impacts of starting up unregistered on firm performance. *Entrepreneurship Theory and Practice* 41(5), 773–799. Doi: 10.1111/etap.12238.

https://doi.org/10.1142/9789811270178_0013

Chapter 13

Sustainability Transformation Journey of Small- and Medium-Sized Enterprises: The Path of a Design Company

Elisabeth Kraut

*Department of Business Administration,
Tallinn University of Technology, Ehitajate tee 5,
Tallinn 19086, Estonia*

elisabeth.kraut@taltech.ee

Abstract

Organizations globally are faced with numerous new challenges in their quest to become more sustainable and environmentally responsible. Challenges arise through institutionalized regulatory measures, environmentally conscious consumers, and sustainability-driven employees pushing corporations to increase their efforts in realizing the transformational change needed in order to preserve the planet. Small- and medium-sized enterprises (SMEs) are indirectly affected by these situational developments throughout the value chain, pressuring them into adherence to the same regulatory measures and ethos of employees and customers. Although SMEs have limited resources available to achieve similar commitments as global corporations, implementing sustainability management is still achievable. SMEs are agile and have the ability to support corporations in improving their own sustainability performance. This chapter proposes a generic framework to SMEs that can aid in their sustainability transformation journey. The study explores the example of one SME, "SCHUMACHER Brand + Interaction Design GmbH" (SCHUMACHER), and what steps it undertook in paving the road toward a sustainability transformation.

13.1. Introduction

As the Brundtland Report described: "Sustainable Development is the development that meets the needs of the present without compromising the ability of future generations to meet their own needs. It is a change process, in which the exploitation of resources, direction of investments, orientation of technological development and institutional change all blend in harmoniously and enhance both current and future potential to meet human needs and aspirations" (Lebel & Kane, 1987, p. 41). At a global scale, fundamental challenges arise with respect to achieving sustainable development, such as "depletion of natural resources, climate change, growing inequality in income and wealth distribution, increasing numbers of people that live in absolute poverty and threats to peace and security are a few examples that illustrate the definitive and unsustainable nature of these developments" (Rockström *et al.*, 2009, p. 1). The study conducted by Rockström on planetary boundaries estimates that some of Earth's "ecological limits, such as rate of biodiversity loss and climate change, have already been exceeded. This imbalance in ecosystems impose imminent threats to the livelihood of humankind" (Rockström *et al.*, 2009, p. 1).

To prevent any further aggravation of these effects, it is essential that sustainability development is regulated by institutes (Gassenferth *et al.*, 2015). The European Commission, for example, has established regulations, such as the EU Taxonomy (European Commission, 2020), and apart from that, the transformation level of companies toward a more sustainable economy is increasing (Kunzlmann *et al.*, 2023; Wadin *et al.*, 2017). More than 20 years ago, Elkington (1998b, 1999) already posited that new business models should be expanded to consider the whole triple bottom line (social, ecological, and economical), regardless of the size of a company. Sustainability is moving closer to the operational management of companies. Increased transparency in the obligations of corporations and the high pressure to deal with these issues have emerged as the main drivers for transformation, as restrictions imposed by regulatory institutions also affect the entire value chain (Kunzlmann *et al.*, 2023). This indirect constraint puts small- and medium-sized enterprises (SMEs) in the same group as large corporate entities. So, regardless of company size, SMEs too need to excel in their nonfinancial performance to meet the requirements that their customers and other stakeholders are facing (Elkington, 1998b; Barbosa *et al.*, 2020, Dentchev *et al.*, 2018). Therefore, it can be said that SMEs also need to provide an excellent nonfinancial performance to meet the requirements their customers and other stakeholders are facing (Elkington, 1998b; Geissdoerfer *et al.*, 2020; Barbosa *et al.*, 2020). This chapter focuses on the example of the small company called "SCHUMACHER," a design company specialized in building brands, and how it has set out to implement sustainability throughout the company.

Starting with an overview of the legal transformation toward a more sustainable economy in Europe, this chapter continues with a short description of the framework and method proposed by Creswell and Clark (2018) that have been used to illustrate how SMEs can introduce sustainability management in their organizational structures, followed by a description of the implementation process and the single steps taken by the example company, SCHUMACHER, in its sustainability transformation journey. In conclusion, a framework is provided with steps for other SMEs to adapt so that they can move toward sustainable transformation and also be pioneers in their industry (Wördenweber, 2017).

13.2. Current Political Changes

In order to understand the tensions SMEs are currently facing, such as exposing their sustainability performance despite the lack of financial, structural, and human resources, it is important to understand the political background. Currently, the regulations regarding the transparency of the sustainability performance of large companies with more than 250 employees are changing. For example, the publication of the supply chain will indirectly affect SMEs as well, as they are suppliers of the large companies. The international and intercontinental political response to climate change is growing. In September 2015, the members of the UN Summit adopted the 17 Sustainable Development Goals (SDGs) as part of a commitment to protect the planet (Agenda 2030, 2021). In addition, the European Union has published the European Green Deal (European Commission, 2019), which aims to guide "the necessary (sustainable) transformative change in our society, economy and industry"

(European Commission, 2019, p. 1) and further provides concrete guidelines toward the climate ambitions for 2030 and 2050, with topics like "clean, affordable and secure energy supply, circular economy, building and renovating in an energy and resource-efficient way, zero pollution ambitions, ecosystems and biodiversity restoration, healthy and environment-friendly food systems and a shift to a sustainable and smart mobility" (European Commission, 2019, p. 3).

In order to achieve the goals set in the Green Deal, the European Commission published, in 2020, the EU Taxonomy to formulate the standards of sustainable management (European Commission, 2020). It is a classification system that categorizes companies' sustainability performances (European Commission, 2020). These definitions will help to measure the extent to which companies' activities are sustainable and aid in the development of sustainable strategies, investments, and lending decisions (European Commission, 2020).

Which and how companies are supposed to implement the EU Taxonomy and what they have to report for were presented on April 21, 2022, by the EU Commission in the form of a directive revision of the Non-Financial Reporting Directive (NFRD) (European Commission, 2014) to the Corporate Sustainability Reporting Directive (CSRD) (European Commission, 2021). The CSRD states that all companies with 250 or more employees are legally required to publish a nonfinancial report of their sustainability performance (European Commission, 2021, 2022); previously, only capital-market-oriented companies with at least 500 employees were obligated to report their sustainability performance (European Commission, 2014). The CSRD also specifies that sustainability reports must be externally audited in the future (European Commission, 2021, 2022). The European Commission expects that, in Europe, the number of companies required to deliver a sustainability report will increase from 39,000 to a total of 50,000 companies (European Commission, April 21, 2021). To express this in terms of time, all previous reportable companies of the NFRD must apply the CSRD as of January 1, 2024, and all new reportable companies as of January 1, 2025, for the retrospective year (European Commission, 2021). Another essential part, besides the CSRD, is the disclosure of supply chains (European Commission, 2021), which is reinforced by the Supply Chain Act (BGB 09/2022). The law aims to improve the protection of human rights in global supply chains (Bundesamt für Wirtschaft und Ausfuhrkontrolle (BAFA), 2022). The Supply Chain Act indicates that companies with at least 3,000 employees from 2023 and those with at least 1,000 employees from 2024 must assume responsibility for human rights due diligence through the activities within their supply chains (BAFA, 2022).

13.3. Initial Situation for the Sustainable Transformation Journey of SMEs

The provided political framework stresses the importance for companies, especially the larger ones, to fundamentally address the implementation of sustainability management in their business processes (European Commission, 2021). Large corporations have the fiduciary responsibility to ensure that their suppliers implement the same values and practices as held by these corporations. For this reason, SMEs are also indirectly inquired about their sustainability performances (BAFA, 2022).

Therefore, there are several reasons why SMEs should also implement and communicate their sustainability strategy, as listed in Table 13.1.

Nevertheless, there are, of course, reasons against the implementation of sustainability strategies, such as reluctance on the part of employees, customers, and management. The reason for skepticism is that a

Table 13.1. Business cases for sustainability based on the work of Schaltegger *et al.* (2012).

Reasons for a sustainable business model for an SME	Exemplary authors
• Better access to certain markets and customers	Ambec and Lanoie (2008)
• New product innovation	Ambec and Lanoie (2008)
• Reducing cost of material, energy, and services	Ormazabal *et al.* (2018, p. 158), Schaltegger *et al.* (2012), Ambec and Lanoie (2008), Schaltegger *et al.* (2012), Christmann (2000), Epstein and Roy (1996)
• Reputation	Schaltegger *et al.* (2012)
• Risk reduction	Schaltegger *et al.* (2012), Schaltegger (2011)
• Attractiveness for employees	Schaltegger *et al.* (2012), Revell *et al.* (2010)

more sustainable business model also causes higher costs (Bocken & Geradts, 2020; Costache *et al.*, 2021; Hueske & Guenther, 2021). But according to a few researchers (e.g., Damanpour *et al.*, 1989; Doppelt, 2008; Deniz, 2016; He & Ortiz, 2021), the process of constructing a sustainable business model and its implementation brings with it sustainable thinking. This way of thinking is innovative in nature and is shown to be a particular strength of SMEs and entrepreneurs (Weissbrod & Bocken, 2017; Hall *et al.*, 2010; Hansen & Große-Dunker, 2013). According to Schaltegger, sustainable activities of SMEs create a positive business impact and economic success through environmental or social activities (Schaltegger *et al.*, 2012, p. 5). In addition, small companies are able to respond more promptly to upcoming transformations due to their relatively smaller company size and flexible organizational work structures (Chesbrough, 2010; Weissbrod & Bocken, 2017). They create new value by incorporating sustainable innovations into the products and services they offer, through which SMEs not only improve their own sustainability performances but also those of their customers (Hansen & Große-Dunker, 2013; Greenberg *et al.*, 2013).

13.4. Method

The aim of this chapter is to provide a framework that illustrates how SMEs can introduce sustainability management in their organizational structures. Using Creswell and Clark's mixed method design approach, shown in Figure 13.1, the author examined the various stages of the process of implementing sustainability in a company. Qualitative and quantitative research methods are combined for this study (Creswell &

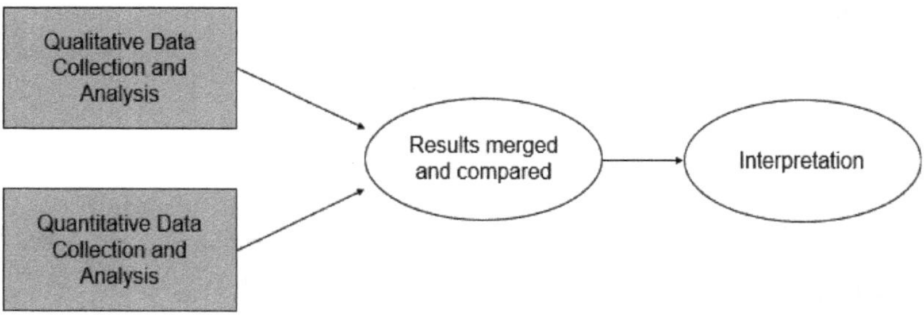

Fig. 13.1. Convergent mixed method design based on the work of Creswell and Clark (2018).

Clark, 2018). In this particular example, data have been collected through the use of quantitative data collection in the form of desk research by screening and analyzing publications from competitors, customers, and suppliers; evaluating workshop results with SCHUMACHER; taking conversation notes; conducting one-to-one interviews; and analyzing internal documents. This is in addition to a qualitative survey of customers, suppliers, and employees. The purpose is to gain a deeper understanding and corroboration (Creswell & Clark, 2018) of the main topics in SCHUMACHER's sustainability transformation.

13.5. Implementation Process of Sustainability Management in SMEs Based on the Example of SCHUMACHER Design

SCHUMACHER Design "develops brands and brand experiences. They are committed to provide their customers with more orientation, identification and relevance in times of change." (SCHUMACHER, 2022a). SCHUMACHER is a small company, comprising 25 employees, and founded in 2003. In its vision of the future, which was further elaborated on in 2021, they intend to make a significant positive impact on the common welfare through their business activities (SCHUMACHER, 2022a). "We see that the communication and design industry has a significant responsibility to provide authentic, transparent and stringent communication. That is why we are already dedicating ourselves to these topics today, in order to be able to serve our customers holistically in the future." says Verena Schumacher, founder of SCHUMACHER Design (Schumacher, 2022f).

13.5.1. *Step 1: Setting a vision*

According to the Deutscher Nachhaltigkeitskodex (DNK, 2022), the first step in implementing sustainability management is setting a vision with related mission statements and targets (2022). In SCHUMACHER's vision of their future, published in 2021, they highlight the opportunities and how they want to promote their values, such as commitment, trust, and sustainability, for their customers (SCHUMACHER, 2021). The company strives to be a "carbon neutral company with a high standard towards their sustainability and ecological responsibility. With its B Corp certification[1] SCHUMACHER has already taken a major step towards embedding sustainability in their company in the future." (SCHUMACHER, 2021).

13.5.2. *Step 2: Setting up a team responsible for sustainability topics*

After formulating the overall commitment ambitions and vision of the company, SCHUMACHER appointed a second person, besides the CEO, with the task of advancing the topic of sustainability (Schumacher, 2022f; Stefanie Wagner, People & Culture, Marketing Manager at SCHUMACHER, 2022).

13.5.3. *Step 3: Framework*

As a third step, SCHUMACHER decided to explore a fitting framework to foster transformation. They chose to get certified by B Corporation (B Corp, 2022), where they presented their performance in the categories of "governance, workers, community, environment and customers" (B Corp, 2022c) in 2022 for the first time. In addition to the verification process by the B Corp analysts, SCHUMACHER must also amend the company's bylaws to officially commit to B Corp values. The B Corp certification takes into account the whole organization and issues its certificate (B Corp, 2022a). Besides the certification, SCHUMACHER voluntarily decided to prepare a sustainability report, despite not being legally required to do so (European Commission, 2021). Their motivation for this is to stringently adhere to their aim of transparent communication with their customers: SCHUMACHER wants to disclose their sustainability engagement to its stakeholders transparently and authentically (Schumacher, 2022f).

---

[1] B Corporation (B Corp) has already certified over 5,000 companies that actively promote a sustainable, social, and fair future. These companies commit to regularly measuring and continuously improving their social and environmental impacts (B Corp Deutschland, 2022).

13.5.3.1. *Results of B Corp certification*

The evaluation of the company's performance by B Corp is currently pending. It is expected that official certification will not be issued by 2022, as B Corp is experiencing capacity shortages (B Corp, 2022b). Despite potential delays, the outlook seems promising. The current B Impact Score, after answering the certification questions, is 90.2 (Table 13.2), with a minimum of 80 points but possibly 181 points to achieve (B Impact Assessment, 2021).

13.5.3.2. *Evaluation and identification of sustainability strategy topics from the B Corp certification*

Taking a deeper look at the B Impact Assessment details, B Corp's evaluations and industry comparisons indicate that SCHUMACHER excels in the following areas:

- Governance (Mission & Engagement and Ethics & Transparency),
- Workers (Health, Wellness, & Safety, Career Development, Engagement & Satisfaction),
- Community (Economic Impact, Civic Engagement & Giving),
- Environment (Environmental Management, Air & Climate, Water, Land & Life),
- Customers (Customer Stewardship).

Table 13.2. Overall B Impact Score: SCHUMACHER.

Category	**Overall score (B impact assessment, 2021)**
Governance	16.7/25
Workers	33.6/56
Community	23.5/50
Environment	11.6/20
Customers	4.6/30
Overall B Impact Score	90.2

On the contrary, areas in which SCHUMACHER still needs to close the gap toward the industry average are:

- Workers (Financial Security),
- Community (Diversity, Equity & Inclusion),
- Customers (Impact Business Model).

The advantage of a B Corp certification is that it provides feedback on the company's own performance and the areas for improvement, as indicated by the feedback structure. This insight can be used to formulate measures which can be directly incorporated into the company's sustainability strategy. With respect to SCHUMACHER, it became clear which areas demand strategic focus.

13.5.4. *Methods to introduce a sustainability strategy*

To successfully introduce a sustainability strategy and implement the resulting changes within the company, it is important to pay attention to the following points. Kurt Lewin proposed a three-stage model, commonly referred to as the Unfreeze–Change–(Re)Freeze method, to understand and manage a change process. In the first stage, the unfreeze period, old behaviors need to be taken out of balance and new behaviors need to be adopted. The second step involves the controlled change of behavioral patterns. Finally, the third stage of change management is the refreeze process. In the first process, the unfreeze period, SCHUMACHER started with making decisions directed toward their own sustainability transformation journey. Corporate sustainability also requires new processes and knowledge that facilitate the acquisition of necessary skills and a way of sustainable thinking (Kuhndt *et al.*, 2004; Deutsches Institut for Normung e.V. (DIN, 2011)). Also, a key to a successful change management process is internal communication about the planned aims of the sustainability strategy (DIN, 2011). During the change process, SCHUMACHER organized several workshops to begin with the implementation of sustainable thinking: "We want to create a business model that has a positive effect, we want to encourage other companies to actively shape sustainability and we want to shape internal initiatives" (SCHUMACHER, 2022b). Employees are also taken into consideration in these initiatives (Schumacher, 2022e). During an internal training, the employees and owners of SCHUMACHER were asked about their understanding of

Table 13.3. Sustainability Definition first employee workshop, $n = 25$ participants (SCHUMACHER, 2022c).

Definition	*N* mentioned
More than ecology	1
Save the planet	2
Long-lasting products & only use as many resources as will grow back	9
Ecological, economic, and social	1
A buzzword	1
Distributional justice	3
Conscious consumption	1
Environment-friendly raw materials	1
Nonprofit projects	1
Reduce carbon footprint and pay more for carbon compensation	3
Sustainable mobility	2
Less plastic	1
Social factor	1
Support and establish natural cycles	1
Conscious confrontation	1
A big topic	1
Social factor	1
Reuse	1

sustainability (everyone was allowed to share as many thoughts as they liked).

The content of Table 13.3 suggests that the Brundtland definition of sustainability is also in the minds of SCHUMACHER's employees. The aim of the training part was for the employees to develop a common initial understanding of sustainability and to bridge their knowledge differences (Schumacher, 2022f), as advised by Conner and Prahalad (1996). So, the unfreeze phase and parts of the change have begun.

In the training sessions topics like challenges, political changes, which fields are becoming relevant for companies, how the importance of sustainaiblity reporting and communication is growing have been discussed. Also if there are new opportunities for SCHUMACHER, as well as the challenge of building sustainability communication in such a way that it does not become greenwashing (SCHUMACHER, 2022b). The employees were asked which SDGs[2] they see as particularly relevant for SCHUMACHER, and every participant was asked to contribute a maximum of three points. It was found that SDG 5 Gender Equality ($n = 10$), SDG 8 Decent Work and Economic Growth ($n = 8$), SDG 11 Sustainable Cities and Communities ($n = 6$), SDG 12 Sustainable Consumption and Production ($n = 9$), SDG 13 Climate Action ($n = 5$), and SDG 17 Partnerships to Achieve the Goals ($n = 5$) are the most important SDGs for SCHUMACHER employees (SCHUMACHER, 2022c). Furthermore, the expectations of the employees regarding the transformation toward a sustainable company were worked out once again in the training session. They wanted a common understanding of corporate behavior and a good exchange between the management and the employees (SCHUMACHER, 2022c), which is part of the change, according to Lewin's model. In SCHUMACHER's sustainability strategy, it should be noted that in the step of knowledge transfer and the involvement of employees, as an important stakeholder and implementer, they need a common understanding of values and that, from their point of view, sustainability is reflected in the conscious use of resources and the reduction of the carbon footprint. As SCHUMACHER has a great influence in the areas of gender equality, economic growth, sustainable cities and communities, sustainable consumption, and their partnerships, this is also where the greatest fields of action lie. Hence, for those fields, a common corporate behavior, including continuous communication, will be developed. After the change process, SCHUMACHER aims for a sustainable thinking culture as the new organizational routine as a new standard (Yang *et al.*, 2021).

13.5.5. *Stakeholder analysis and materiality matrix*

Conducting a stakeholder analysis and a materiality analysis is a crucial step in implementing reliable sustainability management. According to ISO 26000, "an organization should identify who has an interest in its decisions and activities in order to understand what impact they have and how to deal with them" (DIN, 2022, p. 12). This can only be achieved through dialogue with key stakeholders (Deutscher Nachhaltigkeitskodex, 2022).

[2]"The 17 Sustainable Development Goals (SDGs) are political targets set by the United Nations (UN) to ensure sustainable development at the economic, social and environmental levels worldwide." (United Nations, 2022).

Edward Freeman first laid the foundation for stakeholder theory for the development of strategic approaches in 1984. He defined stakeholder groups in such a way that they can contribute to the success of the company or can significantly influence the company; therefore, they should be taken into account in the strategy (Freeman, 2011). This is also the case in the development of a sustainability strategy (Isenmann *et al.*, 2009). In the context of sustainability, there is also the question of what impact the company's activities have on the environmental and/or social challenges (EFRAG, 2022). Also, it shows the other way around: how the future development from an ecological and social perspective influences the company from the outside. (Deutscher Nachhaltigkeitskodex, 2022). Intensive and continuous stakeholder dialogue can become a partnership exchange that can also lead to a competitive advantage by better adapting to the challenges together, sharing knowledge and best practices, and thus keeping transaction costs down (Dyer & Singh, 1998). SCHUMACHER also decided to conduct a stakeholder survey, which they divided into two steps.

13.5.5.1. *SCHUMACHER's definition of stakeholders*

It is important for SCHUMACHER to engage with its stakeholders to find out what their requirements are. Moreover, because SCHUMACHER creates added value for their stakeholders, it is essential for them to know what SCHUMACHER does (Freeman *et al.*, 2010a). During a workshop with SCHUMACHER's sustainability team, the primary and secondary stakeholder groups were identified, as shown in Table 13.4. They are

Table 13.4. Stakeholder analysis.

Primary stakeholders	**Secondary stakeholders**
• Suppliers	• Market companions and competitors
• Customers	• Press and media
• Employees	• The public
• Management	• Cooperation partner
	• Banks
	• B Corp & B Corp network
	• Authorities
	• Stakeholders in the local economy and politics

aligned with the stakeholder theory proposed by Freeman *et al.* (2010a, 2010b).

13.5.5.2. *Benchmark*

To get a feel for the sustainability issues and the requirements of the stakeholders, SCHUMACHER started with an analysis of the environment and, in the course of this, first checked the documents available online from its most important market companions on the subject of sustainability. Among them were three agencies that were analyzed, as summarized in Table 13.5.

In summary, it can be seen that all agencies are climate neutral. They have published a concrete sustainability strategy, and some have already published reports with key figures. In addition, some already offer

Table 13.5. Comparison of Competitives SCHUMACHER (SCHUMACHER, 2022b).

Agency 1	Agency 2	Agency 3	Topic
• Implemented and published sustainability strategy	• Implemented and published sustainability strategy incl. aims	• Concrete outlook for the measures in the coming year	**Sustainability strategy and concrete measures**
• New product innovations: climate-neutral products	• Already has some experience in sustainability reporting		**Now products and innovations**
• Sociopolitical commitment within the region			**Social responsibility**
• Advises clients on how to implement an impactful activity	• Support and advise their clients to create sustainable brands	• Uses their knowledge and experience to inspire their clients	**Consult their own clients**
• Climate-neutral company	• Climate-neutral company & works on consistent improvement and reduction	• Climate-neutral company & wants to be climate positive	**Climate neutral**
		• B Corp certified	**Certifications**

innovative products or, at least, share their experience and knowledge with their customers and advise them on the topics. SCHUMACHER can now include these topics in their own sustainability performance.

13.5.5.3. *Qualitative survey: Materiality analysis*

Based on the above and the topic points from Sections 13.5.1 to 13.5.5.2, a questionnaire has been developed and was used for a quantitative survey of data. The management decided to conduct the survey anonymously for suppliers ($n = 6$), customers ($n = 10$), and employees ($n = 16$) (Schumacher, 2022f). The goal was "to identify issues and expectations from a wider range of stakeholders and sources to embed the outcomes into internal decision-making processes and create a license to operate in the external review" (Hsu *et al.*, 2013, p. 144). The top themes that emerged from the survey from all three survey groups (SCHUMACHER, 2022d) are listed in Table 13.6.

After these topics were consolidated, the following top issues arose for all the stakeholder groups under consideration, which represent internal and external materiality (SCHUMACHER, 2022d):

- pleasant working atmosphere;
- environmental aspects consideration when selecting suppliers;
- environment-friendly innovative solutions;
- transparent, fast, and correct communication with customers;

Table 13.6. Results of the stakeholder survey.

Employees	Customers	Partners and suppliers
• Sustainable behavior • Pleasant working atmosphere • Lively, cooperative management culture • Inclusion as a team member • Access to processes • Flexible locations & working models • Team events • Employee skills development	• Environmental aspects in the selection of suppliers • Transparent, fast, and concrete communication with customers • Waste minimization • Environment-friendly innovative solutions • Pleasant working environment • Diversity in the workforce • Offering CO_2-neutral products • Energy origin	• Energy origin • Recycling • Environment-friendly innovative solutions • Pleasant working climate • Diversity in the workforce • Sustainability communication • Transparent, fast, and concrete communication with customers • Environmental aspects in the selection of suppliers

- diversity in the workforce;
- energy origin.

These are important insights that SCHUMACHER has gained as a result, and they are also the needs that stakeholders are most interested in. Therefore, they should play an important role in SCHUMACHER's sustainability orientation.

13.5.5.4. *Double materiality impact and business relevance*

After all the above steps had been completed, an inside-out analysis (How can I with my business influence or improve our environment and society?) and the business relevance outside-in (How will sustainability topics influence my business in the future?) has been made (EFRAG, 2022). To address the possible risks and look at the main changing potentials, a strategy workshop with the management, the sustainability manager, and an external consulting company was held to reevaluate the matrix

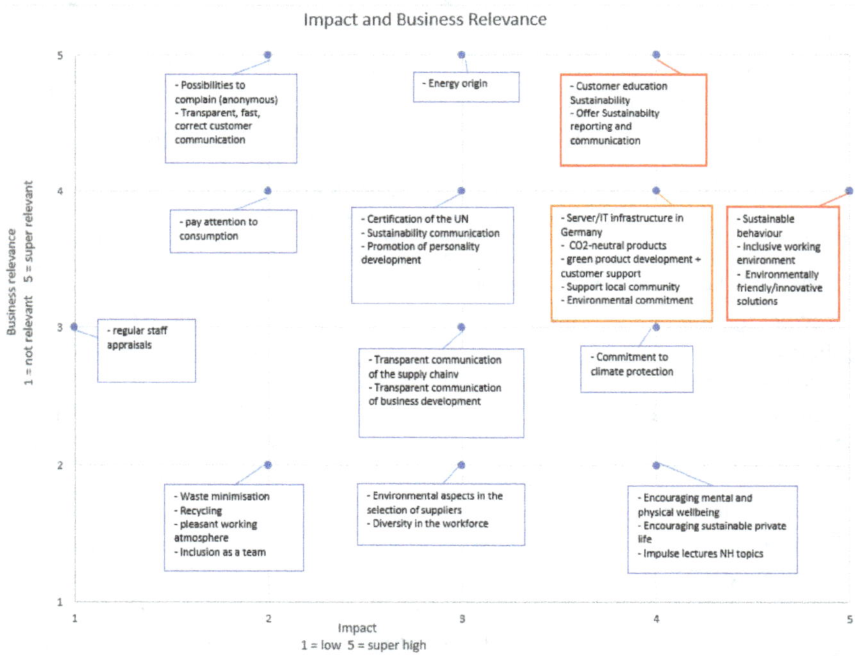

Fig. 13.2. Impact and business relevance.

(SCHUMACHER, 2022d). Figure 13.2 is the result of this analysis of business and impact relevance, which is a new process required by companies who have to apply for the CSRD and, therefore, the new reporting standard ESRS (EFRAG, 2022). The red- and yellow-bordered boxes denote the most important topics that have been evaluated.

13.5.6. *Step 3: Identifying key fields and formulating a strategy*

According to ISO 26000, the "identification of the key fields of action for corporate responsibility as well as principles and approaches for implementing social responsibility" (DIN, 2022, p. 12) is the core discipline for creating a sustainability strategy. Hence, SCHUMACHER applied this instruction to create a unique selling proposition and a competitive advantage (Prieto-Sandoval *et al*., 2019; Schumacher, 2022e). This is the reason why SCHUMACHER looked at both internal and external factors beforehand (Schumacher, 2022e). Like Porter (1985) said, a competitive advantage exists when an organization can provide more value for its stakeholders than its competitors (Prieto-Sandoval *et al.*, 2019). In order to consolidate the analyses and results, the management, the sustainability officer, and the consultants met for a final sustainability strategy workshop.

In this workshop, the high-level themes for an overall strategy have been elaborated upon, and the fields of action have been determined based on the previous analyses. The results are summarized in Table 13.7.

13.5.7. *Further steps: Sustainability report and communication*

Sustainability reporting is important because it ensures the transparent presentation of the company's situation with regard to nonfinancial endeavors and KPIs (DIN, 2022). SCHUMACHER has set out to develop a sustainability strategy and to address the issue fundamentally because, even as a small company, they consider sustainability a central part of their business. At the time of writing this book chapter, SCHUMACHER had not yet started to elaborate on these defined fields of action as a strategy and set concrete action plans behind them. Nevertheless, this is planned as a further step. The drafting of a sustainability report has also been initiated, but only internal documents are currently available (SCHUMACHER, 2022b). However, they plan to start internal and

Table 13.7. Superordinate topics for the corporate transformation of SCHUMACHER.

High-level themes for the company's transformation:

Main topics in this area: B Corp Certification, amending the Articles of Association and committing the management to integrate sustainability as a central part of the company's core (which is also important for the B Corp certification), and establishing internal and external communication about sustainability topics.

Secondary themes: Design for democracy, developing an understanding of sustainability values, giving preference to local suppliers, promoting access for disadvantaged groups, and transparent communication of business development internally and externally.

Engagement	People	Ecology	Value chain/partners	Expertise
Collaboration for sustainability — more partnerships, supporting local communities, expand engagement for the common good, expand donations, volunteering	Employee competencies and promotion of personal development, pleasant working atmosphere through lived values, promoting diversity, encouraging a sustainable private life, involving the team in company decisions, family-friendly company, anonymous grievance mechanisms, expanding the content of onboarding processes, include sustainability in job descriptions, health and well-being offers, designing an inclusive working environment	Commitment to climate protection and the environment, to become a climate-neutral agency, anchor an environmental guideline, climate-neutral meetings, bicycle campaigns	Adapt supplier selection criteria, transparent, correct, and fast customer communication, support sustainable suppliers	Sustainable product innovations, environment-friendly carbon footprint materials CO_2-neutral hosting

external communications in the form of their own website development in 2023 (Schumacher, 2022e, 2022f; SCHUMACHER, 2022b).

13.6. Sustainability Transformation Journey

The aim of this chapter was to use the practical example of SCHUMACHER to illustrate how SMEs of similar sizes and belonging to similar sectors can implement their own sustainability management through a series of steps, which are concisely presented in the following:

(1) **Establishing a vision:** Step 1 involves the creation of a vision that acts as a guiding force behind sustainability engagement. The vision puts into words the impact the company wishes to make. The vision of all stakeholders works toward the same, overarching goals. It also provides a competitive advantage as it helps the company to differentiate itself through establishing a unique selling point (Dermol, 2012). The integrity of a company is essential for it to set into motion the plan and actions to realize that vision. Organizations that do otherwise can quickly be accused of greenwashing (Galpin *et al.*, 2015). Therefore, it is essential for sustainability to be embedded into a strategy so that its holistic effects are truly visible.

(2) **Building a responsible team:** Assigning a responsible person or group is essential to achieving the sustainability transformation (Davis *et al.*, 1997, p. 29).

(3) **Adhering to regulatory frameworks:** Regulatory frameworks foster the urgency for companies to change. Frameworks applicable to this study are the guideline ISO 26000, the certification of B Corp, and the reporting standards of DNK, GRI, SASB, and ESRS. It is important to be aware of which legal regulations apply to the company and then choose the most fitting ones to act accordingly. Though GRI, ESRS, and GRI are mostly used internationally, DNK and ISO 26000 are more applicable for SMEs.

(4) **Promoting team engagement and facilitating knowledge transfer:** Regular training, meetings, and workshops conducted by the management promote sustainable thinking, which, in turn, facilitates sustainable innovation (Kuhndt *et al.*, 2004). In addition to the development of internal knowledge, knowledge-building about sustainability can also be incorporated into the recruiting process, as identified by

SCHUMACHER as a field of action (see Table 13.7), and into employees' target agreements (Galpin *et al.*, 2015). It is the task of managers to create a culture that embraces sustainability. This includes letting employees participate in the development process (Galpin *et al.*, 2015).

(5) **Stakeholder analysis and materiality matrix:** Building upon the triple bottom line principle (Elkington, 1998a), it illustrates that in becoming more sustainable, a vast number of actions can be identified. Companies, therefore, need to manage and address the expectations of their stakeholders (Freeman *et al.*, 2010b) in order to discern what is truly essential. Managers in organizations can achieve this through effective communication with internal and external stakeholders (Desmidt *et al.*, 2011). The active involvement of stakeholder groups can even lead to long-term partnerships (Dyer & Singh, 1998).

(6) **Identifying key areas and formulating a strategy:** The pivotal question to SMEs in this step is "what aspects from the previous steps can we use to identify the key areas of impact?" Once this is answered, SMEs need to come up with measuring instruments and set priorities for what to measure. A common sentence in financial reporting and overall company strategy is: "What gets measured, gets managed" (Davies, 2002, p. 129). This also applies to sustainability strategies. However, what KPIs to consider depend on the type of company, the sector, and its aims (Hristov & Chirico, 2019). SCHUMACHER carried out iterations and enlisted the help of external experts to determine the strategic areas of action and the corresponding measurements and goals to measure the progress of the sustainability transformation. It must be added that SCHUMACHER measures its sustainability performance even today by monitoring its carbon footprint, which can be extended. At this point, it should be mentioned that the support of digital tools for measuring and monitoring sustainability performance can also be useful for SMEs. Especially because the large companies will be subject to machine readability of their sustainability reports in the future (EFRAG, 2022), information from their suppliers, which are mostly SMEs, can be passed on faster and more accurately. For this reason, the digitalization of sustainability data plays a key role in the formulation of a sustainability strategy.

(7) **Internal and external communications:** "You cannot, not communicate," said Paul Watzlawick. Because both external and internal stakeholders want to know how far a company is on its sustainability

transformation journey, the latter is also a part of stakeholder communication. SCHUMACHER introduced internal meetings and workshops to present to employees the current state of its journey toward a sustainable company. Employees' engagement and commitment can increase when they are able to actively participate in the development of the next steps toward more sustainable thinking (Galpin *et al.*, 2015). Preparing its sustainability report is another way in which SCHUMACHER shows external stakeholders its sustainability performance.

13.7. Conclusion

This chapter gives a brief insight into the current process of change toward a more sustainable economy supported by the new legal regulations. The focus is on the following questions: How can these changes affect SMEs? and how can they implement a more sustainability economy in their companies' structures? The following section sets the focus on how these changes affect SMEs and how they can implement a more sustainable economy in their companies' structures. For this purpose, the example of the design agency SCHUMACHER is used. Using qualitative and quantitative data, these steps are supported and lead to the sustainable strategy of the company. This example provides a basis for assuming that similar companies can take the same steps to implement a sustainability strategy in their companies. This generates the sustainability transformation journey for SMEs. By following the steps: first, establishing a vision and building a responsible team; second, being informed about the regulations applicable to the company and its stakeholders; third, promoting team engagement and facilitating knowledge transfer; fourth, conducting a stakeholder analysis and developing a materiality matrix; fifth, identifying key areas based on the stakeholder analysis and formulation of a strategy; and finally, developing internal and external communication plans, managers of SMEs have the means and tools to shape their path toward creating a more sustainable organization. Company culture, effective communication, and stakeholder management are essential to foster sustainable thinking and prompt behavior in employees to make change happen.

The case of SCHUMACHER sets an example for other SMEs. It illustrated how the company followed a series of steps to reach effective sustainability management and, consequently, successfully transform in a holistic fashion into a sustainable organization. Exploring different methodological approaches and cases in the future can help in reaching a better understanding of the sustainability transformation journeys of SMEs. Future studies could investigate the long-term effects of the transformational change journey. Various challenges and enablers in SCHUMACHER's case in the creation of its sustainability transformation journey have been excluded. Further research can examine whether SMEs have different enablers and barriers than corporations.

Acknowledgment

The author is most grateful to SCHUMACHER for being willing to share its information about the sustainability transformation journey and provide access to its proprietary data. Good luck to all SMEs who are embarking on their sustainability transformation journey.

References

2030 Agenda (2021). Die Agenda 2030. Infos zu den SDGs. Hg. v. Global Policy Forum Europe e.V. Forum Umwelt und Entwicklung. https://www.2030agenda.de/de, zuletzt aktualisiert am 29.08.2021, (accessed 31 August 2021).

Ambec, S., & Lanoie, P. (2008). Does it pay to be green? A systematic overview. *The Academy of Management Perspectives* 22(4), 45–62.

B Corp (2022a). B Lab Global Site. https://www.bcorporation.net/en-us, (accessed 13 November 2022).

B Corp (2022b). Delay of BCorp Certification, 27 July 2022. E-Mail to SCHUMACHER Brand + Interaction Design GmbH. E-Mail.

B Corp (2022c). B Impact Assessment. https://www.bcorporation.net/en-us/programs-and-tools/b-impact-assessment/, (accessed 17 November 2022).

B Corp Deutschland (2022). Unsere Mission — B Corp Deutschland. https://www.bcorporation.de/unsere-mission, (accessed 13 November 2022).

B Impact Assessment (2021). SCHUMACHER Brand + Interaction Design GmbH Active Assessment Fical Year End Date: 31 December 2021.

Barbosa, M., Castañeda-Ayarza, J., Lombardo, F., & Denise, H. (2020). Sustainable Strategic Management (GES): Sustainability in small business. *Journal of Cleaner Production* 258, 1–11. Doi: 10.1016/j.jclepro.2020.120880.

BGB (09/2022). Lieferkettensorgfaltspflichtengesetz. LkSG. https://www.buzer.de/s1.htm?g=LkSG&f=1, (accessed 25 September 2022).

Bocken, N. & Geradts, T. (2020). Barriers and drivers to sustainable business model innovation: Organization design and dynamic capabilities. *Long Range Plan* 53, 101950.

Bundesamt für Wirtschaft und Ausfuhrkontrolle (BAFA) (2022). Risiken ermitteln, gewichten und priorisieren. Wirtschaft & Menschenrechte. Eschborn.

Chesbrough, H. (2010). Business model innovation: Opportunities and barriers. *Long Range Planning,* 43(2–3), 354–363. Doi: 10.1016/j.lrp.2009.07.010.

Christmann, P. (2000). Effects of "best practices" of environmental management on cost advantage: The role of complementary assets. *Academy of Management Journal* 43(4), 663–680.

Conner, K. R. & Prahalad, C. K. (1996). A resource-based theory of the firm: Knowledge versus opportunism. *Organization Science* 7(5), 477–501. Doi: 10.1287/orsc.7.5.477.

Costache, C., Dumitrascu, D., & Maniu, I. (2021). Facilitators of and barriers to sustainable development in small and medium-sized enterprises: A descriptive exploratory study in Romania. *Sustainability* 13(6), S. 3213. Doi: 10.3390/su13063213.

Creswell, J. W. & Clark, V. L. P. (2018). *Mixed Methods Research. Designing and Conduct* (3rd ed.). Sage Publications Inc. California.

Damanpour, F., Szabat, K. A., & Evan, W. M. (1989). The relationship between types of innovation and organizational performance. *Journal of Management Studies* 26(6), S 587–602. Doi: 10.1111/j.1467-6486.1989.tb00746.x.

Davies, J. E. (2002). What gets measured, gets managed: Statistics and performance indicators for evidence based management. *Journal of Librarianship and Information Science* 34, 129–133. Doi: 10.1177/096100060203400030.

Davis, J. H., Schoorman, F. D., & Donaldson, L. (1997). Toward a stewardship theory of management. *Academy of Management Review* 22(1), 20–47.

Deniz, D. (2016). Sustainable thinking and environmental awareness through design education. *Procedia Environmental Sciences* 34, 70–79. Doi: 10.1016/j.proenv.2016.04.008.

Dentchev, N., Rauter, R., Jóhannsdóttir, L., Snihur, Y., Rosano, M., Baumgartner, R. *et al.* (2018). Embracing the variety of sustainable business models: A prolific field of research and a future research agenda. *Journal of Cleaner Production* 194, 695–703. Doi: 10.1016/j.jclepro.2018.05.156.

Dermol, V. (2012). Relationship between mission statement and company performance. *Annals of the Alexandru Ioan Cuza University — Economics* 59(1), 325–341. Doi: 10.2478/v10316-012-0022-9.

Desmidt, S., Prinzie, A., & Decramer, A. (2011). Looking for the value of mission statements: A meta-analysis of 20 years of research. *Management Decision* 49(3), 468–483. Doi: 10.1108/00251741111120806.

Deutscher Nachhaltigkeitskodex (2022). Deutscher Nachhaltigkeitskodex — Nutzen des DNK. Online: https://www.deutscher-nachhaltigkeitskodex.de/de-DE/Home/DNK/Benefits-of-DNK, (accessed 13 November 2022).

DIN Deutsches Institut for Normung e.V. (2022). Guidance on social responsibility (ISO 26000) 2011.

Doppelt, B. (2008). The power of sustainable thinking. How to create a positive future for the climate, the planet, your organization and your life. London, Sterling.

Dyer, J. H., & Singh, H. (1998). The relational view: Cooperative strategy and sources of interorganizational competitive advantage. *Academy of Management Review* 23(4), 660–679.

EFRAG (2022). ESRS 2 General, strategy, governance and materiality assessment. ESRS. https://www.efrag.org/Assets/Download?assetUrl=%2Fsites%2Fwebpublishing%2FSiteAssets%2FED_ESRS_2.pdf, (accessed 18 November 2022).

Elkington, J. (1998a & 1998b). Accounting for the triple bottom line. *Measuring Business Excellence* 2(3), 18–22. Doi: 10.1108/eb025539.

Elkington, R. (1999). Cannibals with forks: The triple bottom line of 21st century business. *Choice Reviews* 7, Doi: 10.5860/choice.36-3997.

Epstein, M. & Roy, M. (1996). Managing corporate environmental performance a multinational perspective. Irwin Professional Publ. 1996.

European Commission (2014). Non-Financial Reporting Directive (NFRD) https://eur-lex.europa.eu/legal-content/EN/TXT/PDF/?uri=CELEX:32014L0095 (accessed 5 September 2022).

European Commission (2019). Communication from the Commission to the European Parliament, the European council, the council, the European economic and social committee and the committee of the regions. The European Green Deal. https://eur-lex.europa.eu/resource.html?uri=cellar:b828d165-1c22-11ea-8c1f-01aa75ed71a1.0002.02/DOC_1&format=PDF (accessed 5 September 2022).

European Commission (2020). EU Taxonomie. https://eur-lex.europa.eu/legal-content/EN/TXT/PDF/?uri=CELEX:32020R0852 (accessed 25 September 2022).

European Commission (2021). Sustainable finance package. Corporate Sustainability Reporting Directive (CSRD). Hg. v. European Commission. https://finance.ec.europa.eu/publications/sustainable-finance-package_en (accessed 25 September 2022).

European Commission (21 April 2021). Sustainable Finance and EU Taxonomy. https://ec.europa.eu/commission/presscorner/detail/en/ip_21_1804 (accessed 5 November 2022).

European Commission (2022). Directive of the European Parliament and of the Council 2022 as regards corporate sustainability reporting. https://data.consilium.europa.eu/doc/document/ST-10835-2022-INIT/X/pdf (accessed 25 September 2022).

Freeman, R. E. (2011). *Strategic Management. A Stakeholder Approach.* Cambridge University Press, Cambridge.

Freeman, R. E., Harrison, J. S., Wicks, A. C., Parmar, B. L., & Colle, S. de (2010a & b). *Stakeholder Theory. The State of the Art*. Cambridge University Press, Cambridge.

Galpin, T., Whitttington, J. L., & Bell, G. (2015). Is your sustainability strategy sustainable? Creating a culture of sustainability. *Corporate Governance* 15(1), 1–17. Doi: 10.1108/CG-01-2013-0004.

Gassenferth, W., Da Conceição, C. M., Machado, M. A. S., Pereira, S., & Krause, W. (2015). Gestão de Negócios e Sustentabilidade. *Textos selecionados*: Brasport.

Geissdoerfer, M., Pieroni, M., Pigosso, M., & Soufani, K. (2020). Circular business models: A review. *Journal of Cleaner Production* 277. Doi: 10.1016/j.jclepro.2020.123741.

Greenberg, D., McKone-Sweet, K., & Wilson, H. J. (2013). Entrepreneurial leaders: Creating opportunity in an unknowable world. *Leader to Leader* 67, 56–62. Doi: 10.1002/ltl.20063.

Hall, J. K., Daneke, G. A., & Lenox, M. J. (2010). Sustainable development and entrepreneurship: Past contributions and future directions. *Journal of Business Venturing* 25(5), 439–448. Doi: 10.1016/j.jbusvent.2010.01.002.

Hansen, E. G. & Große-Dunker (2013). Sustainability oriented innovation. *Encyclopedia of Corporate*, Artikel 1.

He, J. & Ortiz, J. (2021). Sustainable business modeling: The need for innovative design thinking. *Journal of Cleaner Production* 298, 126751. Doi: 10.1016/j.jclepro.2021.126751.

Hristov, I. & Chirico, A. (2019). The Role of Sustainability Key Performance Indicators (KPIs) in Implementing Sustainable Strategies. *Sustainability* 11(20), 5742. Doi: 10.3390/su11205742.

Hsu, C., Lee, W., & Chao, W. (2013). Materiality analysis model in sustainability reporting: A case study at Lite-On Technology Corporation. *Journal of Cleaner Production* 57, 142–151. Doi: 10.1016/j.jclepro.2013.05.040.

Hueske, A. & Guenther, E. (2021). Multilevel barrier and driver analysis to improve sustainability implementation strategies: Towards sustainable operations in institutions of higher education. *Journal of Cleaner Production* 291, 125899. Doi: 10.1016/j.jclepro.2021.125899.

Isenmann, R., Gómez, J. M., Amelung, M., Arndt, H., Behrens, B., & Bergmann, U. *et al.* (2009). Internetbasierte Nachhaltigkeitsberichterstattung. Maßgeschneiderte Stakeholder-Kommunikation mit IT, *Erich Schmidt Verlag*, Berlin.

Kunzlmann, J., Edinger-Schons, L., & Kraemer, A. (2023). Sustainability Management Monitor. https://www.sustainabilitytransformation.org/, (accessed 25 September 2023).

Lebel, G. C. & Kane, H. (1987). *A Guide to Our Common Future*. Oxford University Press (Oxford paperbacks), New York.

Ormazabal, M., Prieto-Sandoval, V., Puga-Leal, R., & Jaca, C. (2018). Circular economy in Spanish SMEs: Challenges and opportunities. *Journal of Cleaner Production* 185, 157–167. Doi: 10.1016/j.jclepro.2018.03.031.

Prieto-Sandoval, V., Jaca, C., Javier, S., Baumgartner, R. J., & Ormazabal, M. (2019). Key strategies, resources, and capabilities for implementing circular economy in industrial small and medium enterprises. *Corporate Social Responsibility and Environment Management* 26(6), 1473–1484. Doi: 10.1002/csr.1761.

Revell, A., Stokes, D., & Chen, H. (2010). Small businesses and the environment: turning over a new leaf? *Business Strategy and the Environment* 19(5), 273–288.

Rockström, J., Steffen, W., Noone, K., Persson, A., Chapin, F. S., & Lambin, E. *et al.* (2009). Planetary boundaries: Exploring the safe operating space for humanity. *E&S* 14(2). Doi: 10.5751/ES-03180-140232.

Schaltegger, S. (2011). Sustainability as a driver for corporate economic success. Consequences for the development of sustainability management control. *Society and Economy* 33(1), 15–28.

Schaltegger, S., Lüdeke-Freund, F., & Hansen, E. G. (2012). Business cases for sustainability. The role of business model innovation for corporate sustainability. *International Journal of Innovation and Sustainable Development* 6(2), 95–119.

SCHUMACHER (2021). Zukunftsbild SCHUMACHER Brand + Interaction Design GmbH. Internal Document 2021.

SCHUMACHER (2022a). Agentur — Arbeitsweisen, Team und Kunden — SCHUMACHER Brand + Interaction Design GmbH. Berlin, Darmstadt und Remote. https://schumacher-design.de/agentur/, (accessed 13 November 2022).

SCHUMACHER (2022b). Schulungsprogramme & Erstberatung. Darmstadt, 19 April 2022. Workshop protocol.; *Presentation & Workshop.*

SCHUMACHER (2022c). Auswertungen Mitarbeitenden Workshop. Darmstadt, 30 June 2022. Workshop an Mitarbeitenden SCHUMACHER. Internes Dokument: *Miro Boards*.

SCHUMACHER (2022d). Strategieworkshop, 4 October 2022. Internes Dokument. *Powerpoint*.

SCHUMACHER Design & Wagner S. — People & Culture, Marketing Manager at (2022). Sustainability at SCHUMACHER Brand + Interaction Design GmbH, Darmstadt. *Teams*.

Schumacher, M. (2022e). Sustainability at SCHUMACHER Brand + Interaction Design GmbH. Darmstadt. *Teams*.

Schumacher, V. (2022f). Sustainability at SCHUMACHER Brand + Interaction Design GmbH. Darmstadt. *Teams*.

Seiler-Hausmann, J. D., Liedtke, C., & von Weizsäcker, E. U. (Eds.) (2004). *Eco-Efficiency and Beyond. Towards the Sustainable Enterprise.* Greenleaf Publishing Limited, pp. 64–72.

United Nations (2022). THE 17 GOALS | Sustainable Development. Agenda 2030. Online: https://sdgs.un.org/goals, (accessed 18 November 2022).

Wadin, J., Ahlgren, K., & Bengtsson, L. (2017). Joint business model innovation for sustainable transformation of industries — A large multinational utility in alliance with a small solar energy company. *Journal of Cleaner Production* 160, 139–150. Doi: 10.1016/j.jclepro.2017.03.151.

Weissbrod, I. & Bocken, N. M. P. (2017). Developing sustainable business experimentation capability — A case study. *Journal of Cleaner Production* 142, 2663–2676. Doi: 10.1016/j.jclepro.2016.11.009.

Wördenweber, M. (2017). Nachhaltigkeitsmanagement. Grundlagen und Praxis unternehmerischen Handelns, *Schäffer-Poeschel Verlag*, Stuttgart.

Yang, N. N., Bertassini, A. C., Mendes, J. A. J., & Gerolamo, M. C. (2021). The '3CE2CE' framework — Change management towards a circular economy: Opportunities for agribusiness. *Circular Economy and Sustainability* 1(2), 697–718. Doi: 10.1007/s43615-021-00057-6.

https://doi.org/10.1142/9789811270178_0014

Chapter 14

Conclusions and Outlook

Aive Pevkur*,‡ and Susanne Durst*,†,§

**Department of Business Administration, Tallinn University of Technology, Ehitajate tee 5, Tallinn 19086, Estonia*

†Department of Business Administration, Reykjavik University, Menntavegi 1, 102 Reykjavík, Iceland

‡aive.pevkur@taltech.ee

§susanned@ru.is

Abstract

Throughout this book, the interested reader would have gained insights into different perspectives on the topic of digital transformation for entrepreneurship. The aim of the concluding chapter is to highlight some main takeaways that may initiate the next concrete steps.

14.1. Main Takeaways: Thoughts From Chapters

Digitalization has come to stay and expand further. Entrepreneurial activities, especially those of smaller companies (the younger ones in particular), tend to be more digitalized than more resource-intensive trades or activities, as modern entrepreneurship is often characterized by digitization and agility is achieved or promoted through digital transformation (DT). As digitalization enables companies to pay even better attention to customer needs and feedback, they, especially small- and medium-sized enterprises (SMEs), can make their business models even more service oriented. The increasing number of digital solutions facilitates cooperation and the creation of new digital ecosystems.

Not surprisingly, there are increasing debates about digitalization and DT. These discussions are taking place at different levels. In academic literature, there is a growing text corpus of studies with a normative character. These studies highlight what should be the best DT approaches and what are the positive and negative risks and implications to take into account regarding DT.

In this book, we aimed to present a collection of both theoretical or conceptual analyses and practical examples contributing to the elaboration of DT for entrepreneurship. As regards the latter, these examples are not just from the Global North, which is often considered a role model for other regions of the world, but also from Kazakhstan, a country that has a population that is higher than the ones in the Netherlands, Finland, or Sweden, countries that are often named in conjunction with DT, but with the majority of economies also driven by SMEs.

Implementing DT in companies is a challenging task, even more so in smaller companies due to limited resources and, sometimes, the mindsets of these firms' owner-managers. A systematic approach to knowledge management (KM) may help smaller firms better use their scarce knowledge resources and channel them in a way so that they support not only DT but also other internal and external challenges the company has to cope with.

The COVID-19 pandemic has, however, accelerated the adoption of digital tools and solutions, e.g., the use of e-commerce platforms. Being part of an e-commerce platform has its advantages, but it also might have hidden disadvantages for those smaller companies that have to use the digital platforms without the right to participate in their development or to gain benefits from doing so.

Progressive digitalization generates even more data. Thus, data management, particularly how to cope with the data, has become a further challenge, especially in smaller firms that do not have sufficient personnel with the right skills and expertise; in the worst case, there is none. At the same time, the legal framework to manage data correctly is still weak; thus, there are a lot of expectations and pressure on individual enterprises.

In this context, sustainability requirements must not be neglected. Smaller companies are also increasingly required to disclose their activities in this regard. The sustainability goals address three areas: ecological, social, and economic. How can a smaller company keep an eye on all three areas? And this, when at the same time DT has to be managed along with other challenges such as the shortage of skilled workers, possible succession planning, but also the energy crisis and its consequences for the operational business?

In smaller entrepreneurial firms, there is a tension between agility and a lack of resources and competencies. As regards financial resources, and access to them in particular, recent developments have brought about a number of new forms of financing, such as tokenization or employee equity participation, which can increase agility and the entrepreneurial scope. Fintech companies offer some of these new financial solutions, but one should keep in mind that these companies are new enterprises themselves, where all discussions of challenges and risks associated with smaller (younger ones in particular) firms are relevant.

For new enterprises, all business risks are new. Thus, these firms have to learn to identify, analyze, and manage them. Compared to the older, smaller firms, they do not have experience and thus a history of managing risks or crises. The new digital technologies and DT itself have brought about new types of risks that have to be carefully monitored as well. How do we manage these risks, of which many take place at the same time or lead to others (domino effect)? How do we meld old and new knowledge? How do we know when old knowledge can or should be discarded and when not to? These are questions that ask us to think again in the direction of a systematic approach to KM.

Can everything as a service (XaaS) be a suitable concept for all small businesses? What new forms of collaboration are needed among SMEs as well as other actors in the ecosystem to make this concept fly? How do we establish and maintain, for example, cooperation where some SMEs are producing and others are providing customer-centered services?

All big change initiatives need clear and continued commitment from the top of the company (owners and managers) and must be accompanied by a vision, values, and a strategy that emphasizes strategy implementation. Additionally, justified rules and procedures must be in place not only for internal management but also for relations with external stakeholders; thus, a strategic fit should be strived for.

Giving more autonomy to individual employees or groups of employees is expected to contribute to higher job satisfaction and work performance. SMEs usually do better in this regard compared to larger companies due to less bureaucracy, fewer hierarchical levels, and better relations between founders and staff. DT may have the potential to support SMEs in becoming even stronger in this regard. Continued learning and unlearning should be ongoing activities for all members of the organization; all individuals should possess relevant and updated skills and competencies so that better decisions can be made at all levels.

Highly skilled individuals expect certain incentives. Very high salaries are often not possible in the broad mass of SMEs, but as it is known from research, nonfinancial incentives are rather powerful as well and could be offered in the form of responsibilities or decision-making privileges in certain business areas. Another issue that has been triggered by the pandemic is the well-being of the organization and its members. What can the owner or founder do to keep himself or herself healthy, considering that the world has become even more unpredictable? How can he or she avoid or prevent possible health issues inflicted by DT, namely technostress?

Coming back to the increasing shortage of skilled people, how do we keep hold of the motivated and engaged employees and ensure their loyalty to the company? As regards the individual person in DT, one possible risk is alienation from oneself by becoming a tool or part of the workload. The increasing digitalization of the firms' business operations might create a situation where there is no spare time for individuals, as feedback or orders are received 24/7, thus blurring work and private life — a circumstance to which the founders or owners may be particularly vulnerable.

A special type of entrepreneurship is micro-entrepreneurship. In many countries, it is the main form of entrepreneurship. In connection with DT, where critical aspects are the development of a suitable organizational culture and the training and further education of the organization's members, in micro-firms, there is a question of how to describe the phenomenon of DT in organizational terms. And if there is no organization, what should be the focal point? It appears that in these firms, the education aspect becomes vital in particular. Also, the relevance, i.e., the contributions of these firms to the economies and their prosperity should be evaluated in the given context.

Regulatory constraints seem to be a challenge in many areas of DT and thus DT for entrepreneurship. Especially in Industry 4.0, new technological solutions and practical applications are usually emerging before a regulatory framework is in place. Business operations have become more and more global, yet regulations are (still) local. Even if one country establishes concrete rules and regulations, it does not resolve issues at the international level. With new global digital platforms for financial operations but without a strong regulatory framework for securing or controlling those, SMEs might be vulnerable to losing their resources.

To compound all the complicated and often closely interlinked issues in entrepreneurship and DT, the question of useful and effective education might be a key point to successful DT.

What to do?

- *Transparency*: Be transparent in your aims and objectives, or declare your main values and principles. Be transparent in your financing, as that creates trust.
- *Ethicality*: Be sensitive to your employees; they are the main asset since standardized and repetitive work will be done by machines. Involve them in designing the business and its continued development. Hire people with a growth mindset. Value people who want to develop something together with you and who are creative and also willing to take responsibility.
- *Sustainability*: Build and run a business with a long-term focus in mind.
- *Agility*: Be ready for changes and their consequences. Have entrepreneurial measures in place to act accordingly. Make change a constant in your business.
- *Knowledgeability*: Do not make decisions based on gut feeling alone but continuously develop or buy in relevant knowledge and manage it properly. Actively involve people in decision-making to increase their involvement and thus their sense of belonging. Be prepared to unlearn outdated knowledge and ways of doing things. Be aware of possible risks and their interlinkages, and manage them continuously.
- *Collaboration with different partners or stakeholders*: It is not only a way to overcome resource limitations but also a way to have a continued inflow of new and different ideas, views, etc.

In summary, and as shown throughout the book, DT for entrepreneurship touches all types of smaller entrepreneurially managed enterprises and, in these, all business areas and functions. This means that something has to be done based on a proactive approach. The good thing is that more and more solid, i.e., research-based, findings are available that can support companies in tackling DT in an entrepreneurial way.

We hope that the readers of this book agree with us on these issues.

https://doi.org/10.1142/9789811270178_bmatter

Index

A
activating students' interests, 72
actors in the ecosystem, 245
adoption of third-party digital platforms, 176
affective skills, 76
agile and user-centric thinking, 138
agile philosophy, 123, 130
agility, 247
angel investors, 156
anything-as-a-service (XaaS), 139
approval anxiety, 102
artificial intelligence (AI), 136
attitudes toward technology, 110
autonomy paradox, 101
autonomy to individual employees or groups, 245
availability stress, 102
avoid doing harm, 27

B
B2C online marketplace, 179
basic ethical principles, 17
B Corp, 222
behaviors of leaders, 126
beneficial innovation, 25
better value for money, 139
blockchain, 165
business ethics, 19–21
business ethics framework, 26
business finance, 153, 162–163, 166
business financing, 166
business model attributes, 181
business model innovation, 137
business models, 244
business risks, 245
business transfer, 8

C
capabilities, 175
CARMA model, 123–124, 130
challenges of DT in SMEs, 33
change process, 224
changing the way of doing business, 196
civic morals, 19
classical financing methods, 159
codes of ethics, 20
cognitive skills, 76
collaboration with different partners or stakeholders, 247
collaborative arrangements, 59
commitment, 222

common morality, 27
community, 222
compete for the top positions, 189
competencies for virtual leadership, 129
competencies that entrepreneurial leaders need, 126
competency-based education, 79
competitor analysis, 188
complexity of challenges, 28
concentrated decision-making power, 38
concise transformational strategy, 34
connection overload, 102
constant connectivity, 97, 107
continued learning and unlearning, 246
cooperation, 54
core leadership processes, 129
corporate digital responsibility (CDR), 21, 24
corporate entrepreneurship, 9
corporate responsibilities, 27
corporate social responsibility (CSR), 21, 24–25
Corporate Sustainability Reporting Directive, 218
COVID-19, 101, 118
COVID-19 global pandemic, 118
COVID-19 pandemic, 99
COVID-19 pandemic, stress levels, 96
create fully digital business models, 138
create new business processes, 32
crowdfunding, 156, 158
culture of organizations, 25
customer loyalty, 139
customers, 221–222
customer satisfaction, 41
customer stewardship, 223
customers' trust and loyalty, 28
cyberattack, 51, 62
cyberbullying, 98, 100
cybersecurity, 65

D

data management, 244
decision-making, 229
decision to start a new venture or to take over, 8
deep work, 108
defines digitization, 10
defining, 55
definition, 57
definition of entrepreneurship, 6
definitions of a digital ecosystem, 54
definitions of digital transformation, 11
definitive values of entrepreneurs, 19
deliberative mindset, 124
Deutscher Nachhaltigkeitskodex (DNK), 221
developing capabilities, 188
development of a digital strategy, 40
different modes of entrepreneurship, 11
digital and soft skills, 122
digital
  competence framework, 109
  consciousness and CDR, 27
  Darwinism, 126
  domains, 25
  domains and ethical issues, 23
  economies, 21
  educational technology, 72, 84
  entrepreneurial ecosystem (DEE), 51–52, 56, 59–60, 65
  entrepreneurship opportunities, 137
  ethics, 25
  ethics themes, 27
  framework, 54
  infrastructure, 55
  infrastructure governance, 62
  innovation in SMEs, 197
  Kazakhstan, 201
  leadership, 126, 128
  minimalism, 108

multi-sided platform, 60–61
platform experiences, 177
platforms capability, 179
platforms to advertise and sell their products and services, 198
skills, 108–110
stress, 102
technologies and leadership, 129, 131
technologies at work, 99
technology, 71, 80–84, 110, 119
technology entrepreneurship, 63–64
transition, 178
user citizenship, 61
well-being, 95, 107–108, 111
well-being at work, 107
workplace, 117, 119–120, 130
work practices, 130
digital transformation (DT), 9–10, 31, 53, 110, 117–118, 131, 196, 244
digital transformation for different modes of entrepreneurship, 12
digital transformation for entrepreneurship, 1, 5
digitalization, 9–10, 22, 96, 243
digitalization at workplaces, 119
digitalization risk, 51, 60
digitalization shapes, 119
digitalized work, 120
digitalizing companies, 118
digitization, 9, 22
digitized products and services, 144
disruptive innovation, 138
disruptive service offerings, 143
distributive channels, 199
double materiality impact, 230
DT as a sociocultural process, 25

E

early-stage challenges, 175
early-stage researchers (i.e., doctoral students), 2
e-commerce platform, 181, 244
e-commerce retail sales, 176
educational experience, 82
educational institutions, 84
educational pedagogies, 78
educational process, 77, 79, 84
educational technologies, 83
educational tools, 85
education sector, 78
effective leader in a virtual environment, 131
effective leadership, 117–118, 124–126, 130
EFRAG, 234
e-marketplace entry decisions, 178
emerging business ventures, 157
emerging economies, 196
employee development, 41
employee engagement, 130
employee performance, 97
employee well-being, 96, 108
employee work, 123
employee work engagement, 118
empower, 62
engagement, 222
entrepreneurial
activity, 7, 243
business finance, 151
competences, 72–73, 80
ecosystem, 55
ethics, 20–21
firms, 9, 85
funding, 167
leaders, 117
leadership, 120
learners, 75, 81
mindset, 21, 74
outcomes, 73
settings, 85
skills, 71–72, 74
venture, 153, 166

entrepreneurs, 19, 81, 85
entrepreneurship and ethics, 17
entrepreneurship courses, 83
entrepreneurship curricula, 82
entrepreneurship education, 71–78, 80, 82, 84
entrepreneurship education curricula, 81
entrepreneurship education planning, 84
entrepreneurship education programs, 83
entrepreneurship educators, 75
entrepreneurship ethics in DT, 26
entrepreneurship pedagogies, 82
entrepreneurship students, 72, 76
environment, 222
ergonomic risks, 101
e-skills, 109
ethical challenges at the organizational level, 24
ethical challenges for enterprises, 24
ethical challenges in DT, 22
ethical decision-making, 27
ethical entrepreneurs, 26
ethicality, 247
ethical risks, 25
ethical risks and standards, 27
ethics for entrepreneurs, 27
ethics in entrepreneurship, 20
ethics of entrepreneurial activity, 17
European Agency for Occupational Safety, 100
EU Taxonomy, 218
evaluation of organizational competencies, 40
everything as a service, 136
experiential approaches, 76
experiential learning, 77–78, 81
experimental studies, 85

F

fear of missing out, 102
feelings of isolation and loneliness, 100
felt obligations, 106, 111
financial institutions, 159
financial service, 162
financial solutions, 245
financial technology, 160
financing, 157, 160
financing methods, 163
financing methods for businesses, 152
fintech, 159
flexible work arrangements, 121
formal and informal education and training, 206
formal leaders, 125
forms of entrepreneurial activity, 6
foster entrepreneurship, 13
foundations of ethics in organizations, 25
framework, 31, 217, 233
funding, 155, 163
funding activity, 154
funding methods, 158, 167
future of work, 119

G

generation Z, 79
global digital platforms, 247
governance, 222
Green Deal, 218

H

harmful disruption, 25
higher educational institutions, 80
highly heterogenous segment, 35
highly skilled individuals, 246

holistic risk assessment, 141
how organizations and employees define work, 120
how to engage with their clients behind the computer's screen, 206
huge potential to disrupt the typical purchase and use cycle of product sale, 147
human capital paradox, 127
human flourishing, 27
humanistic values, 21
human knowledge risks, 58
hybrid workplaces, 110

I

ideal worker image, 106, 111
impact assessment, 223
impacting interhuman relations, 26
impact of the COVID-19, 196
implementation, 219
implementing new business models, 197
improved business performance, 33
individual ethics, 19
industrial economies, 21
industry 3.0, 24
industry 4.0, 24, 246
industry 5.0, 25
informal leadership, 125
information and communication technology, 79
information overload, 97–98, 110
initial challenges, 181
innovative service, 135
integrated framework, 52
integrate service innovations, 137
integrative framework, 42
interact with consumers, suppliers, 198
International Labor Organization, 100
Internet of Things (IoT), 136
investing in entrepreneurial ventures, 154
investors, 162
ISO 26000, 226

J

just decisions, 27

K

Kaspi marketplace, 181
Kazakhstan, 175, 179
key business model attributes, 182
knowledge, 225
knowledge ability, 247
knowledge censoring, 51, 59, 63
knowledge leakage, 51, 60–61
knowledge management (KM), 31, 39
knowledge risk, 53, 57–59

L

lack of common standards, 25
lack of formalized processes, 37
larger logic of value creation, 138
leader's roles in digital transformation, 127
leadership, 118, 125
leadership in the digital context, 126, 131
leadership in the virtual world, 127
leadership tactics, 129
leaders of digitalizing companies, 118, 129
learning experience, 85
learning goal mindset, 124
learning process, 77
legal framework to manage data, 244
liability of smallness, 177
"localization" of supply chains, 209
"localization" of their goods' supply chain, 208
long-term partnerships, 234

M

managerial philosophy, 121
managerial practices, 111, 122, 130
managing digital transformation, 178
marketplace-based online merchant, 181
marketplace's platform resources, 189
materiality analysis, 226
materiality matrix, 234
meaningful work, 123–124, 130
mental health, 101–102
mental health problems, 96–97
microenterprise, 204
microentrepreneurs, 195
micro-entrepreneurship, 246
micro entrepreneurship in Kazakhstan, 196
mindful usage of technology, 111
mindful use of technology, 95, 108
modern entrepreneurship, 243
modes of entrepreneurship, 7
modes of entry into entrepreneurship, 7
moral considerations, 27
motivation, 222
motivations to join a marketplace, 181

N

narrow perspective, 6
nature of work, 97
necessity-based entrepreneurship, 8
negative effects of digital transformation, 10
new aspects of working life, 120
new service-based business model, 142
new ways of working, 121
Non-Financial Reporting Directive, 218
normative obligations, 106

O

old and new knowledge, 245
online marketplaces, 175, 177
online platforms, 187
online reviews, 185
operational knowledge risks, 58
operational transparency, 142
opportunity-based entrepreneurship, 9
organic organizational culture, 36
organizational and group norms, 108
organizational culture, 26, 205
organizational inertia, 37
organizational norms, 107
organizational practices, 95, 108
organizational responsibilities, 24
outward mindset, 124
overuse of technology, 97

P

paradoxes in virtual leadership, 127
paradox theory, 128
partnership exchange, 227
partnerships, 226
paucity, 64
perceptual stress, 105
performance, 54
personal obligations, 106
personified ideal worker image, 106
platforms, 158
platform utilization, 175
plurality of morals, 19
poor planning, 37
positive leadership behaviors, 123
positive leadership styles, 123
potential knowledge risks, 59
primary modes of entrepreneurship, 11
principlism, 27
privacy, autonomy, and security, 26
process improvements, 41
process of transformation, 42
productivity paradox, 101

professional activities, 21
professional ethics, 19
promotion mindset, 125
proposed conceptual model, 64
proposes, 61–63

R

recovery from work, 108
regulatory constraints, 246
regulatory framework, 233, 247
remote emotional skills, 109
remote social skills, 109
remote work, 98, 110
remote work skills, 95, 109
resilience of small entrepreneurs to economic shocks, 200
respect the autonomy, 27
responsible team, 233
responsive leadership, 128
right skills and expertise, 244
risk management, 65
risks, 230

S

sedentarysedentary work, 101
selective leaders, 128
self-care skills, 109
service ecosystem, 139
service-oriented business models, 136
shortage of skilled people, 246
shortage of skilled workers, 245
small- and medium-sized enterprises (SMEs), 7, 26, 31–32, 96, 175–176, 180, 215, 243, 245
small and micro businesses, 196
small companies, 178, 243
small entrepreneur, 26
smaller entrepreneurial firms, 245
smart leader, 122, 124
smart leader attributes, 122
smart leadership, 117, 121, 123, 130
smart leadership behavior, 121
smartphone users, 102
smart worker, 122
smart working, 117–118, 121, 130
SME participation, 177
social, 227
social and environmental
sustainability, 28
social connectivity paradox, 101
social isolation, 109–110
socially responsible, 22
social norms, 107
social obligations, 106
soft skills, 108
stagnant leaders, 128
stakeholder analysis, 234
stakeholders, 65
stakeholders transparently, 222
starting a company, 7
start-up, 12
start-ups or more mature microbusinesses, 204
strategic agility, 36
strategic opportunities, 35
strategic revision of organizational knowledge, 40
strategy, 37, 195
strategy-driven, 32
stress, 98–99, 101, 104, 110
stress, anxiety, and depression, 97
stressors, 98, 100, 105
student-centred education, 82
successful digital transformation in
organizations, 126
successful realization of DT, 38
Supply Chain Act, 218
sustainability, 247
sustainability goals, 245
sustainability in a dynamic
environment, 35
sustainability management, 219
sustainability performances, 219
sustainability strategies, 219

sustainability team, 227
sustainability transformation, 216
sustainability transformation journey, 215, 224
sustainable and environmentally responsible, 215
sustainable business model, 28
sustainable development, 216
Sustainable Development Goals (SDGs), 21
sustainable thinking, 233
synergistic leaders, 128
systematically monitored, 42
systematic approach to knowledge management, 244–245
systematic transformational strategy, 33

T

takeover, 8, 12
taking over an already existing company, 7
taxonomy, 57
technical skills, 129
techno-addiction, 102
techno-complexity, 104, 111
techno-distress, 103
techno-distress at workplaces, 103
techno-engagement, 109
techno-eustress, 103, 111
techno-insecurity, 104, 111
techno-invasion, 104, 111
technological-ethical considerations, 26
technological knowledge risks, 58
technology, 71, 79, 152, 160, 165
technology acceptance, 110
technology dependence paradox, 127
technology-free time, 107
technology-induced stress, 108
technology-related stress, 95
techno-overload, 104, 111
technophobia, 103
techno-strain, 102
technostress (TS), 96–97, 101
techno-stressors, 104, 111
techno-uncertainty, 104, 111
techno-work engagement, 107, 111
Third Industrial Revolution, 24
third-party digital platforms, 175, 180
third-party marketplace, 188
third-party online marketplaces, 178
tokenization, 161
tokenization of assets, 165
traditional educational approaches, 75
training and further education, 246
transformational goals, 42
transformation level, 216
transformation of education, 78
transformative technologies, 25
transitioning to a digital business model, 141
transition to digital technologies, 32
transparency, 247
transparent operations structure, 38
triple bottom line, 234
trust building skills, 109

U

unethical situations, 186
unfreeze–change–(re)freeze method, 224
unique selling proposition and a competitive advantage, 231
unlearning, 51, 61

V

venture capital funds, 153
venture creation, 73

videoconference fatigue, 104
videoconferencing, 105, 111
virtual
leadership, 128
leadership styles, 128
marketplace, 188
(remote)work, 110
work, 100, 110

W
work engagement, 123
work–life balance, 110
work-related health problems, 97, 99
work-related stress, 96, 98, 100
work stress, 99, 101–102
work stress prevention, 110

X
XaaS, 245
XaaS model, 145

Z
Zoom fatigue, 104